The Cinema of Tod Browning

The Cinema of Tod Browning

Essays of the Macabre and Grotesque

Edited by
BERND HERZOGENRATH

McFarland & Company, Inc., Publishers
Jefferson, North Carolina, and London

LIBRARY OF CONGRESS CATALOGUING-IN-PUBLICATION DATA

The cinema of Tod Browning : essays of the macabre and grotesque / edited by Bernd Herzogenrath.
    p.   cm.
Includes bibliographical references and index.

ISBN 978-0-7864-3447-3
softcover : 50# alkaline paper ∞

1. Browning, Tod, 1882–1962 — Criticism and interpretation.
I. Herzogenrath, Bernd, 1964–
PN1998.3.B773C56   2008
791.4302'33092 — dc22   2008029412

British Library cataloguing data are available

©2008 Bernd Herzogenrath. All rights reserved

No part of this book may be reproduced or transmitted in any form or by any means, electronic or mechanical, including photocopying or recording, or by any information storage and retrieval system, without permission in writing from the publisher.

On the cover: Tod Browning, circa 1930s (Photofest); (background) poster art for *London After Midnight, Dracula* and *Freaks*

Manufactured in the United States of America

McFarland & Company, Inc., Publishers
  Box 611, Jefferson, North Carolina 28640
  www.mcfarlandpub.com

...again, for Frank

I'd like to address a sincere and heartfelt "Thanx much!" to Janna "Jamni" Wanagas for her invaluable help in all this.

Table of Contents

Introduction: Browning = Poe + Kant + ... = Cinema
BERND HERZOGENRATH ... 1

Undoing Make-Believe: The Magic of Cinema in Tod Browning's Films
EKKEHARD KNÖRER ... 19

In Love with a Nightmare: Disability Imagery and Fascination in *The Unknown*
HIONI KARAMANOS ... 33

Cinematic Torture Machines: Tod Browning and Masochism
LARS NOWAK ... 50

Shaking an Elephant: Sound, Space and Suspense in *The Unholy Three*
MICHAEL LAWRENCE ... 70

The Black Bird: Mocking Duality
F. GWYNPLAINE MACINTYRE ... 84

Seeing Through Seeing Through: The *Trompe l'Oeil* Effect and Bodily Difference in the Cinema of Tod Browning
HUGH S. MANON ... 96

The Big City: All of Browning's Universe in One Film
F. GWYNPLAINE MACINTYRE ... 116

Lost in Proto-Performance: *West of Zanzibar* and the Last Stand of the Primal Father
BJÖRN QUIRING ... 132

You're Better Off Without Your Parents: *Where East Is East* Seen Through a Daughter's Eyes
SARAH DELLMANN ... 139

Tod Browning vs. George Melford: *Dracula*'s Doppelgänger
    FRANK LAFOND   151
Browning. Freak. Woman. Stain.
    EUGENIE BRINKEMA   158
Mark of the Vampire: Seeing Is Believing
    REYNOLD HUMPHRIES   174
An Incident in the History of Surrealism: On a Sequence in
The Devil-Doll
    ADRIAN MARTIN   198
Miracles for Sale and Other Films of Detection and the Occult
    MARCEL ARBEIT   214

Filmography   231
About the Contributors   235
Index   239

Introduction
Browning = Poe + Kant + ... = Cinema

BERND HERZOGENRATH

In a review of Tod Browning's *The Show* in the *New York Herald-Tribune* of March 20, 1927, Richard Watts, Jr., dubbed Tod Browning the "Edgar Allan Poe ... of the cinema."[1] Watts goes on to state that where "every director, save Stroheim, breathes wholesomeness, out-of-door freshness and the healthiness of the clean-limbed, Tod Browning revels in murkiness.... His cinematic mind is a creeping torture chamber, a place of darkness, deviousness and death." Browning, then, like Poe, is seen as a "founding father" of the marriage between mystery and gothic, a visionary and inventor of tales of the macabre and Grotesque, haunted by his own ghosts — a representative of the "Southern Gothic." Those two Southerners — Poe and Browning — share a common lineage of a dark vision in which realism, pastiche and a sense for or of the grotesque combine. The macabre and grotesque, however, are part of what could be described as a "terrible beauty"; it is exactly this morbid romanticism that made Poe — and later Browning — appeal to the French, Symbolists and Surrealists alike: both share more than a faint scent of the *Fleurs du Mal*.

Another point in common between Poe and Browning is the absence of "regionalism" — there are virtually no references to "The South" in their respective work. Poe, who was born in Boston, grew up in Richmond, Virginia, Scotland and England, and who worked in Baltimore, Richmond, New York and Philadelphia, resists any smooth localization within the parameters of an easily identifiable national or regional identity. Browning, born in Louisville, Kentucky, in 1880 as Charles Albert Browning, was a nomad as well, leaving home early, running away with a traveling sideshow at the age of sixteen, and performing as a *spieler* and contortionist for the Manhattan Fair and Carnival Company. In 1920, the *Motion Picture News* stated that in 1901 Browning "was an entertainer — singing, dancing and otherwise adding to the general gaiety in a 'river show' on the Mississippi and Ohio rivers."[2] That Browning ever "added to the general gaity" seems more than only slightly at odds with his cinematic vision, in line with exactly that Southern Gothic of the Poesque nature that Tennessee Williams has described as a "sense, an intuition, of an underlying dreadfulness in modern experience" (quoted in Tischler 302).

Maybe the absence of Browning's regional references can be accounted for by seeing cinematic vision itself as a "swamp thing," as coming to life in the marshes and swamps that are so readily identified with "the Old South." I would like to evoke the well-known scene from Murnau's *Sunrise* here, the famous scene in the marshes where the Man and the Vamp lie in the grass and watch a film of the city projected against the dark sky. That scene almost perfectly doubles the position occupied by the spectator of the movie *Sunrise* when sitting in the cinema — a frame within the frame. Taking place in the fertile swamps — reminiscent also of the fecund part of the acreage of Rancho La Brea christened "Hollywood" in 1886 by H. H. Wilcox — this "cinematic vision" is immediately related to a kind of eroticism and bodily desire, a connection supported by the Woman from the City's ecstatic dancing. The vision is thus a "mutual creation" of the "art of representation" and a very material force, both "bodily" and "swampy." Let me quote Gilles Deleuze here. According to Deleuze, German Expressionism evoked

> a dark, swampy life into which everything plunges, whether chopped up by shadows or plunged into mists. *The non-organic life of things* ... which is oblivious to the wisdom and limits of the organism, is the first principle of Expressionism, valid for the whole of Nature.... From this point of view natural substances and artificial creations, candelabras and tress, turbine and sun are no longer any different.... In all these cases, it is not the mechanical which is opposed to the organic: it is the vital as potent pre-organic germinality [Deleuze, *Cinema I* 50–51].

Read in this way, the vision/film is almost like a reversed Platonic cave-allegory, where the vision is not a minor reflection of an idea "somewhere outside," but originates in matter to begin with. The "vision-of-the-city-film" almost percolates out of that vital and fecund swamp. Thus, in order to become cinematic art with a vital force to move people, the spectacle (Hollywood) has to be inoculated with intensity.

The above quotation, at least to my mind, not only evokes a possible "birth of cinema" from "materiality" — literally, the marshes of Rancho La Brea, metaphorically, born from bodily desires rather than "ideas" — but also seems like a perfect description of the revenge scene in Browning's *Freaks*. Here, the freaks take revenge on Cleopatra and Hercules, and they can be seen as if emerging out of the elements — they creep out of the mud, visible only as shadows in the rain, storm, and thunder. The freaks, armed to their teeth, are shown in (and as) this vital pre-organic germinality — violent, forceful, potent. In their crawling and slithering through the mud, they are involved in a *becoming-animal*, in which the organization of the autonomous subject "dissolves" into the composition of an animal pack that organizes itself, a *non-organic* life in that it is "without organs," without the organization of organs, oblivious to the limits of the organism, a multiplicity that does not add up to a unity, a "sum which does not totalize its own elements" (Deleuze, *Logic of Sense* 267). Like Bakhtin's "grotesque body," the freaks' body-without-organs "...is a body in the act of becoming. It is never finished, never completed; it is continually built, created, and builds and creates another body" (317). "Its logic ignores the closed, smooth, and impenetrable surface of the body ... as a separate and completed phenomenon" (317–18). The freaks, the *ne plus ultra* (because "real") of Browning's obsession with the grotesque body, are also a curious *real*ization of Browning's work with Lon Chaney, whose fascination and experimenting with "what a body can do" Skal and Savada describe as "a living, breathing assault on the boundaries of human personality, experience, and identity as they were commonly understood" (Skal and Savada 67). The freaks "crawling Body|Politic"* "organizes" itself in a kind of "swarm–intelligence." In a decidedly "counter–Adamitic" gesture, an Anti-Genesis, the body is not made out of clay by divine intervention, but emerges out of the mud as a de-centered, dynamic multiplicity — a Body|Politic as a "counterflow of amorphous, undifferentiated fluid" (Deleuze and Guattari 9), a cinematic vision as a "material event," a "swamp thing."

Browning was a Southerner. Immanuel Kant was certainly *not* a Southerner, but, I would argue, there is something Kantian in Browning's obsession with the grotesque body — at least something akin to Kant's more speculative side. In his 1755 cosmology *Universal Natural History and Theory of the Heavens*, Kant, in an appendix, includes speculations about "the inhabitants of the stars [planets]" (Kant 183). Closely related to his attempt to show how "general laws of motion" and "the accepted law of attraction" (Kant 92) can be used to explain the development of the universe out of a primordial chaos, setting out "to discover the systematic factor which ties together the great members of the created realm in the whole extent of infinity" (Kant 81), the appendix is less a curious anomaly, less a pre-critical work of weird "scientific significance" (with Kant predicting the existence of new planets beyond Saturn, none of which had been discovered by the time Kant was writing) than a philosophical testing ground of Kant's theory of the body

---

*For the concept of the Body×Politic, see my "The Monstrous Body/Politic of *Freaks*," *The Films of Tod Browning*, ed. Bernd Herzogenrath (London: Black Dog Publishing, 2006, 181-97), and my study *An American Body/Politic — A Deleuzian Approach* (forthcoming).

as a necessary condition of the possibility of knowledge. Speculating about aliens provides a laboratory to shed light on how "the manner of operating and feeling is bound to the condition of the material with which they are connected and [also] depends on the measure [intensity] of impression which the [external] world evokes in them" (Kant 183–84). For Kant, the body, in its materiality, is not a secondary carrier of, but coextensive with knowledge and cognition.

> Man is so created as to receive the impressions and stirrings which the world must evoke in him through that body which is the visible part of his being, and the material of which serves not only to impress on the invisible soul that dwells in it the first notions of external objects, but also to recall and connect them interiorly, in short [that body] is indispensable for thinking [Kant 186].

What is at stake is not to say that mind and body, thought and movement, are one and the same, but that "the ability to think ... is wholly dependent on the properties of matter" (Kant 186). The specific, contingent materiality of our bodies influences our way of thinking:

> The grossness of stuff and of the texture in the build of human nature is the cause of that sluggishness which keeps the faculties of the soul in perennial dullness and feebleness. The handling of reflections and representations enlightened by reason is a tiresome condition into which the soul cannot place itself without opposition, and out of which the soul would, through the natural inclination of the bodily machine, soon fall back into the passive condition, where the sensory impressions determine and rule all its activities [Kant 187–88].

It follows that, for Kant, the mind cannot function effectively if it cannot interact with wholesome, fresh and healthy bodies, if knowledge becomes "hemmed in and impeded by the obstacles of a crude matter to which they are most intimately bound" (Kant 188). In fact,

> the spiritual faculties disappear together with the vigor of the body: when owing to the slackened flow of fluids advanced age cooks only thick fluid in the body, when the suppleness of the fibers and the nimbleness in all motions decrease, then the forces of the spirit too stiffen into a similar dullness. The agility of thought, the clarity of representation, the vivacity of wit, and the ability to remember lose their strength and grow frigid [Kant 188].

Kant's "Appendix" to his *Universal Natural History* (and it is noteworthy that in corporeal terms, the appendix is of "sluggish corporeal stuff" devoid of function, a "useless supplement" that in fact points at the "grossness" of the body as such) provides a speculation about how difference in bodily set-up logically effects "different ways of thinking." What the aliens are to Kant, I argue, the freaks are to Browning — the grotesque-bodied protagonists of

Browning's cinematic universe are embodiments of a testing ground for how "to think otherwise," whether that's good or bad (and I would argue that such a testing ground also tests notions of such conventional morality).[3] "What a body can do"—that Deleuzian/Spinozist question—is intimately linked to "what a mind can think." And both strands find their convergence in the notion of experiment—film, for Browning, is an experiment in "thinking cinematically." Ultimately, Browning's obsession with the grotesque and the macabre, with the abnormal and the deformed, with the margins of culture (and culturally constructed ideas of "humanity"), is not a mere conjurer's trick (although it is exactly that, too—a spectacle), but a speculation about the workings and abysses of culture and its other. For Tennessee Williams, the "Southern Gothic" expresses a "kind of spiritual intuition of something almost too incredible and shocking to talk about" (quoted in Tischler 302). Ludwig Wittgenstein, in the 7th Proposition of his *Tractatus*, wrote that "[w]hereof one cannot speak, thereof one must be silent." So, if you cannot talk about it, you can either shut up—or show it, screen it! This way, it's more corporeal anyway....

This present volume deals with Browning's work from a multiplicity of vantage points—film history, film studies, philosophy, disability studies, colonial studies, psychoanalysis, and so on, all the "best silver" and strange cutlery with which to taste an exotic and exquisite dish such as the maître's *plat du jour*. It tackles not only Browning's most popular films, but also lesser known ones, providing analyses of particular films, but introducing broader topics as well, such as the importance of the body in Browning's films, the various transitions implicit in his work (e.g. from the Magician's Stage to the Silver Screen, from Silents to Talkies, from novel to film and *vice versa*), his work as a scriptwriter, his collaborations with Lon Chaney, and so on.

In his essay "Undoing Make-Believe: The Magic of Cinema in Tod Browning's Films," Ekkehard Knörer follows one particular subject in three of Tod Browning's films: the performance of stage magic. He argues that Browning's stagings of these performances can be read as allegories of cinema itself, or more precisely, as allegories of a film's relation to its own practice of make-believe. In *The Show*, a stage performance very loosely based on Oscar Wilde's *Salome* presents Jokanaan's beheading as an illusion on the stage. This presentation works—within the film—very similarly to what Tom Gunning has described as a "cinema of attractions." This cinema—Gunning mainly refers to movies from the first decade of the 20th century—has a specific temporal and visual structure described by Gunning as the logic of presence and absence: "Now you see it, now you don't." This logic of attraction is, however, immediately reversed for us, the spectators; the attraction as an illusion is, in other words, undone in front of our eyes—and thereby transformed into a narrative. This, Knörer argues, is what happened when the movies turned from a vaudeville attraction into a narrative form of entertainment based on the production of suspense and continuity, i.e. a very different temporal structure. Whereas in *The Show* this transformation still has to be actively performed by the film itself and in various moments of vicarious insight concerns us as the spectators rather immediately, in *West of Zanzibar* it is a tribe of African natives who have to learn the lesson that stage performances always are part of a story. This film, in other words, completely absorbs the stage performance into its narrative. *Miracles for Sale*, Browning's final film, goes at least one step further by now staging — and thereby revealing — our wish of being duped by something we know is nothing but a trick. The formula of a cinema of attractions is replaced by the magician's formula made explicit in *Miracles for Sale*: "The hand is faster than the eye"—which can be described as exactly the formula of experiencing cinema as the pleasure of willingly believing in an illusion. In his final film, it seems, Browning demonstrates and exposes the spectator's implicit complicity with the cinematic illusion.

Browning's reputation as one of Hollywood's preeminent horror filmmakers endures more than four decades after his death. Themes of monstrosity remain hallmarks of Browning's films and continue to generate interest and appreciation. However, scholarship on horror films generally ignores the prevalence of stereotypical images of disability. According to Hioni Karamanos, characters with disabilities often provide a means of evoking horror, but the relationship between images of disability and responses of repulsion goes largely unchallenged. Distinguishing Browning's films as classics of the horror genre without mentioning physical disability is a disservice, as is investigating his use of disability imagery without considering representations beyond horror stereotypes. Disability studies, a newly emerging field of academic inquiry, provides a framework to investigate such themes and offers opportunities for fresh perspectives and analyses. Disability studies explores the social construct of disability, beyond the level of individual trait or diagnosis, further scrutinizing notions of normalcy and difference. Hioni Karamanos' essay "In Love with a Nightmare: Disability Imagery and Fascination in *The Unknown*" demonstrates that to understand disability as a social construct sheds new light on Browning's work. Disability studies need not necessarily glorify or vilify Browning, but it does enhance means of critique. While Browning's depictions of physical disability often incorporate early twentieth century models that negatively contextualize disability as a moral failing or a defect that must be eradicated, they also confront such stereotypes through imagery more closely linked to exotification than abhorrence. Browning's 1927 film *The Unknown* offers the most striking example of this aesthetic. Browning makes creative use of prejudices surrounding disability and enhances our understanding of their power. Browning's depictions of physical disability surpass horror to venture into the territory of fetish and fascination. Browning's intense focus on the extraordinary bodies of his characters suggests a gaze prompted more by desire than disgust. Examining several key scenes from *The Unknown* reveals the depth and complexity of this gaze. From this vantage point, ways in which Browning's films both rely on and expose the prejudices of his era become clearer, and appreciation for Browning's work both within and beyond popular culture stereotypes becomes possible.

Lars Nowak's essay "Cinematic Torture Machines: Tod Browning and Masochism" argues that Browning's films are not about sadism, as a first glance would suggest, but about masochism, and that the latter perversion is not only dealt with by those films Browning made together with Lon Chaney, like *The Unknown* or *West of Zanzibar*, but also by several other Browning films, such as *The Show*, *Dracula*, and *Mark of the Vampire*. Browning's films reveal masochism's phenomenological aspects as well as its structural logic. Their protagonists combine psychological frustrations and physical deformations with experiences of ecstatic joy. The masochistic interplay of pain and pleasure is intensely expressed in facial affect-images that suspend the flow of time in a typically masochistic manner. Brought about by other characters that represent the law, both the psychological and the physical suffering serve as metaphors for the symbolic castration that is a central element of masochistic fantasies and practices. However, Browning's masochists do not only subject themselves to the law, but also rebel against it. They do so not only by reversing the causal and temporal relations between pleasure and its punishment, but also by perverting the concept of guilt, by annulling the father (even if they take this position themselves) and by preserving the phallus with the help of fetishes. In addition, the masochism depicted by Browning's films predominantly assigns the role of the servant to a male character, and that of the master to a female character, and thus subverts patriarchy's distribution of gender roles. In *Dracula* and *Mark of the Vampire*, vampirism, too, is presented as a kind of masochism, since it is less enjoyed by the vampires themselves than by their victims. Whereas Browning's other films focused on masochism's phallic aspects, the vampire's bloodsucking points at its oral dimension. Though at first sight Browning's vampire films seem to affirm the traditional opposition between vampirism and Christianity, by revealing the masochism that is inherent in Christianity itself, they draw attention to the deep affinity between both phenomena.

While masochism was not at all restricted to the films by Browning, but was also represented by many other pictures of the 1920s and 1930s, such as those directed by Josef von Sternberg or Erich von Stroheim, and those featuring Rudolph Valentino, John Barrymore, or Douglas Fairbanks, Browning's films were unique in that they gave masochistic suffering the radical shape of bodily mutilation. Nevertheless, the true originality of Browning's movies lies in the fact that the masochism represented in them mirrors the masochism inherent in cinematic spectatorship itself. Psychoanalytic theory has repeatedly pointed out the fact that, by masking and displaying themselves, both participants in the masochistic scenario behave like actors on a theater stage. By comparison, theoreticians of film have claimed that the cinematic spectator takes a masochistic position as well, since every narrative film subjects him to an alternation between tension and relaxation, and the cinematic apparatus as such controls his visual and auditory perception to a high degree. Browning's films and those of his contemporaries emphasize the close relation between masochism and theatrical role-play by placing their masochistic subjects on actual stages. But only Browning's pictures make clear that the act of film reception is no less masochistic. For here, the stage performances involve mechanical apparatuses that resemble the cinematic machines, and those who suffer really are not the actors but their intradiegetic spectators. Thus, unlike any other filmmaker of his era, Browning created films that expose the masochism of the cinematic experience itself.

Browning's career as a film director took a significant turn with the commercial and critical success of *The Unholy Three* (1925). The *New York Times* praised the film as one of the ten best of the year, and it marked the first major collaboration between Browning and actor Lon Chaney. The two had worked previously on *The Wicked Darling* (1919) and *Outside the Law* (1921), but it was with *The Unholy Three* that the motifs of their work together began to emerge. Browning had worked in sideshows as a barker, and the centering of the story (based on the novel by C.A. Robbins) on the circus reflected his concern for the carnivalesque. Within the film, Chaney, Hollywood's masterful actor of disguises, plays a ventriloquist who is also the perpetrator of a series of criminal acts, and who therefore has to dress as an old woman to hide his identity. Chaney is not alone in his disguise, for Harry Earles plays a midget who dresses as a baby and, to complete the scam, is even pushed around in a pram by Chaney acting the granny. The "unholy three" is completed by a circus strongman (Victor McLaglen) who pretends to be a son-in-law.

Interestingly, Chaney for once did not modify his body or undergo a dramatic make-up transformation to play another character. The film, though, reinforced the depth of Chaney's acting ability, and it demonstrated his adept handling of a silent screen performance. Chaney's parents were both deaf and dumb, and, as David J. Skal notes, he consequently became skilled "at pantomime in early life." Yet Chaney, against expectations, revealed also his ability for sound performance when he reprised his role for the remake of *The*

Unholy Three (1930), directed by Jack Conway. The remake offers a fascinating opportunity to address the style and sophistication of the manner in which Browning's silent version was made.

Michael Lawrence's essay "Shaking an Elephant: Sound, Space and Suspense in *The Unholy Three*" considers the representation of sound and space in Tod Browning's crime melodrama, focusing on scenes of listening (or hearing) and suspense, and audiences' auditory experiences in movie theaters in 1925, before the transition to synchronized sound film. It re-addresses these issues (sound and space, sound and suspense, sound and spectatorship) by looking at the "all-talking" remake of *The Unholy Three*, directed by Jack Conway in 1930 and released towards the end of the period of transition. Looking at the functions of various noises in the two films, Lawrence's essay thinks through the second picture's augmented version of the story, which repeatedly turns on responses and reactions to audible sounds. The film's concerns with illusion and deception (and with, therefore, knowledge and its manipulation) are considered in relation to the transformation of spectators' cinematic experience by the arrival of the "sound" film's pre-recorded sound effect.

F. Gwynplaine MacIntyre, in his essay "*The Black Bird*: Mocking Duality," comments on two of Browning's favorite stock characters, the grotesque cripple and the confidence trickster. In *The Black Bird*, these two characters are combined into a single protagonist: a confidence trickster whose severely crippled body *is* his confidence trick, because he is not genuinely crippled after all. *The Black Bird* also treats a theme which is extremely common in literature and folklore, yet not typical of Browning's universe: the theme of rival brothers; one good, one bad. And yet here, with his typical wit and irony, Browning puts his distinctive cynical twist upon that theme: in *The Black Bird* the rival brothers are the same person, sharing two identities in one body. MacIntyre's essay also dives into the theme of split personality, in terms of fictional precedents to *The Black Bird* (such as Jekyll and Hyde) and real-world examples (such as the bizarre case of Deacon Brodie, the criminal who inspired the original Jekyll and Hyde). Further, this essay explores differences between Browning's film *The Black Bird* and the anonymous novel *The Mocking Bird* which was produced simultaneously to that film: the distinctions between these two works reveal much about Browning's production methods and the development of his plotlines.

In "Seeing Through Seeing Through: The *Trompe l'Oeil* Effect and Bodily Difference in the Cinema of Tod Browning," Hugh S. Manon analyzes how Browning's films repeatedly evoke what Jacques Lacan calls the "triumph of the gaze over the eye," a pleasure in seeing reality trumped by representation, and in recognizing the illusory nature of signification. This essay employs Lacan's discussion of *trompe l'oeil* to understand Browning's representation of bodily difference in *The Unknown* (1927), as well as *The Unholy Three* (1925) and *West of Zanzibar* (1928). According to Lacan, it is not having-been-tricked per se, but the gap between penetrating skepticism and suspension of disbelief in which the pleasure of *trompe l'oeil* resides. But whereas the *trompe l'oeil* of painting plays the two-dimensional plane of the canvas against an illusory depth, Browning's films invite a scopic alternation between the real physical bodies of his actors and the costumes, make-up, and disguises in which they are clothed. In *The Unholy Three*, little person Harry Earles dons the frilly uniform of a two-year-old and spends much of his time hiding out in a baby carriage. As various characters fail to see that the cute child is actually a twenty-three-year-old man, viewerly pleasure emerges in the gap between the costumed criminal-as-deceiver and the real physicality of the actor's body, in which there is no deception. At such moments, Browning traps viewers at the very surface of his representations. By foregrounding cinema's indexical relation to real bodies, the director invites a decidedly non-narrative form of distraction, and it is precisely this redoubled "seeing through" which stabilizes the viewer's relation to Browning's frequently hyperbolic content.

For F. Gwynplaine MacIntyre, *The Big City*, one of the "legendary lost films," is Browning's most typical film — not his best, he argues in "*The Big City*: All of Browning's Universe in One Film," but the film which most fully embodies the various themes which define Browning's fictional universe: the rivalry between crooks, redemption, the confidence trick, the magical illusion, even the physically grotesque. The strengths of *The Big City* tend to be the strengths of Browning's films in general. The most extreme flaws of *The Big City* are, similarly, the most extreme flaws of most of Browning's films throughout his career: his barely plausible tendency to impose sudden reformations upon characters established as life-long criminals, and Browning's totally implausible tendency to have these criminals receive total or near-total amnesty for their crimes merely as a result of making a confession and expressing penitence. Because *The Big City* has been cited as a so-called "lost" film, this essay also details how the author was able to view a print of this film, and further addresses the tendency of film scholars to characterize a film as "lost" when, in fact, they have merely failed to look for it properly. He cites several specific examples of "lost" films which have been rediscovered in recent years, and which are now easily available for viewing and study.

At first sight, Browning's *West of Zanzibar* (1928) seems to be a typical (if somewhat extreme and extravagant) colonial melodrama feeding on racist phantasms. However, for Björn Quiring, the enduring interest of the film lies in the fact that it constantly mirrors its own phantasmatic status into itself and plays with it in the typical Browningian fashion. As he shows in his essay "Lost in Proto-Performance: *West of Zanzibar* and the Last Stand of the Primal Father," the film's reactionary surrealism is both saturated and subverted by the fact that the movie depicts Africa itself as a series of vulgar and blatant arrangements of exoticism created by whites for the white gaze: The main protagonist, a sideshow magician, has been lost in a primal scene he fabricated himself within the parameters of a tragic family romance, and subsequently becomes everything he ascribes to his phantasmatic "brutish" enemy. Reconstructing himself within the colonial context, he takes on the role of the "hyperreal man" beyond the law, the phantasmatic primal father. But just like Mr. Kurtz in Joseph Conrad's *Heart of Darkness*, he thereby only manages to represent the colonialist experience to itself, unintentionally yet fatally.

Sarah Dellmann, in "You're Better Off Without Your Parents: *Where East Is East* Seen Through a Daughter's Eyes," does exactly this. In her essay, Dellmann examines the film *Where East Is East* with regard to feminist theory and carnival background. She stresses the potential for power-critical analysis given by the carnival tradition, searching a concept that grants pleasure for the daughter. To do so, she leaves psychoanalytic interpretations behind and turns to the carnival as interpretative background of Browning's films instead. After a short reconstruction of Mikhail Bakhtin's analysis of the medieval carnival tradition, she takes his anti-hierarchical concept of "degradation" as an element inversing the official order and adapts it for another view of family structures. The potential of this approach is juxtaposed to the limited possibilities that Freudian psychoanalysis, especially the theory of the oedipal stage, can offer feminine characters, here the daughter — a theoretical background chosen by many film critics for analyzing Browning/Chaney films. As feminist (film) critics have pointed out, the daughter's position within oedipal constructions obstruct the way to autonomy and satisfaction, as she remains incomplete and dependent on the male. He, in turn, is defined as being complete in himself and in possession of what the female lacks. (Even if roles were inversed, the myth that does not grant liberty and fulfillment in desire for everyone would be reinstalled.) With Teresa di Lauretis, Dellmann argues that Oedipal interpretations provide a consistent description of desire and identity, but cannot offer autonomous fulfillment of the daughter's desire. In contrast, the carnival logic understands identity as performative and vacillating, and is therefore more useful for rearrangements of family structures, gender roles and yet unknown possibilities of expression desire. Animals, if not seen as a regressive solution to Oedipal development but as grotesque elements in the fairground tradition, open up ways for rearranging family settings and interpersonal relations. For her analysis of the film *Where East Is East*, Dellmann uses the appearance of animals as second interpretative background, their relations to the characters and their positions of power, concluding that the feminine characters take and keep an active role in defending and living their desire. Traditional roles are inverted, and neither the family nor the father seem to be manifestations of patriarchal power or masculine supremacy: male characters figure rather as objects, not subjects of desire. In her conclusion, Dellmann argues for opening our mind up to other perceptions of family structures and interpersonal relationships to allow a lustful life for everyone — including all daughters.

Along with James Whale's *Frankenstein*, also released in 1931, Browning's *Dracula* is a landmark in the history of the talking horror film. Yet another adaptation of Bram Stoker's story was simultaneously filmed by Universal, using the same sets as well as the same screenplay. The resulting picture, directed by George Melford for Spanish-speaking audiences, works as a good instrument for a better understanding of Browning's. Through a close comparison of both versions and the original shooting script, Frank Lafond, in his essay "Tod Browning vs. George Melford: *Dracula's* Doppelgänger," examines Browning's *Dracula* from a wild array of angles: narrative choices, which at times emphasize the idea that our civilization is contaminated by the East; direction and editing (for instance, the frequency of a certain kind of close-up); the use of music or sound (and, concomitantly, their lack); and acting (notably how the portrayal of the living dead character by the two actors differs). Finally, the essay aims at defining with precision Browning's conception of the horror genre at work in his film. If some of the elements studied here have sometimes been used in favor of the film's so-called staginess, they are also — and above all — quite revealing of the way the supernatural aspects of Bram Stoker's novel are handled throughout it. Browning's *Dracula* offers a conception of the horror genre that is more restrained and demanding from the audience than its Spanish-speaking counterpart — a conception that, without completely following Tzvetan Todorov's definition of the fantastic, nevertheless relies more often on a play with the off-screen space than on direct representation of the monstrous and the abject.

Browning's movies, in particular with their obsession with bodies and mutilations, have invited psychoanalytic approaches. What insights does a psychoanalytic reading provide into Browning's films, both as separate entities and a motley assortment of works that have intertextual connections? How might psychoanalysis help us theorize the distorted and distended bodies of Browning's works? For Eugenie Brinkema, these questions necessitate a turn away from Freudian concepts — castration, the uncanny, and Oedipus — to the work of Jacques Lacan. Lacan's concepts of anamorphosis, the gaze, and courtly love allow us to theorize a complex interaction in Browning's films: the relationship between women and "freaks." Her essay "Browning. Freak. Woman. Stain" focuses on the triad of Woman-Freak-Stain in *Freaks*, *The Unholy Three*, and *The Unknown*. Taking the Lacanian concept of anamorphosis (or stain), Brinkema argues that both the Freak and the Woman in Browning's films can be thought of as visual and structural disruptions. Inherent in the perception of both the freak and anamorphosis is a visual and constitutive trickery. The pleasure of anamorphosis is not simply in seeing an image emerge, but also in deciphering the exact details of its construction. What is produced as surplus in the picture is the image of our own negation. Hence, what the freak points to is our own freakery. The horror freaks inspire, then, is not merely the horror of the composite or the ambiguous body, but the unambiguous relationship between the freak and the gaze. Freaks and anamorphosis pull us into the picture and locate us in the insecure position of being visually interrogated. So too does the figure of the Woman in Browning's films prompt such a returned gaze. Woman figures as a stain — the site of a new way of seeing and a disruption to the field of vision itself. The primary love relationships in *The Unknown*, *The Unholy Three*, and *Freaks* consist of two men, at least one of whom is somehow freakish, and an inaccessible woman. This endless and impossible erotic prolongation is the source of the pleasure of Browning's films. The love pairings in Browning's films are of interest to the spectator for the affair that never happened and could never possibly happen. What makes these suspended films fascinating is in how the freakish couple is *de-formed*. In the logic of Browning's films, the freak as fantasy object participates in creating freakishness in the subject who looks. The introduction of sexual signifiers onto the figure of the freak does not function to exploit the desired objects; what is at stake in *Freaks* is how our desiring cripples, distorts, and stains us.

According to Reynold Humphries' "*Mark of the Vampire*: Seeing Is Believing," Browning's 1935 film has often been dismissed as a cheat because of its revelation that the story is all an elaborate plot to confound a murderer by making him believe vampires exist. If the spectator of the film has been fooled up until the moment the truth is revealed, then the film's overall narrative structure is incoherent. We are privy to scenes that do not enter into the play put on by Professor Zelen and Inspector Neumann, whose concern is to prove that Baron Otto is the murderer of Sir Karell. *Mark of the Vampire* includes many elements that can easily be explained by the fact that the story is an elaborate hoax, of which most, but not all, of the characters are a part. Hence the fascination the film exerts: we identify with characters who are playing a role and with others who take everything they see and hear at face value. As such, the film is a remarkable *mise en abyme* of what it means to be the spectator of a film, with Browning using point-of-view shots and editing to force the spectator to participate unwittingly in a charade, much as we do when identifying with characters in a "straightforward" drama, and so on. A comparison with *London After Midnight* (1927), of which *Mark* is a more elaborate remake, will allow us to work through this aspect of the later film. However, *Mark* does indeed include scenes that must perforce be seen as deliberately cheating the spectator in order to keep the make-believe going until its true nature is unveiled. These incoherencies must not prevent us from highlighting the fact that *Mark* also prolongs a crucial dimension of Browning's own *Dracula*: how characters (and spectators) disavow the testimony of their senses (particularly that of sight) and of knowledge in order to hide unpleasant truths from themselves. Thus, aspects of the plot of *Mark* escape the conscious control of its makers and signify in ways that reveal the pertinence of Freud's theory of disavowal: maintaining a belief in something one knows to be false or not to exist. Freud saw this in the context of sexual difference and hence castration, a notion intimately linked to the way the human subject relates to mortality on the one hand and to the Oedipal complex on the other: how they are resolved, yet leave traces never completely overcome. Thus we shall show that the horror felt by the heroine, which cannot be attributed to vampires (as she is part of the plot), is due to the incestuous relationship she had with her now dead father.

Adrian Martin's essay "An Incident in the History of Surrealism: On a Sequence in *The Devil-Doll*" provides another link between Browning and Surrealism — this time close to the end of Browning's career. Although the production of Browning's penultimate film *The Devil-Doll* (1936) was grossly interfered with by MGM, the resulting movie remains a fascinating, haunting, and at times delirious work. Martin's essay proposes that the best way to appreciate the film is to adopt an approach borrowing the premises of the Freudian "dream-work"— attempting to locate the traces of what drew Browning to the project, and what draws us, today, as viewers. In particular, taking further the dream-work cue, the essay relates the film to the precepts of a cinema-based Surrealism. The legacy of Surrealism today suffers from a neglected and frequently misunderstood or misrepresented version of its history. Surrealism in cinema is not just about visual weirdness or an absorption in dream sequences. The vision of the "marvelous" in Surrealism, and its philosophy of a permanent revolution in everyday life, have provided the basis for a complex cinematic theory and aesthetic practice, from Buñuel to Ruiz, stopping by many flowerings of B cinema and special forms, such as animation and Surrealist documentary. In short, Surrealism offers cinema a dialectical relation between the recorded presence of everyday life, and the magnifying and transforming power of the film medium itself (as theorised by Jean Epstein in his notion of *photogénie*). The history of the cinema–Surrealism connection is outlined, and *The Devil-Doll* (as a B-grade fantasy-horror movie) is placed sympathetically within the canons of Surrealist sensibility and taste. Surrealism must be understood in two broad ways in relation to cinema: as an idea for aesthetic practice, and as an account of the "intoxicated" film-viewing experience, of a particular kind of spectatorial sensibility that was cultivated by the Surrealists, especially in the cinematic realm. In line with the Surrealist taste for the "privileged moment," Martin's essay concentrates on a special sequence early in *The Devil-Doll*— the demonstration of scientific shrinkage techniques on humans and animals.

Miracles for Sale (1939), Browning's last directorial item, is one of his most underestimated and least analyzed movies. While originally taken as a comedy melodrama, now it is primarily discussed in the context of the detective genre. The film is based on Clayton Rawson's novel *Death from a Top Hat* (1938), the first crime mystery from the author who was later to become famous for his blending of the criminal and the supernatural. His amateur detective is the Great Merlini, a connoisseur of magic tricks, but a nonbeliever in the occult. He helps the New York City police solve "impossible" crimes involving rooms locked from the inside, mysterious escapes and vanishing murder weapons. Police investigators (in *Death from a Top Hat* it's Inspector Marty Gavigan) play Dr. Watson to the Sherlock Holmes–like gifted amateur. The genre connects the book's adaptation with another neglected Browning movie, *The Thirteenth Chair* (1929), and to a certain extent also with *Mark of the Vampire* (1935) and its silent predecessor, now lost, *London After Midnight* (1927), where the illusion of the supernatural is used to get the confession from a criminal. Hints in Rawson's novel show that the author was familiar with Browning's earlier *oeuvre*; Rawson mentions Count Dracula, Lon Chaney, and freaks, from whom impersonators sometimes learn their methods. One time Inspector Gavigan is likened to an actor; in another scene, magicians are compared to filmmakers. Some scenes seem to have been changed simply because they were influenced by earlier Browning movies, and to shoot them as they were sketched would have forced the director to imitate himself— for instance, those using hypnosis and ventriloquism. Rawson, like Browning, had a rich personal experience with the world of tricks and magic, being a practicing magician for a while. Marcel Arbeit's essay "*Miracles for Sale* and Other Films of Detection and the Occult" carefully scrutinizes the differences between the novel and the film. These differences start with the characters: the Great Merlini was renamed Michael Morgan (in an adaptation of another Rawson novel, *No Coffin for the Corpse*, by director Herbert I. Leeds, Merlini was even replaced by Mike Shayne, the red-headed Irish detective conceived by Brett Halliday); the original narrator, the journalist Russ Harte, was removed; and the character of the beautiful damsel in distress, Judy Barclay, was put in the forefront. The screenwriters even introduced a new comic character, Morgan's father, freshly arrived in New York from Indiana. While the novel deliberately draws on John Dickson Carr's *The*

Three Coffins (1935), the movie simplifies the locked-room mystery plot and develops the romantic potential of the story. Another point of Arbeit's interest is the use of the supernatural in *Miracles for Sale*. Although Mike Morgan is very skeptical about ghosts and communication with the deceased, he finally consents to participate in a *séance* in which the mysterious medium Madame Rapport "interrogates" the victim, a master of the occult named Dr. Cesar Sabbatt. At this time Morgan stops ridiculing occult practices and uses their outcome in solving the murders. What was on the verge of a parody of esoteric rituals gradually loses its comic aspect. Ridiculing the supernatural and taking it seriously at the same time creates an interesting tension in the movie. Similar ambiguity can already be found in Robert Dale Owen's influential book *Debatable Land Between This World and the Next* (1872). Browning also stresses the moral aspect of Rawson's novel: even though ghosts might exist, the evil, whatever dirty tricks it uses, is always connected with humans. Following this idea, *Miracles for Sale* is compared to *The Thirteenth Chair*, based on Bayard Veiller's 1916 theater play, also a locked-room mystery with séances and a fake medium, but *Miracles'* use of the supernatural can be traced back to *The Mystic* (1925). With the silent movie *The Mystic*, *The Thirteenth Chair* and *Miracles for Sale* form a loose "occult trilogy."

In 1953, in the only retrospective article dealing with Browning's work published in Browning's lifetime, author George Geltzer praised the "unexpected scenes of sheer pictorial beauty in almost all of Browning's films" (416). He then observed that Browning's "techniques and devices for thrilling and chilling audiences have been copied by directors all over the world" (416). This remains true, and almost sounds prophetic (50 years after Geltzer's statement, there is a case to be made for Browning's influence on directors such as David Lynch and John Waters). The freaks peopling the movies of Alejandro Jodorowsky seem to have sprung from Browning's cinematic universe, and the "body horror" of David Cronenberg owes much to Browning's and Chaney's experimentations with "what a body can do." So far, only some of Browning's movies have been made accessible on DVD by Warner Bros. and Universal; thus, there is still plenty to be discovered in the cinematic universe of Browning's tales of the macabre and the grotesque.

Notes

1. More specifically, Watts describes Browning as "the combination of Edgar Allan Poe and Sax Rohmer of the cinema"— Sax, not Eric, Rohmer!!— a strange hybrid of high and low culture, and aesthete of pulp cinema.
2. *Motion Picture News*, December 25, 1920 (no pagination).
3. And it is yet another matter of speculation of how much Browning's 1915 car crash (he

was drunk) that nearly disfigured Browning's own body triggered his obsession with bodily dismemberment.

Works Cited

Deleuze, Gilles. *Cinema 1: The Movement Image.* Trans. Hugh Tomlinson and B. Habberjam. Minneapolis: University of Minnesota Press, 1986.
_____. *The Logic of Sense.* Trans. Mark Lester, with Charles Stivale. Ed. Constantin V. Boundas. New York: Columbia University Press, 1990.
Deleuze, Gilles, and Félix Guattari. *A Thousand Plateaus: Capitalism and Schizophrenia.* Trans. B. Massumi. Minneapolis and London: University of Minnesota Press, 1993.
Geltzer, George. "Tod Browning: He Made Great Horror Films Because He Believed Horror Is Naturally Cinematic." *Films in Review* 4: 8 (October 1953), 410–6.
Kant, Immanuel. *Universal Natural History and Theory of the Heavens.* Trans. Stanley Jaki. Edinburgh: Scottish Academic Press, 1981.
Skal, David, and Elias Savada. *Dark Carnival: The Secret World of Tod Browning, Hollywood's Master of the Macabre.* New York: Anchor Books, 1995.
Tischler, Nancy. *Tennessee Williams: Rebellious Puritan.* New York: Citadel Press, 1961.

Undoing Make-Believe
The Magic of Cinema in Tod Browning's Films

Ekkehard Knörer

Legend has it that the scandal surrounding his film *Freaks* (1932) was Tod Browning's undoing as a successful Hollywood director. The films he made — and was, with increasing distrust from the studios, allowed to make — after *Freaks* are generally regarded as an ever dimmer twilight of his career.[1] Legend seems to have it wrong, however, as there is little doubt that Browning's career had been in decline already before the film, harshly cut, even mutilated by the studio, reached movie theaters and failed to leave an impression at the box office. The story, I think, has to be told differently, then. And yet I would argue that there is a story here, a plot that connects Browning's career in intriguing ways to the trajectory of Hollywood's history from 1910 to 1940, roughly the thirty years of Browning's rise, his triumphs and his fall in the movie industry.

A short look at his career before and in Hollywood therefore seems in order. As was the case with so many of the film industry's later protagonists, Browning's professional life had not exactly been very reputable before his arrival in Hollywood — which, of course, has a lot to do with the fact that in the 1910s working for the movies itself was not exactly a reputable way of earning your living. The exact border between myth and fact is not always clear concerning Browning's early years as a performer in carnival, vaudeville and traveling stage shows; there seems little doubt that one of his routines was a so-called "Hypnotic Living Corpse" stunt, in which the performer was buried alive and miraculously stayed six feet under for up to 48 hours — based on a trick involving sliding tubes and ventilation ducts (see Skal and Savada 25–26). Browning also claimed — no proof seems to exist — to have been associated with the famous magician Leon Herrmann who, with lots of orientalist embroidery, performed the "bullet catch," which was dangerously based on a sleight-of-hand exchange of real and fake bullets reminiscent of the exchange of swords in Browning's film *The Show* (see Skal and Savada 27–28). It is a fact, however, that Browning came into contact with the movies in 1913, where, still in New York, he met David Wark Griffith, joined Biograph Films as an actor, and soon accompanied the director to California. Griffith there became the director of the Reliance-Majestic company, for whose subsidiary, Komic Company, Browning developed a routine as a comic actor. He turned into a director already in 1915 when he produced one- and two-reelers for Griffith's Reliance-Majestic company.

Browning had arrived in Hollywood in its early heydays of formal experimentation, when David Wark Griffith not only facilitated the establishment of the narrative feature film, but also invented or developed major elements of what came to be regarded as the basic grammar of film, from the close-up to sophisticated techniques of montage. Browning himself never was, nor claimed to be, a formal innovator, neither in respect to the history of cinema as such, nor even in the course of his own cinematic trajectory. It was, on the contrary, one of the most common complaints about his movies that they were nothing but variations on a very limited set of motifs and plots. It is certainly true that his films remained deeply steeped in his gaudy and grand-guignolesque vaudeville and performance roots.[2] This is obvious thematically, with the omnipresence and never-ending repetition of tricks and mediums, carnivals and vampires, stage shows and magicians, its sensationalist melodrama with incestuous undertones and obsessively recurring threats and actual perpetrations of mutilation and murder. Although Browning, after a short phase as a scriptwriter, never was the single author of his films' scripts, there was something like a trademark Browning film, at least in the second half of the twenties.[3] He had by then acquired a reputation as the unflinching director of plots coming back time and again to a core set of sensationalist constellations, reaching his pinnacle with the series of films he made with the actor Lon Chaney, most famously *The Unholy Three* (1925), *The Black Bird* (1926), and *The Unknown* (1927).[4]

In this essay, I want to concentrate on one recurring Browning motif, a motif that, at first sight, seems to be a less prominent one in his oeuvre: the motif of magic and the magician's show. Only three films Browning directed explicitly focus on magic and magicians.[5] The protagonist of *The Show* (1927), one of Browning's most interesting works, is vaudeville "ballyhoo" Cock Robin, who performs in a stage show that reenacts Jokanaan's beheading at Salome's request. *West of Zanzibar* (1928) takes the magician's show into the exoticist life of tribes in Africa, where revenge and escape are acted out in scenes of a magician's performance. Browning's final film, *Miracles for Sale* (1939), is the apotheosis of all this, if, as befits a curtain call, an apotheosis in farcical form. In a move very typical for the director it opens with a scene that cannot be taken at face value. The murder mystery serving as a basic plot plays out among a congress of magicians. Things and people appear and disappear following a simple, but magical, logic: You can never believe your eyes.

This thematic recurrence has, I want to argue, systematical reasons, insofar as the logic of magic can be read as the structural logic of Browning's films. His *mise-en-scène* very often is not directed at producing, but rather at staging and revealing the production of the kind of make-believe that enables the audience to passively identify with what happens on the screen. He repeatedly shows scenes of trickery that question exactly this kind of make-believe. Matthew Solomon has pointed out that the ambivalent position towards "artful deception" was prefigured in a thoroughly modern brand of vaudeville illusionism (see Solomon). He quotes from James Cook's study on P.T. Barnum, who certainly has always been the paramount example of the impresario of the bizarre as a master of all kinds of dirty tricks and sleights of hand: "As Barnum often noted in his own self-defense, no producers of such entertainment who wanted to stay in business for long simply fooled their viewers without also drawing attention to the act of fooling—or at least the possibility thereof" (Cook 17, quoted in Solomon 63). This makes perfect sense, of course, in a context of attractions which are supposed to create rumors—which then create curiosity. This sensationalist "aesthetic" of deception as an art of innuendo can even turn, as Cook makes clear, into the sensational revelation of the trick by the magician himself (see Solomon 64).[6] Explaining the arts and techniques of deception can, in other words, become an attraction as well as the deception itself. It is certainly true that Browning and his use of magic in his films can be seen in this tradition. Whenever Browning shows magic in his films he unfailingly also shows what is going on behind the scenes. The undoing of make-believe is part of all scenes of presenting and staging illusions in Browning's films. This does not mean, at least not necessarily, that his films are self-reflexive in an avant-garde or post-illusionist way. I would rather argue that the magician's show in Browning's films serves as the allegory of a pre-illusionist cinema—a vaudeville that is a late variety of what Tom Gunning for early cinema has called a "cinema of attractions." The Browning version of this "cinema of attractions," however, is "reflexive" in at least one way. By coming back time and again to the magician's show (or its vaudeville equivalents), it tends to produce and reproduce allegories of make-believe that are at the same time allegories of the dangers of make-believe and allegories of (never quite) undoing make-believe.

In a medium on its way to narrative illusionism this tendency must lead to ambivalent and therefore irritating, even contradictory, results. How this structure can turn into disappointment becomes most clear probably in two films in which magic is not the subject at all. In Browning's lost silent movie *London After Midnight* (1927)[7] and its sound film remake *Mark of the Vampire* (1935) the vampire story is rather brutally revealed as nothing but a trick late in the film.[8] This is exactly the structure of a disillusioning undoing of make-believe I will analyze in the following close readings of the role of magic in the three films mentioned above, by which I hope to show in which ways his films reflect Browning's position as *the* exemplary director of transition between the movies' beginnings and their times of illusionist and classical glory.

Foreplay: "Now You See It, Now You Don't" (The Show)

In his essay "'Now You See It, Now You Don't': The Temporality of the Cinema of Attractions," Tom Gunning explains the temporal structure of cinematic attractions: "In effect, attractions have one basic temporality, that of the alternation of presence/absence that is embodied in the act of display. In this intense form of present tense, the attraction is displayed with the immediacy of a 'Here it is! Look at it!'" (Gunning 76). This, Gunning adds, is the temporal logic of vaudeville, circus and also the magic show, forms of entertainment where sequences of presence and absence are produced without attempts at narrative connection or closure. The attraction attracts in and of itself, it is displayed for a short span of time and then it disappears again. A curtain is drawn back and then it is closed again. A scene is opened to a public gaze and then it is hidden again. Early cinema, i.e. the one- and two-reelers that were produced before directors like D.W. Griffith started making attempts at cinematic narrative, should be regarded, Gunning argues, as mimicking this kind of attraction. This "cinema of attractions," then, has its own logic and should not be regarded, from a necessarily teleological perspective, as a not yet developed forerunner of later narrative feature films. It has its own different logic of display and the spectator's gaze, too, Gunning argues, a logic that is openly exhibitionist and mutual, implying a visible look at visible things rather than, as is the case in illusionist cinema, a voyeuristic gaze based on an invisible look at private and invisible scenes. Moments of such a cinema, it must be added, resurface in later forms of cinema where narrative time is bracketed and an attraction seems to take precedence — in action sequences of Hollywood genre films, or, coming from a somewhat different tradition, even in the picturizations of Bollywood cinema.

In an early sequence of Tod Browning's film *The Show* we enter a vaudeville show and are introduced to its—and the film's—protagonist, Cock Robin. He is the ballyhoo at this show, and he very literally opens curtains and speaks the "Behold!" that marks the logic of a display of attractions: "Here it is! Look at it!" What we see first are attractions of the freakish kind, the Living Hand of Cleopatra, Zela the Half Lady, Arachnida the Human Spider. At first sight, it might seem as if we, as the spectator, are subjected to the simple logic of the surprised or shocked or awed gaze. We follow the ballyhoo's and the movie camera's imperative: "Behold!"—and, lo, we behold. We do not know, at first, if there is a trick or if the freaks we see are "for real." The same is true for a magician's performance that follows the display of the freaks. A woman seems to fly without strings attached to her body. We do not learn how this might be possible. The curtain falls and we do not see what lies behind it. This, however, is not the end of it. Something else has already come into view. We, the spectators, have entered the picture, however vicariously. Browning insistently shows an audience that gazes with amazement at the things that are presented. What is at display here, then, is not (only) an attraction but the structure of the presenting of attractions.

This structure, at first sight, does not seem specifically cinematic. The spectators are present at the scene—whereas the audience at a movie theater remains at a distance, safely savoring vicarious pleasures of identification, or so we have learned to think. The attractional logic of early cinema must be conceived of in different ways. The answer to the "Behold!" cannot be a silent voyeuristic pleasure but only a direct involvement that produces immediate—and, very precisely, not vicarious—affects. There is always the structural danger that we are caught in the act (of gazing). Browning demonstrates that most drastically later at the vaudeville when another protagonist is introduced as a most poisonous reptile jumps from the stage into the crowd of onlookers and literally attacks a man and kills him. Such are, one could argue, the dangers (or pleasures) of a cinema of attractions that seeks to affect its spectator directly and openly, or, more precisely, that seeks to involve her/him in the seemingly two-sided logic of interactive display where s/he cannot hide—and must not hide in order to be affected. The spectator and her/his response are always part of the picture. The foundational legend of the onlookers fleeing from the Lumière train threatening to run them over, and the revolver aimed at the audience, in Edwin S. Porter's *The Great Train Robbery* (1903) can easily be read as emblematic scenes of an attractional logic of early cinema that, of course, covers for the loss of the literal immediacy still found in the vaudeville show. At the movies, the onlooker as direct bystander is always already on her/his way to a dark movie theater, following the logic of the screen and a representation that in the last instance can never—or only allegorically or in imaginary misrecognitions — return to a breaking down of the fourth wall that separates the scene of the action from the scene of the watching.

In *The Show* things are complicated further soon enough. We are introduced to another scene, the scene of a dance on a stage, Salome's dance that is followed by a beheading. The beheading is shown not *ob-scoena*, as would befit classical theater, but on the stage as an attraction.[9] For the audience the beheading is an illusion that works: Jokanaan's head seems to fall and is put on a platter and handed to Salome.

This time we, the movie audience, are let in on the trick by way of a multiplicity of perspectives: We are presented with a different set of spectators who look at the scene from the side of the stage, and with their eyes we see — and it is even explained to us in title card writing — that the real sword is replaced by a fake sword. We see the contraption that produces the illusion we therefore don't share. We are, so to speak, distracted, let in on the workings of the magic of the attraction by way of a complicated installation of different and incongruent perspectives. The illusion of a presence that governs the workings of the attraction presupposes a certain sequence of actions — "Now you see it, now you don't" — facilitated also in this case by the opening and closing of a curtain. It also presupposes a certain and continuous distance, a stable configuration of the exhibited attraction and the gaze that desires to be attacked by the attraction. In *The Show* Browning disrupts this configuration and retroactively even dispels the illusions from the very beginning.

The "letting in on the trick" is a change to the backstage perspective, an elaboration on the "Now you don't (see it)" aspect of the attraction. Just as Zela the Half Lady seems to not have an abdomen, the attraction seems to work by making the (idea of a) backstage disappear. What we see backstage and behind the curtain, however, is that Zela and all the other "freaks" are no freaks at all but only actors who, within a carefully staged illusion of make-believe, appear to be what they are not. What happens when we enter the backstage is the undoing of the attractional logic of make-believe: "Now you see, what you don't see" — and what, moreover, makes the attraction as a very specific organization of a scene on a stage and a gaze stabilized by and tied to this organization possible.

The magic, then, necessarily disappears. *The Show* is a careful choreography of this undoing. First, we see the attraction of the illusion. Then we are shown the illusion in its context of a curious and fascinated audience; i.e. we as the spectators can see how we get into the picture, can even see how we are "duped" by the illusion. Then we are distracted to the side and the back and see the "making of" the illusion of make-believe, the staging of an attractional logic. What is cinematic about all this, one could argue, is exactly this very fluid change of perspectives, from the front to the back, from the show to the audience, from fascination to observation, from the illusion to its undoing by the demonstrated explanation. This, however, is no longer simply a "cinema of attractions," or rather, it is a second order observation of exactly this kind of cinema. But it turns out to be more than that. The change of perspectives most easily translates into an "attraction" of a different, more contemporary kind: a narration. The movement from the front to the side and the back of the stage, and even onto the stage, turns into a plot that evolves exactly from connecting the multiple places and gazes and actions into a narrative that is a play with this multiplicity: of spaces and of layers of illusionism.

The trick that magically *awes* the naive audience — i.e. the exchange of the swords — becomes a plot point that *thrills* the second order observers — i.e. us — as the major event in a whole different story. The Greek, Cock Robin's jealous rival for Salome's heart, has illegitimately slipped into the beheader's role — as we, and only we, have seen in a backstage event — and by *not* exchanging the sword, by literalizing, by un-doing the trick, threatens to *really* kill. This breach between the stage and its back produces what is called dramatic irony: the actors on the stage almost fatally lack an important piece of knowledge which we possess. This imbalance and surplus of knowledge, however, changes our position from fascination or awe (the spectator position of the "cinema of attractions") into a disposition of thrill and suspense (the spectator position, one could say, of narrative cinema). If the spectator in a "cinema of attractions" desires to be attacked by what awes him (the poisonous reptile), the spectator in narrative cinema sees himself vicariously put into somebody else's (here: Cock Robin's) place.

The magical trick as an attraction is explained and thereby undone, but in its undoing turns into a magic of a different kind, into the illusional make-believe of narrative cinema. In Tod Browning's *The Show* this trick seems to be rather irreversible and even infectious. All the stage actors seem to assume a second life offstage in a second plot that circles around what Hitchcock would have called a McGuffin — the most simple one, actually: a lot of money that everybody wants to have. This desire sets into motion a choreography of observation and eavesdropping, of murder and pursuit. The movement, however, stops and stabilizes into a second drama when Cock Robin goes into hiding in the Salome actress' apartment.

Browning's direction leaves no doubt that a second "stage" is established here, but it is a stage that turns all the props and constellations of the first stage into a pure narrative of happy misrecognition. In a subplot that transforms the stage tragedy (of sorts) of a threatened beheading into the melodrama of an actual hanging (and an actual poisoning), it even naturalizes the naive audience's lack of knowledge into literal blindness. The rather complicated story on the second stage goes like this: "Salome's" father is actually blind and takes Cock Robin for his son, whom he wrongly imagines to be in the army—but who, in fact, will be hanged in the prison yard that can be seen from the apartment's window. What happens in front of this window is almost an event on a third stage, visible only to Cock Robin and Salome, and to us. The blind father is, and remains, in the position of the spectator of an illusion—which goes to show, of course, that this position is actually a position of blindness, of a rather willing suspension of disbelief. The explicit contrasts and parallels between the "show" in the apartment and the actual stage show go even further. There is a sword also in this "play," but no magical trick to be done with it. It is part of the father's military attire—and, in a complete reversion of the stage show's logic, the dramatic irony of misrecognitions must not be explained to him. It is exactly his mistaking Cock Robin for his son that makes the father happy, so happy, in fact, that he can die peacefully. Salome, on the other hand, in this turn of the melodrama of make-believe, recognizes the true—i.e. honest—Cock Robin, and in revealing (and until then not having revealed) herself as being the blind man's daughter makes him recognize her magnanimous character. Even the reptile—domesticated by narrative—plays its role perfectly in this plot, killing the evil Greek before itself being killed by a policeman. There is no undoing of make-believe on this second stage. Every change of perspective and position only adds *another* perspective to the *same* story, and is another step in the unfolding of the plot, not the undoing of an illusion. *The Show* enacts a complete transformation, from a "cinema of attractions" demonstrating staging and the dissolution of make-believe to a cinema of melodramatic narrativity reveling in an aesthetic ideology that knowingly turns misidentification into recognition, money into love, and blindness into the spectator's perfect disposition.

Interplay: Suspension of Disbelief (West of Zanzibar)

In the first shot of *West of Zanzibar* we see a coffin, upright on a stage. The first words we read are: "Ashes to Ashes, Dust to Dust." Then Phroso, the magician (Lon Chaney), enters the frame; we see the audience watching what we now have realized is a magician's performance. A fast change of camera perspective enables us to see a young woman enter the coffin from the back, and we are shown the simple trick—a revolving door—that does the magic of a seeming transformation from death to life. The film's ending, happy to a degree, will be a repetition of its beginning—but with a difference. There will again be a coffin, on a somewhat different stage; the audience is, once again, very much in the picture; Phroso, however, being burnt to ashes and dust, will leave the frame, opening the narrative for a young woman (the daughter) who — through the same revolving door we saw at the beginning — leaves the coffin into a bright, yet fatherless, future.

This is the story's arc; the coffin's back very literally is the entrance and exit door to and from a once again very bloody narrative of love, jealousy, rivalry, misrecognition and revenge. Immediately after the stage show the magician Phroso loses his wife Anna (Jacqueline Gadsden) to his rival, Mr. Crane (Lionel Barrymore). In a fight between Phroso and Crane the magician is paralyzed from the waist down. Crane and Phroso's wife elope, and a few months later Phroso finds his wife dead in a church, next to a newborn child. Eighteen years later we meet Phroso in East Africa, where he is called "Dead Legs" now, revered as a god by the African savages, and out for revenge on Crane, who has become an ivory trader. Maizie (Mary Nolan), whom Dead Legs takes to be Crane's and his dead wife's daughter, has become an alcoholic and prostitute, also living in East Africa. Crane is killed, and Maizie, as part of a savage African ritual, has to die as well. This is the point where Phroso, having in the meantime learnt that Maizie is, in fact, his own daughter, has to come up with a last coffin trick to let her escape.

In *West of Zanzibar* we never gaze at an attraction. From the first moment, and with only the slightest ado of a camera movement that brings the stage into view, we are the privileged audience of a (convoluted) narrative that, from the first shot to Phroso's last performance, simply unfolds in front of our eyes. In contrast to the introduction sequence in *The Show*, with its putting into perspective of displays and attractions, in *West of Zanzibar* the very moment we see the coffin and the stage we already are within a narrative. *West of Zanzibar* is, quite literally, a film about a magician and a show that lose their magic — and in a last gasp still manage to do the trick of saving a life and redeeming a villain. The show itself is not staged as an attraction, and therefore there is no gesture of undoing the magic, and no transformation is necessary, or possible, from a "cinema of attractions" to a purely narrative cinema. In the blink of an eye we move from the stage to its back — but in this seemingly unproblematic movement the stage is defined as the same kind of place as its back: the space of a narrative. What follows is a double gesture of storytelling that contrasts most strikingly with the unity of time and place that governs the two stages of *The Show*. We jump ahead in time — eighteen years, no less — and we jump away in space, to East Africa, no less. But we move and jump in the pure space and time of a story that asks for the only thing we are used to being asked for by fictional stories — in Coleridge's words: the suspension of disbelief within the frame of consistent and plausible make-believe. (This frame may, admittedly, be a bit ragged and loose in *West of Zanz-*

ibar, but within the trademark genre of a Browning film all the jealousy and attempts at murder arguably make perfect sense, or at least are what is to be expected.)

In the end, the magic, as the creation of an illusion, no longer works. Phroso tries to dupe the Africans with his coffin trick, but the answer is not the spellbound reaction of an audience to a fascinating attraction. This is confirmed, as in the beginning, by Browning's direction; the scene is torn between the daughter's hastening away and the movie's hastening ahead to the cannibalistic feast. There is no time and no need to dwell on the magician's performance, as the knots in the plot have already been undone.

What remains is another and final undoing, the revengeful undoing of magical make-believe by the natives. In the short moment of a last doubt the daughter manages to escape into a future where she will live happily ever after. But then it dawns on the natives what tricks Phroso has been playing on them. As the African chief succinctly puts it: "No believe." Phroso's show fatally aborts with the natives' insight. It's a diagnosis of the history of media reception: Even the unsuspecting spectators are now media savvy enough to not spoil their meal (i.e. their pleasure in the happy ending of a story). Phroso, the magician, has to learn it the hard way.

Afterplay: The Hand Is Faster Than the Eye (Miracles for Sale)

Tod Browning's last film, *Miracles for Sale*, is bracketed by two performances by its protagonist, Morgan, the magician. Both are instances of what is at stake throughout the movie: a constant confusion of tricks and facts transformed into a narrative of mysteries and their revelation. The movie is a whodunit among magicians and mystics, a "who killed who" of serious practitioners of make-believe and dubious true believers. Morgan is the enlightened magician *cum* detective, the movie's medium of entrapment as detection by sleight of hand.

The film's first scene confronts us with a demonstration of one of Morgan's new tricks, but it is almost a reversal of the display of a "cinema of attractions" we see in the beginning of *The Show*. It is not presented by the words and gestures of a ballyhoo, it is not "presented" at all, but rather looks like the kind of illusion in which we believe when we watch a fictional film. This first scene is, in other words, not marked as an attraction. We hear the noises of a war and we see a woman being shot into halves. We are put, in the very beginning, *in medias res*, into a scene that, at first, is not framed as being staged. In order to take this scene, the atrocious killing of a woman, at face value, we have to suspend our disbelief in almost exactly the same way we had to suspend it in Browning's films of the middle to late twenties. It is a horrid and improbable event, but everything is possible in a Browning film. We may have to actively refrain from disbelieving, but we might just as well do it. This investment into the suspension of disbelief, however, very soon turns out to have been misplaced. The atrocious murder we seemingly witness is, eponymously, nothing but a miracle for sale. It is revealed, immediately afterwards, to have been nothing but the staging of a new trick, which Morgan wants to sell to a producer. We, however, have been framed, we have believed our eyes — and have therefore been a bit embarrassingly exposed in our willingness to be taken in by the crudest kinds of make-believe.

The second performance, placed at the ending of the film, also is not exactly what it seems, although in a different way. What we experience here is another sleight of hand. This time, the revelation is threefold, and the performance is, therefore, three things at a time. It is, firstly, a performance of the "bullet catch" trick, one of the better known standards of stage magic. This first trick is, secondly, explained to the movie's (not the actual show's) audience in quite the same way in which the "beheading" trick in *The Show* was revealed to us. All this, however, then turns out to have been primarily in the service of revealing a double murderer's identity. It is no accident, either, that the whole film is a farcical whodunit.

Suspense is the kind of thrill we experience when we suspend our disbelief in order to follow a narrative; it is a thrill very different from the fascination we experience when we let ourselves be overwhelmed by the display of an attraction. What we experience in *The Show* is, in the undoing of make-believe, a transformation of our experience from the latter into the former, from display into suspense — by way of turning a magic trick of beheading into the narrative of an attempted murder. What we see in the somewhat happy ending of *West of Zanzibar* is the undoing of a completely narrative (i.e. intradiegetic) suspension of disbelief as a final gesture of poetic (as cannibalistic) justice. The natives no longer believe in what they see — and when, at this point, they reach our, the spectators,' level of insight, the narrative comes to an abrupt ending.

What we experience in *Miracles for Sales* is, again, something different. I would argue that the first and very easy move out of the magic illusion (i.e. the revelation that what we saw and took at face value in the first scene was really nothing but an illusion), is the signature movement of Tod Browning's final film. We move into and out of illusions fast — but the film is not about these revelations or the transformation of trick into narrative, as in the earlier movies; it is, rather, about the movement itself and, more exactly, about the speed with which it is performed. Morgan, the magician, explicitly gives the aesthetic formula: "The hand is faster than the eye"—which is, as we can say without any exaggeration, the formula of cinema as the pleasure of willingly believing in an illusion. (This is true on the most basic technical level: Film as an illusion only works because the projection is faster than our eye.) An illusion, we know of course, is nothing but a trick. We believe in it not because we are easily duped. We have awoken, like the Zanzibarian natives, from our naive slumber into the kind of enlightenment that takes revenge on the trickster they still believed in a moment ago. In this context it also makes perfect sense that what has to be refused—and is refused so steadfastly by Morgan exactly because he is a magician—is the belief in the supernatural. Ghosts have to be exposed as nothing but make-believe, as the wrong kind of illusionism. In *Miracles for Sale* we are shown how we heartily welcome the trickster and his tricks; we know that his miracles are for sale, but we are most glad to buy them. And we do it because we, very simply, agree to be duped and demand to be duped. And Morgan, "the famous unbeliever" (to quote again from the dialogue), teaches us to gain pleasure not so much from seriously not believing, but rather from gladly renouncing our right to suspend the disbelief in the narrative illusion. We believe in what we see because we know that we don't have to. We enjoy the trick knowing that it is a trick. And what we enjoy most, therefore, is virtuosity in the performance of the trick. (What really turns us off, on the other hand, is the attempt to seriously make us believe in apparitions.) *Miracles for Sale*, then, is not only a film that moves fast, a film that propels its *whodunit* plot and funny/romantic dialogue forward at the breakneck speed of screwball comedy, but rather a film *about* the pleasure we take from the virtuosity of performances in which "the hand is faster than the eye."

This is magic of a kind very different than in *The Show* or *West of Zanzibar*. In *The Show* we can see a reflexion on the fascination with which the audience used to gaze at the display of attractions; but we also see the transformation of such a "cinema of attractions" into the kind of narrative cinema in which we suspend our disbelief in order to get into the illusion of fiction and feel the suspense that ensues from it. In *West of Zanzibar* we see—embedded into this suspenseful illusion from the very beginning—a moment of enlightenment in which the audience reveals the illusion as a trick. *Miracles for Sale*, finally, switches to a kind of second order observation that focuses on the illusion and its undoing *at the same time* and boldly claims that the contemporary audience takes its pleasure from being in the illusion and out of it at the same moment; the final demonstration, in which the murderer is revealed by his hidden actions in a performance of magic, demonstrates that the difference between stage and backstage has collapsed—the backstage of the hidden action of magic is demonstrably on stage and the stage is shown to be the place of backstage machinations.

If one can suspect that Tod Browning had fallen from grace with the mass audience in the early years of sound cinema because his — however self-reflexive — nostalgia for a "cinema of attractions" was in discordance with the realism that had started to dominate the movies, then one must perhaps assume that with his final film, *Miracles for Sale*, he managed to get ahead of his time by now exactly reflecting and — only in this kind of second order observation — fulfilling this wish for escaping into a narrative illusion. Times had changed, not only in the profession of stage magic but also in the directing of movies. As we read in Skal and Savada's monograph *Dark Carnival*, Browning got into trouble with the representatives of the trade he portrayed: "Loew's, Inc., had received a complaint from the Pacific Coast Association of Magicians, objecting to the revelation of stage-magic techniques in the film" (Skal and Savada 203). The trouble he finally ran into with the general audience might have been trouble of a similar kind.

Notes

1. There seems little doubt that contemporary critics shared this impression. To quote a few examples from Skal and Savada: The *New York World-Telegram* on *Mark of the Vampire* (1935): "'Mark of the Vampire' emerges as an inconsequential little piece of synthetic moviemaking, which will probably go on record as the horror film to end all horror films" (307); the *New York Herald-Tribune* on *The Devil Doll* (1936): "In *The Devil-Doll*, Mr. Browning is hardly at his best" (308). Reviews of *Miracles for Sale* (1939) seem to have been a little more friendly.
2. For an examination of the relationship of Browning's movies to the *Grand Guignol* tradition, see Diekmann and Knörer.
3. The most famous example of a Tod Browning script today probably is *The Mystery of the Leaping Fish* (1916), a Sherlock Holmes persiflage harping on the detective's cocaine addiction, now available again as a bonus on the DVD edition of the F. Richard Jones–directed Douglas Fairbanks film *The Gaucho*.
4. Very often Browning received the story credit, and there is little doubt that his influence on the choice of the literary texts from which the screenplays would be adapted, and the development of the scenario, was enormous, at least at the height of his career.
5. There is a magician in *The Black Bird*, too, who is part of a variety show. He is, however, not one of the film's protagonists.
6. See also Solomon's comparison of Browning to stage magician Marvin Smith, who loved to reveal his techniques immediately after he had presented his magic deceptions (52).
7. In 2002, film reconstructionist Rick Schmidlin produced a 40-minute restoration of *Mark of the Vampire* for Turner Classic Movies, based on the surviving stills.
8. The same structure can be found in the revelation of disguises. Solomon writes, "In a number of Browning's later films with (Lon) Chaney, performed transformations lay bare the deceptive process of disguise" (56).
9. Solomon compares this to Charles Bryant's 1923 film version of *Salome*, "in which the beheading of Jokanaan takes place off-screen and the kiss of Salome is shielded from direct view" (61).

Works Cited

Cook, James W. *The Arts of Deception: Playing with Fraud in the Age of Barnum.* Cambridge, MA: Harvard University Press, 2001.

Diekmann, Stefanie, and Ekkehard Knörer. "The Spectator's Spectacle: Tod Browning's Theater." (Herzogenrath 69–78).

Gunning, Tom. "'Now You See It, Now You Don't': The Temporality of the Cinema of Attractions." *Silent Film.* Ed. Richard Abel. New Brunswick, New Jersey: Rutgers University Press, 1996, 71–84.

Herzogenrath, Bernd. *The Films of Tod Browning.* London: Black Dog Publishing, 2006.

Skal, David J., and Elias Savada. *Dark Carnival: The Secret World of Tod Browning.* New York: Anchor Books, 1995.

Solomon, Matthew. "Staging Deception: Theatrical Illusionism in Browning's Films of the 1920s." (*The Films of Tod Browning* 49–67).

In Love with a Nightmare
Disability Imagery and Fascination in The Unknown

Hioni Karamanos

> *Specular investments are central to the workings of visual imaginaries ... The eye of the viewer is directed to "read" the [image] in meaningful ways. But as with any cultural trope, the pornographic gaze, and its ideological and libidinal supports, is contradictory and oscillating (68–69).*
> — Berkeley, Kaite, *Pornography and Difference*

Tod Browning's reputation as one of Hollywood's preeminent horror filmmakers endures more than four decades after his death. His films resonate throughout popular culture with themes of shock, terror, and monstrosity. Within this spectrum, images of disability permeate his works. Yet, rarely are these motifs evaluated beyond their most transparent meanings. Characters with disabilities often appear, yet many film analyses overlook the relationship between horror and the exploitation of people with disabilities. Understanding how Browning's films both define and defy traditional notions of horror requires deeper investigation. Examining disability as a social construct, and Browning's films in relation to that process, provides a novel viewpoint. Browning's disability imagery makes creative use of disability prejudices, enhancing our understanding of their power. Browning's depictions of physical disability in *The Unknown* (1927) surpass horror to venture into the territory of fetish and fascination. The emerging field of disability studies provides a framework to explore Browning's aesthetic use of physical disability beyond reinforcing ideas of disability as horrific. Inherently interdisciplinary, disability studies fosters dynamic scholarship by exploring the social construct of disability beyond the level of an individual trait or diagnosis. In *Claiming Disability,* Simi Linton presents a concise outline:

> Disability studies takes for its subject matter not simply the variations that exist in human behavior, appearance, functioning, sensory acuity, and cognitive processing but, more crucially, the meaning we make of those variations. The field explores the critical divisions our society makes in creating the normal versus the pathological, the insider versus the outsider, or the competent citizen versus the ward of the state [2].

Disability studies challenges the construct of "normal" to augment social and theoretical analyses. In *Extraordinary Bodies: Figuring Disability in American Culture and Literature*, Rosemarie Garland-Thomson provides additional insight:

> [D]isability is a representation, a cultural interpretation of physical transformation or configuration, and a comparison of bodies that structures social relations and institutions. Disability, then, is the attribution of corporeal deviance — not so much a property of bodies as a product of cultural rules about what bodies should be or do [6].

Images of disability have varied widely over the years, but most depend on age-old myths. According to basic Western cultural constructions, disability degrades the individual. Being or becoming disabled compromises or negates personhood. From this standpoint, any individual with a disability is innately abhorrent. Thus, disability becomes a literal representation of evil.

The social construct that generates this disparaging view is identified as The Moral Model of Disability by current scholars. From this perspective, any perceived physical flaw signifies moral weakness or the consequences thereof. At the very least, the person with a disability is a perpetual victim. The supposed (and imposed) suffering of people with disabilities serves as a moral lesson and warning. Examples of characters with disabilities abound in the cinema and reflect these attitudes throughout history. From the vengeful villain whose unattractiveness motivates evil schemes, to the pitiful child whose disfigurement signals the degeneracy of its parents, characters with disabilities show audiences that moral and immoral behaviors have direct, physical consequences. This model waned through the latter part of the twentieth century as understandings of science, technology, and social responsibility began to define disability in more discrete terms. The resulting social construct, known as the Medical Model of Disability, focuses on individual defects, which must be eradicated in all humanity. Removing the stigma of abhorrence is possible if the individual becomes an inspirational figure by striving to overcome "invalid" status. However, this feat does not achieve equality. Rather, the person with a disability becomes an example of scientific and personal triumph. Viewers come to understand an essential link between normalcy and happiness. Paul Darke extrapolates these findings in his thesis *The Cinematic Construction of Physical Disability*:

Disability is, thus, in the *Medical Model*, a "personal tragedy" rather than anything to do with society or its social processes. It is pathological. Many disabled people, and the organisations that they have founded, are highly critical of such a definition as it de-socialises a condition that they perceived as being socially constructed.

In contrast to the Medical and Moral Model of Disability, a new worldview is developing. Often called the Social Model of Disability, this newest model recognizes that human beings exhibit varying degrees of functionality in life. The Social Model emphasizes human variation and the influence of social constructs. Being or becoming a person with a disability is understood through the social phenomena of environmental barriers and the stigmatization of difference. Accommodating and integrating people with disabilities in society calls for a greater appreciation of diversity.

Each model represents a distinct viewpoint upheld and expressed throughout society. The terms "moral," "medical" and "social" describe modes of thinking, not specific institutions. The Medical Model is not exclusive to laboratories and hospitals. It outlines influential attitudes about disability, as shaped by larger cultural constructs of science and medicine. Likewise, the Social Model of Disability does not reject medicine, science, or technology. Instead, it advocates changes in the philosophies behind their use. Darke explains succinctly:

> The *Social Model*'s definition of disability is based on the fact of discrimination and the social exclusion of people with impairments, grounded in the assumption that the disabled are socially constructed as abject and not the natural results of a physical limitation or difference within any given individual. [T]he *Social Model* [calls for] a form of equality that accepts difference; for [the] nexus impairment is different, but not inferior, and it is only when this factor is accepted that equalising action will be given as of right and not as charity.

Disability studies seeks to promote critical thinking on the subject of disability as a social construct. More than a specific set of physical circumstances, disability is a concept reflected in popular culture in much the same way as more widely recognized social constructs, for instance race or gender. Such thinking exposes not only stereotypes and prejudices, but also the fluidity of cultural categories. Thanks to academics and activists, a shift toward understanding disability as a social construct is mounting. For example, even the clinical handbook *Orthopaedic Examination, Evaluation, and Intervention* acquaints readers with the three major theoretical models. While it might seem that such clinical texts would have little use for engaging in social history and commentary, it further states, "[d]isability ... encompasses a wide range of issues, from very specific topics to the basic question of what it means to be human" (Dutton 140).

While a great deal of work remains, on every level of social and theoretical interaction, evidence of powerful and profound change is clear. As the Social Model gains prominence, disability studies offers the chance to evaluate and advance the place of people with disabilities in society. It also investigates representations contributing to our attitudes and perceptions. In his seminal essay "Screening Stereotypes: Images of Disabled People," Paul Longmore highlights these challenges:

> The scholarly task is to uncover the hidden history of disabled people and to raise to awareness the unconscious attitudes and values embedded in media images. The political task is to liberate disabled people from the paternalistic prejudice expressed in those images and forge a new social identity. The two are inseparable [16].

It might seem that the outdated Moral Model of Disability could continue to flourish only in extreme and intensely faith-based venues. However, most horror films continue to grant it legitimacy in the popular imagination as well. From the "mad scientist" to the inhuman "monster," such films rely on disability stereotypes to generate feelings of horror. In the introduction to *Framed: Interrogating Disability in the Media*, Ann Pointon demonstrates the power such representations still hold:

> Although cinema has developed conventions of its own, much of its treatment of disability is rooted in a culture that has for centuries used the impaired body to signify sins past, sins present, and the threat of future evil. It is easy to manipulate metaphor ... it is much less easy for people, whether they are movie-makers or shopkeepers, to connect these internalised and discomfiting images with those real disabled people who are increasingly on the streets and who expect to be treated like one of themselves [7].

The negative, exploitive nature of most portrayals is undeniable. As films characterizing people with disabilities as villains, Browning's works may appear typical. Clearly, they demonstrate the pervasiveness of the Moral Model of Disability in Browning's time. However, looking closely at Browning's framing of physically disabled characters presents more questions than answers. While Browning's films do not demonstrate an awareness of disability issues comparable to that of current activists and theorists, the Social Model of Disability offers opportunities to both analyze and appreciate Browning's work in more profound ways. By focusing on the social construction and representation of disability in Browning's films, as well as in some analyses of them, a broader sense of discourse emerges.

Browning's intense focus on the extraordinary bodies of his characters suggests a gaze prompted more by desire than disgust. Examining several key scenes from *The Unknown* reveals the depth and complexity of this gaze. Through these sequences, one glimpses ways Browning's work destabilizes stereotypes it might otherwise promote. Seeing his characters with disabilities as merely repulsive makes his work easy to dismiss. In contrast, viewing them as objects of desire and affection increases the possibilities for criticism and appreciation. Tensions between representations of "normal" and "abnormal," between "beauty" and "ugliness," are useful for evoking traditional shock responses in a horror film. Even so, they may also serve to critique and subvert boundaries between such categories. Contextualizing Browning's use of disability imagery in terms of the social construction of disability as horrific reveals much. However, evaluating Browning's depictions of disability in terms of fascination and fetishism proves more intriguing. Few would argue that distinguishing Browning's films as classics of the horror genre without mentioning disability is a disservice. At the same time, investigating his use of disability imagery without seeking to identify representations beyond horror stereotypes is equally problematic. Highlighting such themes need not re-classify Browning's films as more closely linked to pornography than horror; nonetheless, it demonstrates how tropes more erotic than horrific are often at work.

The tradition of viewing disability as a manifestation of evil is present in Browning's work, but his approach routinely flouts such categorization. In fact, Browning's use of physical disability as vital to identity keeps his work relevant. While Browning's films occupy a specific cultural and historic space, in which the Moral Model of Disability is the most prominent, current rethinking of disability as a social construct allows analysis of his films from both within and beyond those representations. Browning's films are by no means budding representations of the Social Model, but they demonstrate the importance of looking at representations of disability from a perspective more conscious of how social constructs emerge. Browning's characterizations of people with disabilities confuse normal/abnormal or good/evil dichotomies. They also illustrate aesthetic techniques of enhancing characterization through physicality. Browning's films often appear more determined to confound expectations than rely on stereotypes to hold up the plot. In *The Cinema of Isolation*, Martin F. Norden underscores a vital distinction of Browning's work: "More of interest is Browning's unwillingness to go along with the dominant curability trend—a refusal that was to characterize all his many films of disability" (83). Browning's presentation of physical disability as part of the identity of his characters sets him apart. Without including notions of cure in the representation, any sense of redemption cannot come at the expense of disability or difference. His films may still appeal to notions of disability as disquieting, but they do not go so far as to imply that normalcy—or the struggle to attain it—is necessary or noble. Characters who demonstrate incurable deviance add to the sense of villainy and pathology associated with disability, but they may also present notions of disability as identity in a way that appeals to concerns over larger social issues and constructs. To look more closely at Browning's use of disability, particularly in *The Unknown*, requires an investigation of media other than film. Historic shifts in the social construction and representation of disability at the beginning of the twentieth century, especially in terms of live entertainment, play an important role. Much of the intense fascination with the disabled body that distinguishes Browning's films stems from the American phenomenon of the freak show. Browning worked the carnival circuit prior to his filmmaking career and often made films based on stories about freak show performers. The sensationalism and exhibition that characterized freak shows pervades his films.

Browning's films are often recognized and promoted through freak motifs. However, these techniques may work as much to draw the audience in as to question and undermine assumptions. As Matthew Solomon argues in *Authorship and Film*, references to Browning's sideshow work remain enigmatic:

> [A] critical and biographical cliché that requires further interrogation.... Although this particular biographical construct informs most contemporary studies of Browning's films, it is one of many that could be applied.... Placed within a much larger complex of biographical determinants, Browning's identification with the sideshow is seen less as a series of straightforward recollections than as a self-conscious strategy for authoring Hollywood films [236].

While the oppressive and degrading nature of freak shows can scarcely be overstated, it is also important to note the construction of "otherness" that informed such displays. The significance given to physical variations differs radically from current understandings of science, humanity, and culture. Exhibitions of human "oddities" often sought to elicit a sense of wonder, awe, or even erotic titillation. Such exhibits did not present performances designed to evoke fear, disgust, or horror exclusively. For example, Rosemarie Garland-Thomson's introduction to *Freakery: Cultural Spectacles of the Extraordinary Body* notes the process of "enfreakment," a term coined by writer and photographer David Hevey. Garland-Thomson offers dramatic illustrations of how the public display of people with physical disabilities shaped a range of attitudes:

> Enfreakment emerges from cultural rituals that stylize, silence, differentiate, and distance the persons whose bodies the freak-hunters or showmen colonize and commercialize. Paradoxically, however, at the same time that enfreakment elaborately foregrounds specific bodily eccentricities, it also collapses those differences into a "freakery," a single amorphous category of corporal otherness. By constituting the freak as an icon of generalized embodied deviance, the exhibitions also simultaneously re-inscribed gender, race, sexual aberrance, ethnicity, and disability as inextricable yet particular exclusion-

ary systems legitimated by bodily variation — all represented by the single multivalent figure of the freak. Thus, what we assume to be a freak of nature was instead a freak of culture [10].

Understanding this method sheds light on Browning's methodology. Browning distinctly incorporates enfreakment — generating manifestations of aberrance with unique personal appeal. Instead of focusing solely on responses of horror, his films also depend on disability to evoke fascination. Browning's films offer a glimpse into this complex theatrical dynamic because, as a filmmaker, he works both sides of the freak show — creating and controlling the spectacle as simultaneous participant and observer. As John McCarty argues in his essay on Browning in *The Fearmakers*:

> The ghoulish plots of these and other Tod Browning films of the silent and early sound period have led to the critical conclusion that here was one fearmaker who truly let his hair down and revealed his dark side to us ... conjuring up a picture of the man as the first great twentieth century American Gothic artist and the cinematic inheritor of the mantle of Edgar Allan Poe.... [However], I see him not as a purveyor of dark themes who consistently let loose his private demons ... but as a pioneer in the craft of exploitation filmmaking, whose artistic credo rang with the call of his step-right-up carnyman career .... It's not in the submerged contents of his films where the "real" Tod Browning is to be found but in their sensational, amazingly upfront, and often taboo-breaking concepts [3–4].

Browning's use of disability imagery prompts recognition of harmful stereotyping, yet its intricacy highlights otherwise neglected aspects of disability history and presentation. Effective analysis requires more than bringing its "negative" aspects to light. Yet, themes of fetish and fascination are not necessarily "positive." Nonetheless, identifying those aspects in his filmmaking illuminates ways "difference" and "deviance" may motivate art and reveal commonly ignored social tensions. Michael Chemers notes this persistent controversy in "Le Freak, C'est Chic: The 21st Century Freak Show, Pornography of Disability or Theatre of Transgression?":

> [T]he impulse to exclude the freak show [from scholarship] is not one grounded in a sensitivity to issues confronting the marginalization of disabled persons; in fact, it is a symptom of essentialist and positivist ideologies that only further that marginalization. The omission of freaks from American theatre history unduly privileges the able-bodied performer by erasing the history of disability in performance and replacing it with the notion that *any* disabled body in performance must necessarily be the subject of degenerate exploitation, indeed of pornography. [T]his notion is grounded in an impulse to restrict the types of behavior the abnormate body should be *allowed* [303].

Such viewpoints prove the need to examine Browning's work more closely. However, applying such reasoning to re-evaluate Browning's films need not provide an excuse to render the harmfully stereotypic acceptable. Efforts to bring greater awareness to the phenomenon of freak performance must remain vigilant against re-popularizing the dehumanization of people with disabilities as a form of entertainment. While much of Browning's work demonstrates a level of familiarity with such imagery that few other horror films incorporate, the ambiguity of such motifs warrants further consideration. Instead of either celebrating or criticizing Browning's films simply because they indulge in the use of disability imagery, it is important to note the way these images contribute to Browning's legacy. The presence of continued debate and discussion shows how complex and conflicting notions of disability enhance Browning's mystique. In *Dark Carnival: The Secret World of Tod Browning*, David J. Skal and Elias Savada note the keen disparity that persists:

> [To some he was] a kindly and generous man who displayed no signs of the dark sensibility revealed in his films. But to others, he was a classic Hollywood son of a bitch with a morbid streak a mile wide, who used the film medium to indulge his unhealthy obsession with physical disability and human predation [6].

Such a statement indicates how strongly performance, perception, and enigma continue to define the legend of Browning's life and work. A classic example of the "unhealthy obsession" critique appears in *The Hollywood Professionals*. Critic Stuart Rosenthal's chapter on Browning includes the following characterization:

> He is inevitably attracted to situations of moral and sexual frustration ... [and] with ... patterns of human repulsion and attraction. What sets Browning apart is his abnormal fascination with the deformed creatures who populate his films — a fascination that is not always entirely intellectual, and one in which he takes extreme delight [9].

Unfortunately, for all their insight, critiques like Rosenthal's also reflect the assumption that attraction to people with physical disabilities is pathological. Rosenthal's discussions of Browning's work demonstrate a critical bias, which greatly dehumanizes Browning's films and characters. Rather than recognizing ways Browning's films often expand the range of worthy characters and subjects, Rosenthal determines that such representations are entirely undesirable. Instead of considering the bold, if not always flattering, representation of people with disabilities in Browning's films, Rosenthal suggests they are not even human:

> The typical Browning protagonist is a man who has been reduced to the state of an animal. In almost every instance, he displays a physical deformity that reflects the mental mutilation he has suffered at the hands of some element

of callous society.... His overwhelming psychic pain is channelled [sic] into a search for revenge that dominates him in the same manner that an instinct governs an animal's actions.... A Browning hero would never feel compulsion to symbolically relive a moment of humiliation. Instead of taking the philosophical route of subjugating himself to his frustration, [he] opts for the primitive satisfaction of striking back, converting his emotional upheaval into a source of primal strength [11–20].

While mindful of Browning's unique approach, such analyses ignore larger issues of disability and presume a completely "normal" and able-bodied audience. From this perspective, there is no choice but to view Browning's films, and the cinematic representation of people with disabilities, as gruesome spectacles worthy of little more than shame and disdain. Framing Browning's work thusly casts even greater aspersions on people with disabilities themselves, because it directly links disability, and the representation thereof, to notions of human misery and degradation. Pointon illustrates the dehumanizing effect of such assumptions:

> A case in point is the vast literature on the monster genre, in which there are assumed to be no parts of an audience who will be decoding these "monster messengers" rather differently from the producers or the non-disabled audience. Disability is rarely mentioned, except, perhaps, when the subject of Tod Browning's *Freaks* comes up, yet still the language of the discussion tends to call the disabled actors who took part "freaks" and not disabled people; they have acquired a reality as something other than human even when not in role [7].

Nevertheless, such analyses prove that Browning's films are aesthetically unmistakable. Browning's portrayals of physical disability remain etched in stark relief upon the narrative, in contrast to more traditional depictions. With such grandiose and indulgent displays of physical difference, the aura of "deviance" surrounding Browning's work suggests a very personal sense of style. This hint of private obsession continues to intrigue critics. In *The Monster Show*, David J. Skal unearths a quote from *The New York Herald-Tribune* in 1927 reflecting this sentiment: "The case of Mr. Tod Browning is rapidly approaching the pathological" (71). Oddly enough, the same might apply to the perspectives Skal highlights most in his works on Browning. Skal's diligence and attention to detail in researching Browning is unsurpassed. Without his documentation, a great deal of information on Browning would remain hopelessly obscure. However, much of Skal's biographical material tends to echo the sentiments of critics who remain content to view physical disability as purely metaphoric, rather than as a diverse representation of the human condition.

The resulting portrait of Browning's life and career often reduces its characters and imagery to the same degrading stereotypes it might otherwise question or, at least, examine in greater depth. For example, Skal distills

Browning's worldview thusly: "To Tod Browning, the ultimate image of a human being ... (is) an armless, legless bag of guts wriggling through the muck of existence" (228). Skal's commentary dutifully details and enhances Browning's reputation, but is far from exhaustive. It is still possible, especially in *The Unknown,* to locate perspectives that extend beyond such a limited view. In presenting such an unconventional story, Browning solidified his reputation as an *auteur.* His unique vision demanded exceptional actors. As was often the case in Browning films, Lon Chaney was able to bring an unmatched vitality and depth to his portrayals. Norden provides key examples in his description of their working relationship:

> Browning ... saw him as the perfect facilitator for his art. Said he of Chaney in a 1928 interview, "I'm particularly lucky in carrying out my ideas by having an artist like Lon to take on guises and disguises of the most grotesque nature. He will do anything, permit almost anything to be done to him, for the sake of his pictures'" [92].

The Unknown gave Browning and Chaney a chance to expound on the theme of the dramatic spectacle of a person with a physical disability in profound ways. Despite this novelty, critical reaction to the film remains substantially negative. For example, in a 1997 article from *The Village Voice,* reviewer Gary Dauphin quotes a review, from its original release, calling the film "an offense to every normal-minded movie-goer." Dauphin then adds, "The evaluation holds true today" (Discovery 61). Such sentiments verify that Browning's films continue to confront concepts of normalcy, and disrupt social constructs of what is desirable, as much as ever. Dauphin's remarks epitomize the standard approach to films featuring characters with disabilities. Instead of evaluating the portrayal of people with disabilities as they would any other recognizable minority, most critics focus on "abnormality" for its own sake. They assume that the meanings of such terms are timeless and concrete. In doing so, they perpetuate a view of disability as isolated and exceptional. People with disabilities remain excluded from social discourse and are presented only in extreme circumstances. The perpetuated normal/abnormal dichotomy highlighted in such reviews raises numerous questions about the continued stereotyping of people with disabilities. An evaluation declaring that all "normal-minded" moviegoers will take offense assumes a highly homogeneous audience. Regrettably, suggesting that a film stands as an affront to all that is "normal" evokes and maintains many of the same prejudices about disability supposedly warned against with such a negative review. Questioning the willingness of critics to assume the worst in Browning's representations of disability does not negate their conclusions. Indeed, to claim that such analyses appear shortsighted need not declare Browning's work free of negative stereotypes. On the contrary, Browning's films are rife with prejudices. Shock and horror often depend on the device of disability. His characters with disabilities never lead "normal" lives. However, viewing such portrayals strictly as horrific, and judging such characters as simply villainous, leaves no possibility for exploring the more creative aspects of Browning's work or for contextualizing disability as a social construct. It is this narrow approach, ignoring the social construction of disability, which leaves such reviews seeming unduly harsh and unsympathetic to the range of human diversity. While Browning's representations of physical disability depend largely on negative stereotypes, they also use such motifs to engage in broader social critiques. *The Unknown* especially demonstrates Browning's willingness to explore the tensions between "normal" and "abnormal." Furthermore, his scenarios depend on the fluidity of such constructs. By linking disability to identity in his characterizations, Browning's images of disability offer a broader spectrum of potential interpretations and reactions. Browning's films do not completely dismantle traditional stereotypes of disability, but they do reconstruct them quite creatively.

The Unknown tells the story of a performer desired for his perceived disability, who thus finds disability desirable. Browning himself devised the plot for *The Unknown*, and it is the best example of his aesthetic and fetishistic use of disability. On the one hand, it appears a sordid, exploitive drama designed to display Lon Chaney's legendary physicality. On the other hand, it stands as extreme metaphor — celebrating not only deviant desires, but also the desire of deviance. If disability were simply a shock device or shorthand representation of evil to Browning, then *The Unknown* would not exist in his repertoire. In *The Unknown*, "Alonzo the Armless" earns a living by performing as a knife thrower. The ability to appear armless brings him fame, fortune, and romance. The circus owner's daughter, Nanon (played by Joan Crawford), has an extreme phobia of male arms and is thus infatuated with Alonzo. Nanon's fetish forces Alonzo to integrate disability into his identity both onstage and off. Physical disability becomes increasingly desirable to him, especially as the plot complicates when Alonzo, unbeknownst to Nanon, kills her abusive father. The rare distinction of having a double thumb on one hand makes him easily identifiable. Only by becoming the disabled person he has pretended to be can Alonzo hope to avoid persecution and attain love. Ironically, while he is away having his arms surgically removed, Nanon falls in love and becomes engaged to the circus strongman, Malabar (played by Norman Kerry). Alonzo plans to remove his rival by sabotaging Malabar's act to tear Malabar's arms from his body. Then, in a moment of remorse, Alonzo sacrifices himself so that the couple may — perhaps — live happily ever after.

Such plot elements have the potential to delight moviegoers and theorists of all stripes. With so much to ponder, no single reading can be definitive. Nonetheless, the presentation of physical disability as socially (and erotically) desirable is noteworthy. One might argue that the story exploits disability as bizarre, strongly reinforcing the idea that people with disabilities are incapable of anything but "perverse" relationships. All the same, such a level of horror is far more sophisticated than basic disgust toward disfigurement. Shock, disgust, and pity may still emerge, but to infuse the story with notions of desire complicates boundaries between "normal" and "abnormal." If characters without physical disabilities are also "abnormal," then perceptions of with whom the audience should sympathize begin to shift. Extraordinary protagonists offer the opportunity to redefine values and categories. Norden highlights Chaney and Browning's reported aspirations:

> Chaney viewed the film mainly as his latest attempt to instill redeeming qualities into people ... considered the dregs of society. "I've tried to show that the lowliest people frequently have the highest ideals," said he. "In the lower depths when life hasn't been too pleasant for me I've always that gentleness of feeling, that compassion of an underdog for a fellow sufferer." ... Browning likewise minimized any [standard] subtext: "When I am working on a story for Chaney, I never think of the plot.... For instance, on *The Unknown* I started first only with the idea of an armless man. 'Let's see,' I thought to myself. 'What are the most startling situations for such a deformity?'" [96].

Unexpectedly indulgent displays of physical disability are the grandest attributes of *The Unknown*. As noted Chaney biographer Michael Blake points out, in *Lon Chaney: The Man Behind the Thousand Faces*, Alonzo's feet are not always Chaney's, but those of talented armless performer Peter Dismuki (195). This level of attention to detail demonstrates Browning's commitment to the presentation of exotic spectacle. Instead of minimizing shots of Alonzo performing, Browning shows him executing a variety of tasks, suggesting that armlessness is neither repulsive nor debilitating. While building up audience fascination with spectacular performance, Browning also manipulates Alonzo's act to lead the audience on. Once Alonzo has won crowds over as an inspirational figure, the audience learns that he does indeed have arms. However, instead of simply cutting to a scene with him out of costume, the intimate details of his gaff are exposed. This sequence dramatically illustrates how Browning destabilizes traditional responses to disability imagery. Removing Alonzo's costume requires taking off several layers of clothing and unfastening a complex leather corset. This forces the camera to linger on his body long enough to suitably impress — and titillate — the curious audience. Instead of exposing Alonzo's pseudo-disability like a pratfall, Browning presents it more like a striptease. The audience catches a private glimpse of him and must share in the suspense and torment brought on by his trickery.

Additional insight into the aesthetic function and importance of such a scene, particularly as a hallmark of Browning's cinematic approach, appears in Oliver Gaycken's "Tod Browning and the Monstrosity of Hollywood Style." In establishing Browning's status as a filmmaker, Gaycken draws attention to critical points of inquiry:

> Browning's works fall squarely inside classical Hollywood's definitional boundaries and can be explained in the same terms as other classical films, but, at the same time, his films challenge those boundaries numerous places and open up the Hollywood style from the inside, exposing the freakishness inherent in the classical mode [75].

Gaycken then cites the work of David Bordwell, explaining the self-referential and reflexive techniques of artistic motivation described as "baring the device." This occurs when an artistic work reveals its methods of construction. When art bares the device, spectators recognize that it cannot be a direct reflection of reality. Filmmaking can "lay bare the device" through special effects, lighting, dialogue or whatever the filmmaker may wish. This reminds the audience that they are participants in a conscious manipulation. With respect to Browning's methodology, Gaycken draws intriguing conclusions:

> What makes Browning remarkable beyond his repeated use of this device is his integration of this "disruptive" element into the fabric of his narrative system, his elevation, in other words, of deception to the level of form and his display of the trickery that is the cornerstone of cinematic storytelling. Instead of producing a classically closed text, Browning's films consistently comment on the freakish nature of cinematic illusion and thereby enable a different, more skeptical spectator.... Browning's interest in the disabled body, in the unusual body, in the boundary between the human and the animal, in, in other words, the limits of humanity is not just or simply voyeuristic, it is also heuristic, insofar as it contains an implicit critique of Hollywood's obsession with the beauty of perfect bodies, by which I mean not only the bodies of performers but also the perfect body of the classically constructed film [77–81].

Taking Gaycken's discussion a step further, one may argue that Browning's use of disability is far more than a "special effect" by which he "bares the device" of moviemaking. Continuing the idea of art that exposes its own underpinnings, disability itself becomes a device, which Browning repeatedly lays bare. For example, in exposing the intricacies of Alonzo's performance of disability, Browning "bares the device" of the freak show performer. He complicates matters further with the nexus of desire surrounding disability and its presentation. By introducing the character of Nanon, with her unabashed arm fetish, Browning also "bares the device" of fascination, making plain the otherwise suppressed or denied carnal motivations of many a freak show (or movie) attendee.

It is also worth noting, especially in examining how the "device" of disability serves the film, that Alonzo's assistant, Cojo (played by John George), is a performer of short stature. Their partnership creates a number of interesting contrasts in the representation of disability. For instance, both are professional freak performers. This calls into question the assumption that all members of a freak show are necessarily disabled, as well as the notion that physical disability alienates individuals and prevents them from having peers. Cojo is not without his critiques of Alonzo's methods. He also makes it clear that his loyalty is out of friendship rather than coercion. He is not an "inferior" character, nor does his "real" disability serve to vilify him more than Alonzo. While the presence of Cojo enhances the sense of uncanny spectacle in the film, he remains a sympathetic character — never becoming stereotypically sinister. He helps Alonzo maintain a state of armlessness for performance, and stands by him through surgery, but Cojo does nothing malicious, nor does he participate in any vengeful schemes. While Cojo literally "bares the device" of Alonzo's act, he also "bares the device" of Chaney's performance, demonstrating the range of difference possible between both freak show professionals and people with disabilities. Alonzo's armlessness represents more than a show-biz gimmick or clever disguise. Almost immediately, his "Alonzo the Armless" identity is required at all times. Moreover, once this identity makes him desirable to Nanon, her attentions become his primary motivation. Alonzo cares deeply for Nanon and wants to possess and protect her. His determination to become her champion and remain the object of her affection far outweighs any concern for his personal safety or professional standing. The depth of emotion captured by the camera compels viewers to sympathize in his quest for her devotion.

Browning's cast of characters insures a plot that decries convention even at its most sentimental. In sympathizing with Alonzo, the audience must place the "abnormal" character in the position of "hero." Malabar also vies for Nanon's affections; yet, while he appears less dramatically disfigured than Alonzo, his physique is also exotic. Even if audience sympathies ultimately lie with Nanon and Malabar as the heroic, romantic couple, they are far from "traditional" in attitude and appearance throughout the film. Although tempting to read as the "cure" for Nanon's "abnormal" arm fetish, her love for Malabar puts her in no more "conventional" a coupling than she would have been with Alonzo. With no "normal" main characters in *The Unknown*, the standard metaphorical dichotomies of good/evil as non-disabled/disabled do not apply. By infusing profound disability imagery into a classic love triangle, Browning challenges audience expectations of romance and allure from multiple angles. It is clear throughout the film that, whether or not Alonzo becomes an object of love, fear, or disgust to other characters, the camera's fascination never falters. The care and attention evident in the gaze of the lens forces the audience to identify with Alonzo. Thus, they look deeper into his character than expected. Lingering close-ups on his facial expressions and carefully staged displays of armless stunts abound. This strong sense of intimacy and familiarity elevates Alonzo's status as both hero and villain. Were disability and desire not so skillfully integrated into the plot, it would be little more than a simplistic and predictable crime drama. Only in the hands of Tod Browning could the story achieve a sustaining level of notoriety. *The Unknown* remains the subject of controversy and continues to evoke passionate reactions. Browning's incorporation of disability and the desire of difference makes *The Unknown* a unique and gripping film.

If Browning's primary intention was to establish physically disabled characters as inhuman villains and cinematic representations of pure evil, scenes of such a delicate nature would not appear in his films. As Skal and Savada note in *Dark Carnival*, film editor Basil Wrangell found Browning's work representative of a highly personal interest:

> I imagine that's why he picked those kind of subjects.... I think it was part of that streak in him because he always dealt with oddities — the misformed kind of people. I think he got a bang out of seeing those crippled characters [171].

In conclusion, the distinct physicality of Browning's characters with disabilities makes it difficult to confine discussions of his films to standard representations of disability. By using disability imagery as an aesthetic element, Browning's work expresses a distinct sensibility. Instead of adopting traditional stereotypes of disability to simplify the process of creating a horror film, Browning uses physical disability to enhance their identities. While reflecting cultural attitudes of disability as horrific, Browning's films also rely on disability imagery to evoke responses that are more complex. With the Social Model of Disability emerging now, along with disability studies as a mode of academic inquiry, greater attention to the representation of the social construct of disability is possible. From this vantage point, ways in which Browning's films both rely on and expose the prejudices of his era become clearer. Given the capacity to examine disability as a social construct, an appreciation for Browning's work within and beyond popular culture stereotypes becomes possible. Disability studies need not necessarily glorify or vilify Browning, but it does enhance means of critique. Certain aspects of *The Unknown* rely on negative stereotypes of people with disabilities to induce shock and horror. At the same time, these representations often engage reactions other than repulsion. It would be foolish to argue that Browning's films do not utilize and reinforce prejudices against disability. Furthermore, it would be equally ridiculous to imply that — by complicating and confounding traditional "horrific" representations — Browning's physically disabled characters represent a "positive" view of disability. However, scenes from *The Unknown* clearly exploit views of the disabled body from the perspective of fascination. Thus, Browning's films appear to counter notions that disability is wholly undesirable.

Defining Browning as a horror film icon through his use of physically disabled characters is not without merit. Such discussions broaden our understanding of disability as a social construct. Many contemporary critics remain content to see Browning's work as comment on the human condition through the exhibition of physical deformity. Unfortunately, this approach restricts the outlook on disability to tragic allegory. Reinforcing both the Moral and Medical Models of Disability, these perspectives confine representations of disability to the realm of frustrated metaphor. From this viewpoint, beholding characters with disabilities "degrades" us to a common level where "imperfections" cannot be ignored. Elevating the level of "abnormality" attributed to the human condition thus unites us in shared "repulsiveness." While the gratuitous displays of extraordinary bodies in *The Unknown* lend themselves to this interpretation, they also defy traditional responses of fear and pity.

Browning prompts us to challenge, and expand, the boundaries of beauty/ugliness, able/disabled, and hero/villain. Because Browning's films feature such dramatic depictions, they call for deeper contemplation. Perhaps, rather than lamenting the impossibility of "beauty," his films promote an alternative notion of what is "attractive." From this angle, Browning's aesthetic glorifies difference and reveres deviance. By infusing elements of identity and notions of desire into representations of disability, Browning's work continues to evoke not only reactions of shock and horror, but sentiments akin to those of Duchess Josiana in Victor Hugo's *The Man Who Laughs*:

> I love you, not only because you are deformed, but because you are low. I love monsters, and I love mountebanks. A lover despised, mocked, grotesque, hideous, exposed to laughter on that pillory called a theatre, has for me an extraordinary attraction. It is tasting the fruit of hell. An infamous lover, how exquisite! To taste the apple, not of Paradise, but of hell; such is my temptation. It is for that I hunger and thirst. I am that Eve, the Eve of the depths. Probably you are, unknown to yourself, a devil. I am in love with a nightmare [Book the Seventh, Chapter IV, par. 15].

Works Cited

Blake, Michael F. *Lon Chaney: The Man Behind the Thousand Faces.* New York: The Vestal Press, Ltd., 1993.

Chemers, Michael M. "Le Freak, C'est Chic: The 21st Century Freak Show, Pornography of Disability or Theatre of Transgression?" *Modern Drama* 46:2 (2003), 285–304.

Darke, Paul. *The Cinematic Construction of Physical Disability as Identified Through the Application of the Social Model of Disability to Six Indicative Films Made since 1970:* A Day in the Death of Joe Egg *(1970),* The Raging Moon *(1970),* The Elephant Man *(1980),* Whose Life Is It Anyway? *(1981),* Duet for One *(1987) and* My Left Foot *(1989)*. 1999. "Title and Contents." Last accessed August 1, 2007. <http://www.outside-centre.com/darke/paulphd/intro.htm>

Dauphin, Gary. "The Unknown." *The Village Voice.* January 28, 1997, Discovery 61.

Dutton, Mark. *Orthopaedic Examination, Evaluation, and Intervention.* New York: McGraw-Hill/Appleton & Lange, 2004.

Enns, Anthony, and Christopher R. Smit (eds.). *Screening Disability: Essays on Cinema and Disability.* New York: University Press of America, 2001.

Garland-Thomson, Rosemarie (ed.). "Introduction." *Freakery: Cultural Spectacles of the Extraordinary Body.* Rosemarie Garland-Thomson. New York: New York University Press, 1996, 1–19.

_____. *Extraordinary Bodies: Figuring Disability in American Literature and Culture.* New York: Columbia University Press, 1997.

Gaycken, Oliver. "Tod Browning and the Monstrosity of Hollywood Style." *Screening Disability: Essays on Cinema and Disability.* Eds. Anthony Enns and Christopher R. Smit. New York: University Press of America, 2001, 73–85.

Gerstner, David A., and Janet Staiger (eds.). *Authorship and Film.* New York: Routledge, 2002

Hugo, Victor. *The Man Who Laughs.* 1869. *Project Gutenberg.* Last accessed August 1, 2007. <http://www.gutenberg.net/etext/12587>

Kaite, Berkeley. *Pornography and Difference.* Indianapolis: Indiana University Press, 1995.

Linton, Simi. *Claiming Disability: Knowledge and Identity.* New York: New York University Press, 1998.

Longmore, Paul. "Screening Stereotypes: Images of Disabled People." (Enns and Smit 1–17).

McCarty, John. *The Fearmakers: The Screen's Directorial Masters of Suspense and Terror.* New York: St. Martin's Press, 1994.

Norden, Martin F. *The Cinema of Isolation.* New Brunswick, New Jersey: Rutgers University Press, 1994.

Pointon, Ann. "Part One: Cinema Portrayal — Introduction." *Framed: Interrogating Disability in the Media.* Eds. Ann Pointon and Chris Davies. London: British Film Institute, 1997, 7–9.

Rosenthal, Stuart. "Tod Browning." *The Hollywood Professionals, Volume 4: Tod Browning and Don Siegel.* New York: Tantivity Press, 1975, 9–20.

Skal, David J., and Elias Savada. *Dark Carnival: The Secret World of Tod Browning, Hollywood's Master of the Macabre.* New York: Anchor Books, 1995.

_____. *The Monster Show.* New York: Faber & Faber, 2001.

Solomon, Matthew. "Reframing a Biographical Legend: Style, European Filmmakers, and the Sideshow Cinema of Tod Browning." (Gerstner and Staiger 235–46)

Cinematic Torture Machines
Tod Browning and Masochism

LARS NOWAK

—for Katja

In Tod Browning's film *The Unknown*, a circus performer named Alonzo is desperately in love with Nanon, the female partner of his circus act, who has a strong aversion to men's arms. Alonzo hides his arms with the help of a corset, but hesitates to marry her since matrimonial intimacy would consequentially lead to his exposure. In a scene in which he discusses this problem with his assistant Cojo, Alonzo's face goes through a remarkable series of different, even opposing expressions. The series starts with a widening of the eyes that could express terror as well as enthusiasm. Alonzo then looks to Cojo, while his lips mould into a transfigured smile. Suddenly, however, his eyes are filled with tears and stare into an imaginary distance. Following this, a chuckle slowly commences and grows bigger and bigger until Alonzo bursts into an infernal laughter. All this serves to express how Alonzo gradually comes to the incredible decision to *actually* have his arms amputated. When Alonzo returns from the operation and meets Nanon to ask for her hand, his face is subjected to a change of expression that is even more radical than the one just described. The reunion begins with a close-up of Alonzo's face smiling at Nanon with tears in his eyes. Obviously, Alonzo is happy to see the girl he loves again and looks forward to marrying her, but at the same time suffers from his memories of their long separation due to the operation. Then, to Alonzo's great surprise, his rival Malabar appears on the scene. When Malabar takes Nanon into his arms, Alonzo's face twists into a hateful grimace; but whenever they look at him, Alonzo smiles again, concealing his anger. The two lovers tell Alonzo that during his absence Nanon has managed to overcome her dislike for male arms and is now planning to marry Malabar. Since this makes the sacrifice of his arms pointless, Alonzo is driven to utter despair, which he also tries to mask; but as his tension increases, his smile turns into a grotesque grin, and, finally, he breaks down, his face streaming with tears.

Alonzo is played by Lon Chaney Sr., Browning's favorite actor, with whom the notorious Hollywood director made no less than ten films. As Stuart Rosenthal has observed, the ambiguous miming, the rapid oscillation or even simultaneous expression of varying affects, that Chaney displays here is characteristic of all collaborations between Browning and Chaney (20–23).[1] What Rosenthal leaves out is that in the two scenes from *The Unknown*, the multiplicity of expressions can be reduced to a binary opposition between crying and laughing, and that generally, Chaney's face is torn between expressions of suffering and joy. The combination of these two affects in the same subject, also called algolagnia, is an essential requirement for masochism. That the roles played by Chaney are consistently masochists has already been observed by Gaylyn Studlar, who writes that "Chaney's characters inevitably emerge as willing victims, the masochistic centerpiece around whom the films' combination of sentimentality and brutality revolves" (*Mad Masquerade* 214, see also 202, 213). Among the films Studlar cites as evidence for Chaney's predilection for masochistic roles are *The Unknown*, *The Black Bird*, and *West of Zanzibar*, all of which were directed by Browning.[2] However, the representation of masochism is not restricted to those films Browning made in conjunction with Chaney. It is also present in his other films, like *The Show*, *Dracula*, and *Mark of the Vampire*, in which the masochists are played by other actors, such as John Gilbert, Dwight Frye, and Helen Chandler.[3]

Because a masochist is able to combine his suffering with pleasure, he accepts it, desires it and even brings it about himself. At first sight, some of Browning's suffering characters do not seem to fit this description. Instead, they obsessively try to avenge themselves on those they hold responsible for their suffering (Rosenthal 31–32; Garsault 43; Studlar, *Mad Masquerade* 211, 213, 232). In *The Unknown*, Alonzo tries to take revenge on Malabar by having two horses rip his arms off. Here, the revenge is exactly matched with the very grounds upon which it is founded, namely the amputation of Alonzo's own arms made useless by Malabar's taking Nanon away from him. Phroso/Dead Legs, the protagonist of *West of Zanzibar*, suffers a fate similar to that of Alonzo. He loses his wife, Anna, to Crane, and is injured so severely in a fight with his rival that he cannot move his legs anymore. His desire for revenge is not restricted to the character responsible for his misfortune but also includes this character's supposed offspring; for apart from having Crane killed by a tribe, Phroso/Dead Legs also debases Maizie, whom he believes to be Crane's daughter, in every way possible. However, in both *The Unknown* and *West of Zanzibar*, the attempt at revenge fails and is replaced by the avenger's fatal self-sacrifice. When Nanon tries to calm the horses that threaten to mutilate Malabar, Alonzo pulls her away and thus saves her life, but is consequentially trampled to death himself. After Dead Legs has learned that Maizie is actually his own daughter, he protects her from being executed by the tribe and, instead of fleeing with her, stays behind and is killed by the infuriated Africans.

Even before the failure of their plans for revenge, the protagonists of *The Unknown* and *West of Zanzibar* strive for their own suffering. Right at the beginning of *West of Zanzibar*, Phroso appears on a variety stage as a clown to be laughed at. He is especially ridiculed by a spectator who tauntingly calls him a "professor" and tries to provoke him by asking him if his female assistant, who is also his wife, has a "friend."[4] In *The Unknown*, it is Alonzo himself who wants his arms to be amputated. It is he who pursues this idea against Cojo's advice, and it is he who blackmails a surgeon into executing the amputation. The amputation, in fact, is not necessary to win Nanon over, nor to conceal Alonzo's past crimes, which include the murder of Zanzi, Nanon's father. Alonzo could have waited, as Malabar did, until Nanon was able to overcome her aversion to men's arms, and in order to hide his crimes, it would have been sufficient to amputate one of the two thumbs on his left hand that would reveal him as the culprit. Finally, in *The Show*, a revenge for John the Baptist's decapitation is not even attempted. Instead, a freak show staging of the beheading is repeated three times. It is also well known that this beheading was provoked by John the Baptist himself, just as Cock Robin, the actor playing the prophet, has not been forced into, but has consented to, the staging of the decapitation. Hence, Browning's suffering characters are also masochists insofar as they are generally responsible for their own misery.

The suffering a masochist desires and combines with pleasure is often imagined exclusively as physical pain. However, a masochist's displeasure is not always physical, but is sometimes psychological in nature. It should be clear from what I have said thus far that in Browning's films both kinds of masochistic suffering are to be found. Phroso/Dead Legs is not only derided during the variety show at the beginning of *West of Zanzibar*, but also later in the film by Crane, who explains to him that Maizie, to whom he has extended his revenge, is not Crane's daughter, but his own. There are other kinds of psychological suffering in Browning's films, such as fear, feelings of guilt, or compassion, but the most severe, which has already been mentioned, is defeat in an Oedipal rivalry, as represented in both *The Unknown* and *West of Zanzibar*. The frustrated man is played by Chaney, not only in the former, but also in the latter of these two films. Studlar has noted that this, too, was characteristic of Chaney's roles in general. According to her, Chaney was typically cast as "a man who ... is an inappropriate, inadequate match for the woman he loves," so that "disappointment in desire seems inevitable" (*Mad Masquerade* 213, see also 210).

Physical suffering in Browning's films principally takes two forms. The first one, as indicated above, is deformation. In *West of Zanzibar*, Phroso's legs are paralyzed; in *The Unknown*, Alonzo's arms are cut off; and in *The Show*, John the Baptist is beheaded. Some of these disabilities, respectively mutilations, are only staged, while others are real, and often a staged malady is nearly or even actually turned into a real one. The reader will remember that Alonzo at first only apparently, but later actually, lacks arms. Similarly, the staging of John the Baptist's decapitation is almost transformed into an actual beheading of the actor Cock Robin by the latter's rival, "the Greek." Though a physical deformation is not essentially a negative phenomenon, in Browning's films it actually *is* one, as it is accompanied by physical pain in both its staged and actual manifestation. Phroso's deformation is caused by a very painful fall, for instance, and Alonzo conceals his arms with the help of a corset which hinders his blood circulation. The second form of physical suffering particularly important in Browning's films is death itself. As I have remarked above, both *The Unknown* and *West of Zanzibar* conclude with their protagonist's death. In *West of Zanzibar*, this is already anticipated when, after his deformation, Phroso declares himself partially dead by changing his name to "Dead Legs." In *The Show*, John the Baptist continues to speak after his decapitation, but will finally die as a result of it.[5] Here, Browning's masochists even submit themselves to the death wish on which, according to the late Sigmund Freud, masochism is based ("Economic Problem" 163–64). In *The Unknown*, Alonzo's physical and psychological pains are closely intertwined. Apart from the fact that they occur simultaneously several times, and that the psychological suffering is caused by the physical one, the latter also serves as a metaphor for the former. When Alonzo collapses in front of Nanon and Malabar, as described above, he explains this breakdown by declaring that "[i]t was just something in here that stung like the lash of a whip."

Browning was not the only director of the 1920s and 1930s whose films dealt with masochism. On the contrary, masochism was a common subject in the cinema of that time. Siegfried Kracauer already considered it a typical consequence of the Germans' ambivalent attitude towards authority, as expressed in Wilhelminian and Weimar cinema (Kracauer 32–33, 122). And when, in the 1980s, psychoanalytic and feminist film theorists debated the relation between film and masochism, they drew many of their examples from the same period by referring to films by Erich von Stroheim and Josef von Sternberg (Schlüpmann; Koch; Studlar, *Realm*), as well as those starring Rudolph Valentino, John Barrymore, and Douglas Fairbanks (Hansen, "Valentino"; Hansen, *Babel*, 243–94; Studlar, *Mad Masquerade*). Regarding the kinds of masochistic suffering depicted, Browning's films are similar to, as well as different from, these other films on masochism. On the one hand, the motif of demeaning oneself by appearing on stage as a clown to be laughed at is not only used in *West of Zanzibar*, but also in *The Blue Angel* (1930) by von Sternberg, *He Who Gets Slapped* (1924) by Victor Seastrom, and *Laugh, Clown, Laugh* (1928) by Herbert Brenon.[6] On the other hand, it would be difficult to find the physical deformations Browning's masochists suffer from in other masochistic films of that era. Studlar has drawn our attention to the fact that the disfigured characters played by Chaney mark his "masculinity as profoundly different within an era that might have been fascinated with pain but nevertheless still preferred to glorify the perfect male body" (*Mad Masquerade* 215, see also 201, 248). Chaney played these physically deformed men not only in the films directed by Browning, but also in those made by other directors. However, in only a few of these films is physical deformation related to masochism. Thus, Browning's representation of masochistic suffering as bodily mutilation was clearly ahead of its time, and it took more than half a century to return in Rainer Werner Fassbinder's masochistic films *In Einem Jahr mit Dreizehn Monden* (1978) and *Berlin Alexanderplatz* (1979–80), which also "take as their initial project the subordination of the male body to physical degradation and literal dismemberment" (Silverman 216, see also 217–44).

Browning's films are not limited to a representation of masochism's phenomenological surface, but also reveal its structural logic, which is, at the same time, a subversive one.[7] As can be gathered from the examples given above, Browning's suffering characters seldom bring about their displeasure in an autonomous way, but generally have other characters inflict it upon them. Even when Alonzo puts on his painful corset, he is aided by Cojo. Hence, Browning's films do not deal with auto-aggression but with masochism proper, which requires a victim and a culprit, a servant and a master.[8] Often, the master who imposes the pain is a particularly powerful individual or a larger social group. John the Baptist's beheading is ordered by King Herod, while Salome's brother is hanged in prison. Alonzo is beaten by Zanzi, the director of the circus for which he works. Phroso/Dead Legs, as stated before, is jeered at by a theater audience and executed by an African tribe. It can be added that this execution is a punishment for his violation of the tribe's law that in the event of a man's death his wife or daughter must be killed as well. Thus, putting it in Lacanian terms, in Browning's films the pain is caused by a small other representing the big Other. Correspondingly, the two most important kinds of suffering in Browning's films, the frustration of desire within an Oedipal triangle and the disfiguration of the body, point towards the symbolic castration imposed by the big Other. According to Theodor Reik, castration is symbolized by all kinds of masochistic suffering, and sometimes even given direct expression in masochistic fantasies and, in an attenuated form, in masochistic practices (41, 56–57, 126–28, 149, 184, 227). In Browning's films, almost all deformations take the form of physical deficiencies. In *West of Zanzibar*, this deficiency is only functional in nature, as Phroso's legs are made unusable yet are not cut off. However, in *The Unknown*, Alonzo's body is not simply paralyzed but is mutilated. This is ironically made explicit by Nanon, who does not know anything about Alonzo's amputation but, upon embracing him after his return, tells him that he seems to have "lost some flesh." *The Show* draws the viewer's attention to symbolic castration's connection with primal repression, since here the detached member is the head. The sword used for the decapitation is not only an instrument of political power, but is also a signifier of paternal authority, as a similar one is a part of the uniform Salome's father dons in order to welcome Cock Robin, whom he mistakes for his returned son. Yet another aspect of symbolic castration is emphasized in *West of Zanzibar*. According to Jacques Lacan, being symbolically castrated means adopting the *non/m-du-père*, and this signifier, just as any signifier, is the murderer of the object it designates. The fact that Phroso turns his name into "Dead Legs" after having been deformed does not only anticipate the character's eventual death, but also expresses this symbolic murder.

However, Browning's masochists do not only subject themselves to the big Other's symbolic castration; they also rebel against it in several ways. For one thing, they violate the laws and attack the authorities. In *The Show*, Cock Robin has to hide from the police because he has embezzled the money of his girlfriend Lena, while John the Baptist is known to have condemned Herodes Antipas for his adultery with Herodias. In *The Unknown*, as indicated above, Alonzo commits several crimes and therefore has to hide from the police as well. He also mocks the policeman who investigates Zanzi's murder. Aside from this, Alonzo forces the surgeon to amputate his arms by way of a blackmailing letter that, like the masochistic contract, totally perverts the concept of guilt.[9] Though actually being the creditor, Alonzo takes the position of the debtor, because, unlike Shylock, the creditor of Shakespeare's *Merchant of Venice*, he does not demand a pound of flesh from his debtor but gives "some flesh" away himself.[10] In *West of Zanzibar*, Dead Legs tries to usurp the position of the tribe's magician. When this fails, he does not exactly abolish the tribe's law, but reverses it by way of his self-sacrifice; now it is not the daughter who is sacrificed for the father, but the father who sacrifices himself for the daughter.

This takes us to the next point. Deleuze has noted that masochism aims at an annulment of the father (*Coldness and Cruelty* 57–68). This annulment, too, recurs in Browning's films. It will be remembered that in *The Unknown* Alonzo kills Zanzi, who is not only Nanon's real father but also

Alonzo's symbolic father. Alonzo then usurps the paternal position by taking care of Nanon and claiming to do so on Zanzi's behalf; just as in *West of Zanzibar*, Dead Legs tries to usurp the magician's position. Though it could be objected that Alonzo's usurpation of Zanzi's role not only annuls, but also acknowledges the idea of fatherhood, this objection does not apply to Dead Legs' self-sacrifice at the end of *West of Zanzibar*. Here, the father the masochist wants to annul is not another person, but the masochist himself, since Dead Legs is Maizie's real father. This corresponds, however, to the fact that the masochist, through his suffering, wants to strike out at the father in himself (Deleuze, *Coldness and Cruelty* 60–61, 66, 99–100). From this perspective, it is also possible to solve the aforementioned contradiction between the masochism of Browning's suffering characters and their desire for revenge. If in the Oedipial struggle for Nanon and Anna, Alonzo and Phroso/Dead Legs are defeated by Malabar and Crane, the latter two assume the position of the symbolic father. Therefore, Alonzo and Phroso/Dead Legs' desire to take revenge on Malabar and Crane is also a desire to eradicate the father. Thus, Phroso/Dead Legs, the masochistic subject of *West of Zanzibar*, negates the father not only once but twice. By having the African tribe first kill Crane and then himself, he exterminates his own symbolic father as well as Maizie's real father.

In *The Unknown*, the symbolic castration is also denied by fetishizing Nanon and thus preserving the phallus that otherwise would be detached from the subject's imaginary body. While Sadism involves destruction of the fetish (Deleuze, *Coldness and Cruelty* 72–73), masochists create and use fetishes (*Coldness and Cruelty* 32–33, 72). In Sacher-Masoch, the two most important fetishes are articles of clothing and whips (*Coldness and Cruelty* 33). Textiles are fetishized in von Sternberg's masochistic films as well, while fetishized whips recur in those with Valentino (Hansen, *Babel* 285). In Browning's *The Unknown*, Nanon is fetishized by being provided with special clothing *and* a whip, as well as by having her body itself turned into a fetish. Though this masochistic fetishization is repeatedly negated by a sadistic removal of the fetishized clothing, it eventually prevails. The film opens with a circus act in which Alonzo, using only his feet, partially undresses Nanon by shooting and throwing knives at her. But this defetishization is immediately compensated for by her fetishistic posing. After the performance, even the vestural fetishes are restored as Alonzo returns the clothes he removed from her and also gives her a mantilla. This cape is jerked from Nanon's shoulders by her father, Zanzi, but after the father has been killed by Alonzo, the whip with which the former had beaten the latter reappears in Nanon's hands. At first, this happens only metaphorically when Alonzo, as remarked above, compares his frustration over Nanon to "the lash of a whip." But during the final variety act in which Nanon tortures Malabar, she drives the horses to tug at his arms with the utilization of a real whip.

The contradiction between a submission to and a subversion of the psychosexual law in which Browning's masochists are caught up helps to elucidate the way in which pleasure and pain are related to each other in masochism. This relation is not referential but causal, since the suffering is not the object of the pleasure, but rather a condition of it (Reik 79, 271). This causation is a humorous reversal of the causal relation which the psychosexual law constructs between an illegitimate pleasure and its punishment. Instead of being punished for a past pleasure, the masochist justifies his pleasure by having himself punished first (Reik 119–23; Deleuze, *Coldness and Cruelty* 87–90).

There are more subversive aspects of masochistic pleasure. Apart from its polymorphous perversity and its sterility, masochism also subverts patriarchy and the incest taboo, since it fills the position of the master with a woman who symbolizes the oral mother, and that of the servant with a man who symbolizes the son. According to Reik, "masochism as a perversion is rare among women while it certainly is the prevailing perversion among men" (214, see also 243). It is no surprise then that Richard von Krafft-Ebing, in his *Psychopathia Sexualis*, described more cases of male masochism than those of female masochism, and also named this perversion after a man's name, that of Sacher-Masoch (Silverman 189). The male masochist's partner is usually a woman, and according to Deleuze, this masochistic couple is modeled on the mother-son-dyad (*Coldness and Cruelty* 57–68).[11] In comparison, sadism generally consists of a woman's subjection to a man, which symbolizes the daughter's subjection to her father (*Coldness and Cruelty* 59–60, 67–68).

In Browning's films the sexual distribution of roles is handled in a way similar to the treatment of fetishism in *The Unknown*. Just as the fetish is alternately affirmed and negated but finally maintained, the roles of servant and master at first oscillate between the sexes but are eventually distributed in masochistic fashion. This reversal of roles does not indicate, though, that Browning's films are "sadomasochistic," as David Skal and Elias Savada have suggested (112), but that sadism and masochism struggle with each other and that this struggle ends with masochism's triumph.[12] In *The Show*, Salome, the biblical character, and Salome, the actress, are in a weaker position than John the Baptist, respectively Cock Robin, insofar as their desire for them is not reciprocated—but then the tables are turned. The former Salome avenges herself by having John the Baptist decapitated, and Cock Robin, who treated the latter Salome badly, finally throws himself at her feet and asks her forgiveness. A woman is also temporarily subjected to a man in *The Unknown* and *West of Zanzibar*. While in *West of Zanzibar* Dead Legs torments Maizie, the circus act at the beginning of *The Unknown* depicts Nanon not only being undressed but also exposed to the danger of being injured, mutilated or even killed by Alonzo. Here, the male aggressor is also linked with the father since Alonzo is assisted by Zanzi who escorts his daughter to the pedestal on which the act is staged. In *West of Zanzibar*, the aggressor is actually the father, since Maizie is Dead Legs' own daughter. However, Nanon is not actually injured, since Alonzo skillfully aims off his target, whereas his own corset causes him real pain. Besides, since both smile at each other, the situation is obviously enjoyed by both. Hence, sadism is not seriously practiced here but ridiculed from a masochistic point of view, as it is in Sacher-Masoch's fiction (Deleuze, *Coldness and Cruelty* 39–40).

In addition, *The Unknown* and *West of Zanzibar* differ from *The Show* insofar as subject and object of the sexual frustration are reversed. For here, as mentioned above, it is not a woman's desire for a man but a man's desire for a woman that remains unrequited. *The Unknown* even represents a son's frustration by his mother since Nanon shows much concern for Alonzo's well-being and therefore does not only relate to him as his symbolic daughter but also as his symbolic mother. At the end of both films the man also sacrifices his life for that of a woman. The female culprits in Browning's films also fulfill Sacher-Masoch's ideal of the masochistic mistress in which coldness and cruelty are combined with sensitivity and tenderness (*Coldness and Cruelty* 50–51). In *The Show*, the frustration of the biblical Salome's desire for John the Baptist is mirrored in the present Salome's unrequited love for Cock Robin. But while the former Salome takes cruel revenge on the prophet, the latter one saves Cock Robin from the Greek's attack and also hides him from the police. In *West of Zanzibar*, Anna deserts Phroso but is unable to tell him that she will do so. And after Phroso has been disfigured by Crane she leaves the latter as well. In *The Unknown*, Nanon adopts an ambivalent attitude towards both Alonzo and Malabar. On the one hand, she favors Malabar over Alonzo as an erotic partner and shows this very clearly to Alonzo after his return from the operation. On the other hand, she displays friendly and motherly feelings for Alonzo, as I have already pointed out. She also chooses Malabar only after a long period of aversion. Since this aversion disappears in a surprising and unmotivated manner (Garsault 44; Tesson 47), its explanation as a phobia against men's arms is easily unmasked as one of those rationalizations with which masochism often tries to dissimulate itself (Studlar, *Realm* 22, 117–20). The aversion is much better explained by the masochistic mistress's coldness. It also only disappears to be replaced by cruelty, since in the variety act towards the end of the film Nanon even, if only apparently, tortures Malabar.[13]

Having thus far focused my analysis on Browning's films *The Show*, *The*

Unknown and *West of Zanzibar*, I will now turn to *Dracula* and *Mark of the Vampire* in order to show that in these films vampirism, too, is understood as a masochistic fantasy. Here, the role of the culprit is taken by the vampires; that of the victim by the human beings. The latter are psychologically tormented by the former, because they fear being bitten and having their blood sucked out by them, and thus turned into vampires themselves. As this fear sometimes becomes a reality, the human beings also suffer physically. Being transformed into a vampire means entering a state between life and death, which, as Count Dracula himself announces with an expression of pain on his face, is even worse than dying, the second of the two forms of suffering typical of Browning's other films mentioned above.

At first sight, the subjection of the human beings to the vampires could be considered sadomasochistic as well. Rhona Berenstein, for example, reads *Dracula* as a "conflation of sadism and masochism" because the bloodsucking Count combines paternal and maternal features (238). In addition, human beings and vampires exchange their roles, since on the one hand a vampire's bite turns a human being into a vampire and on the other hand Dracula opens his arm so that Mina can drink his blood as well. There are even two aspects that seem to indicate straight sadism. First, the vampires are predominantly men, while the mortals victimized by them are mostly women. Second, the mortals' subjection is brought about by the vampires, who use hypnotism for this purpose. However, there are also female vampires and male victims in both of Browning's vampire films. In addition, as Linda Williams has argued, the male vampires themselves are feminized on the levels of both gender and sex ("Woman" 89). Finally, *Dracula* and *Mark of the Vampire* are generally not narrated from the perspective of the vampires but from that of the human beings and therefore represent fantasies of the victims, not the aggressors. The masochistic nature of these fantasies is demonstrated by a peculiar distribution of pleasure and pain between both groups. The vampires do not derive any pleasure from their bloodsucking but simply follow their survival instinct. The satisfaction of this drive prolongs a kind of existence that is referred to as being worse than death by a visibly suffering Dracula. The expression of pain on Dracula's face becomes even more severe as the Count bows down to bite Mina. Here, Dracula seems to suffer not only from his own fate, but also from the fact that he imposes it on his victims. In comparison, the human beings combine their suffering with pleasure. They do not only fear but also desire to be attacked by the vampires (Berenstein 237). This desire is only reinforced by its satisfaction, because the more the vampires' victims are turned into vampires themselves, the more they resist the measures taken by others to protect them from their persecutors. It is Renfield himself who makes his way to Dracula's castle and who does so in spite of the resistance of the local population. Even more fascinated by the vampires are the women. When Mina and Lucy (in *Dracula*), as well as Irena (in *Mark of the Vampire*), go into raptures about Dracula and Mora respectively, the expression on their faces is no less enthusiastic than that on Alonzo's face during his decision to amputate his arms. The fact that Mina and Irena's fascination induces them to break off their respective engagements proves that this fascination is an erotic one. In *Mark of the Vampire*, the vampirism is even brought about by the human beings themselves, as it is simply the result of two intradiegetic stagings here.

As Dracula and Mora are counts, the latter also being the father of the female vampire Luna, both personify the law. Therefore, the pain they inflict represents the symbolic castration, just as the bodily disfigurations in the other Browning films did. At the same time, all vampires are fetishes equipped with more fetishes (Dadoun 54–55) and therefore take the position of the masochistic mistress. The fact that they torment their victims by sucking out their blood corresponds to the infantile fear of being devoured by the oral mother, on whom, as the reader will recall, the masochistic mistress is based. Thus, while the earlier Browning films focused on masochism's phallic aspect, the vampire films complement it with the oral one.[14]

Since vampires can be deterred with the help of a crucifix, vampirism is traditionally opposed to Christian faith. However, Reik and Deleuze consider Christianity a paradigmatic instance of social masochism because it propagates the affirmation of suffering "with so much equanimity and even joy" (Reik 340). While this affirmation of pain is expected of every adherent of this religion, Christianity's masochism is most obviously exemplified by its founder Jesus Christ, by Cain and Job, his predecessors in the Old Testament, and by the Christian martyrs, ascetics, and hermits (Reik 77–78, 123–24, 137–39, 145, 340–59; *Coldness and Cruelty* 11–12, 96–100). The affinity between masochism and Christian faith is not only mirrored in von Sternberg's films (Studlar, *Realm* 150–53), but also in those by Browning. As I have repeatedly stated above, a recurring theme of *The Show* is the beheading of John the Baptist, the martyr who baptized Jesus Christ. Since John the Baptist suffered at the hands of Salome, a lascivious woman acting as his masochistic mistress, his masochism was not only social but also erotic in nature (Reik 333). In *The Show*, this eroticism is emphasized by the fact that during the staging of the decapitation, Cock Robin, who plays the prophet, flirts with several female spectators. The film also contains two direct allusions to Christ, one of them being a crucifix attached to a door in the apartment of Salome, the actress. The crucifix recurs in *The Unknown* where it hangs on a wall in Alonzo's apartment so that it is more closely associated with the masochistic character. Finally, in *West of Zanzibar*, the masochist is even identified with Christ. Phroso/Dead Legs swears his revenge on Crane in front of a statue of the Holy Mary holding the baby Jesus on her lap. Because of the paralysis in his legs he can only crawl on the floor and therefore resembles Anna's baby who lies next to him. The baby, in turn, corresponds to the infant Jesus on Mary's lap since both children have a different father than is first assumed. This mediated identification between Phroso/Dead Legs and Jesus is reinforced at the end of the film when the former, like the latter, is executed by heathens.[15] Browning's *Dracula* and *Mark of the Vampire* seem to adopt the conventional opposition between Christianity and vampirism. In both films, the human beings try to protect themselves from the vampires by carrying crucifixes and making the sign of the cross. In *Dracula*, the crucifix is particularly used by the vampire expert Van Helsing, whom Barbara Creed has called "a pillar of patriarchal Christian society" (123). The gypsies of *Mark of the Vampire* also appeal to the Virgin Mary. However, the opposition between Christianity and vampirism is subverted by the fact that both phenomena participate in masochism. This unity is made clear by the fact that the vampirism is actually not feared but desired and enjoyed by the vampire's Christian victims, which, as I have already shown, applies to Browning's vampire films as well.

The masochist exposes his suffering and his pleasure to be gazed at by the big Other whose law he transgresses (Reik 72–83, 136–46; Studlar, *Realm* 72–73), but he himself also casts a fetishistic gaze upon his mistress. Thus, both participants of the masochistic scenario are on display. At the same time, the masochist's subjection to his mistress is frequently effected by way of a roleplay in which the latter takes a ruling part and the former a degrading one (Deleuze, *Coldness and Cruelty* 10–11).[16] Masochism therefore involves display as well as masquerade, both of which connect it with theater. Masochism's theatricality is made explicit in several masochistic films of the 1920s and 1930s, in which the servant, the mistress, or both appear on an actual stage. Among these films are not only *Laugh, Clown, Laugh*, *He Who Gets Slapped*, and *The Blue Angel*, which have already been cited, or von Sternberg's *Morocco* (1930) and *Blonde Venus* (1932), but also Browning's films. As indicated above, *The Show*, *West of Zanzibar* and *The Unknown* put their masochistic scenes on the stage of a freak show, a variety theater, or a circus respectively. At the beginning of *The Unknown*, the visibility of Alonzo and Nanon's circus act is not only heightened by the fact that they are lifted from the ground on a platform but also by the fact that this platform is set in rotation. Additionally, the reunion between Alonzo, Nanon and Malabar takes place on the same variety stage that is later used for the number with the horses. Furthermore, both the amputation of Alonzo's arms and the examination of Lucy's apparently dead body in *Dracula* are carried out in an anatomical theater. During two of these theatrical demonstrations the auditorium is not really filled with, but only refers to, an audience; but in masochism the spectator is often only imagined as well (Reik 78). Finally, in *Mark of the Vampire* the whole story about vampires, as I have said above, is invented by two intradiegetic stagings.

In a modified form, the problem of masochism's relation to theater also gained access to psychoanalytic-feminist film theory, which in the 1980s not only looked at the representation of masochism in film, but also at masochism's relation to the *reception* of a film. According to Mary Ann Doane ("Masquerade" 80) and Raymond Bellour (Bergstrom 97), masochism was exclusive to female reception. This view obviously proceeded from the contradiction between Laura Mulvey's claim that classical narrative films exclude women from the position of the subject of a pleasurable gaze, and the fact that women nevertheless watch these films and therefore must take some pleasure in them. This pleasure, it was argued, could only result from a masochistic identification with the passive female characters on screen. Doane added that even melodrama could only be enjoyed in a masochistic sense by female viewers, because this genre granted the female characters their own gaze, while at the same time de-eroticizing it ("Woman's Film" 69, 77–79), and this opinion was more or less shared by E. Ann Kaplan (28) and Williams ("*Stella Dallas*" 320). The masochism inherent in female film spectatorship was criticized as a repetition of precisely that kind of pleasure to which women were generally limited in our patriarchal society.

In contrast, David Rodowick tried to demonstrate that male film reception could be masochistic as well (7–9). Referring to the analogy between the dualities of sadism/masochism and voyeurism/exhibitionism drawn in Freud's *Three Essays on the Theory of Sexuality*, he maintained that a woman's identification with a female character was only masochistic if the latter was the object of a voyeuristic male gaze. But according to Mulvey's essay "Visual Pleasure and Narrative Cinema," this voyeuristic gaze was just one of two looks men were allowed to cast at women by classical cinema, the other being fetishistic. While Mulvey connected the voyeuristic look with sadism, such a connection to another perversion was missing in the case of the fetishistic look. This gap, Rodowick suggested, could be filled with masochism. Thus, while Doane and Bellour considered masochism a female complement to the sadism of the male spectator, in Rodowick's perspective it was an alternative to this sadism for the man himself. Having already pointed out the importance of fetishism for masochism, and identified the latter perversion as a typically male phenomenon, I basically approve of Rodowick's view. However, since I did not deny that masochism can also occur in a female subject, I want to draw the reader's attention to two masochistic aspects of cinematic spectatorship that seem to be independent of the spectator's sexual identity.[17]

The first aspect concerns the relationship between pleasure and displeasure in the reception of narrative films. According to Studlar, every such film provokes a masochistic alternation between tension and relaxation in the spectator, since it constantly presents conflicts and then solves them (*Realm* 181). This affective ambiguity is especially characteristic of two particular film genres. I have already mentioned that within psychoanalytic film theory, melodramas have been accused of putting their viewers into a masochistic position. Similarly, the horror film has been described as sadomasochistic by Williams ("Film Bodies" 6, 8–9) and Berenstein (235–45), as only secondarily sadistic but primarily masochistic by Carol Clover (18–19, 61–62, 179, 209–30), and as completely masochistic by Creed (131). For lack of space, I cannot discuss the rather complicated reasons all four authors have given for their respective views, so I must settle for offering a much simpler justification for the claim that both genres in question address masochistic spectators. Both genres evoke unease (sadness in the case of the melodrama, fear and disgust in the case of the horror film), and at the same time are enjoyed by their fans (which in the case of the melodrama are primarily women, but in the case of the horror film are mostly men).

The other masochistic aspect of film reception that, in my view, includes both sexes is connected to the relation between activity and passivity in the cinematic apparatus as such, and can be revealed by amending two widely shared but actually inappropriate beliefs. On the one hand, we must discard the idea that a masochist is a completely passive object. Actually, masochism is a paradoxical combination not only of pleasure and displeasure, but also of activity and passivity. The masochist is passive only in a situation he has actively desired and brought about himself, because it is he who looks for, chooses, educates, instructs, and fetishizes his mistress (Reik 84, 86, 90–91; Deleuze, *Coldness and Cruelty* 18–19, 20–22, 32–33; Smirnoff 666–70; Žižek 92).[18] Masochism is therefore closer to auto-aggression, its origin, than is generally believed. On the other hand, we should abandon the assumption that watching is an entirely active phenomenon, because it really is, as Dennis Giles has put it, "as much an action as a passion" (38). It appears active only in comparison to being watched. However, if we compare it to acting, its passivity is revealed instead (Žižek 73–74). Lacan has argued that this passivity exists on both the physical and the psychological level. Physically, the beam of light connecting the perceived object with the perceiving eye is not cast on the object by the eye but runs from the former to the latter (94). Psychologically, the looking is not controlled by the viewer but by the world that is being viewed, as there are certain objects that attract the subject's eye and others that repel it (75–76, 92, 96, 107). Hence, seeing is not so different from hearing, whose passive character is already made clear by the fact that the ear cannot even be opened and closed at will. According to Laplanche, the paradigmatic example of the passivity of seeing and hearing is the primal scene in which a child is not actively spying on his or her parents' sexual intercourse but is passively overwhelmed by the visual and auditory indices of this parental activity (172–73).

This masochistic combination of passivity and activity also applies to that instance of audio-visual perception that is cinematic reception, as has convincingly been argued by Studlar: "The cinematic spectator passively surrenders to the filmic object of desire in much the same way that the masochist surrenders to his/her object of desire. But like the masochist, the spectator's passive position masks activity" (*Realm* 192). The cinemagoer is active insofar as he is usually not forced to go to the movies but decides to do so himself, and as it is he who gives meanings to the images and sounds he perceives there (*Realm* 183). However, he is passive insofar as these images and sounds are presented to him by the film (*Realm* 183), which, by way of selecting, ordering and combining these sensory elements in a particular way, controls his seeing and hearing to a degree even higher than the world outside the cinema does. There are certain aspects of the cinematic apparatus and certain codes of classical narrative cinema, such as the central perspective or continuity editing, that provide the film recipient with the illusion of assuming a transcendental position. But actually, by entering a film theater, the subject gives up a large part of his perceptive control that might still be left for him in his everyday life, and he agrees to this surrender of control by purchasing a ticket, just as the masochistic subject agrees to the subjection to his mistress/her master by signing the contract with her/him (*Realm* 181–82).

Studlar already developed these ideas on the affinity between film reception and masochism in her early book *In the Realm of Pleasure*, which was primarily concerned with the representation of masochism in von Sternberg's films with Marlene Dietrich. However, her findings about the masochism represented in films and that experienced in film reception remained rather unconnected. This might have been different if Studlar had come back to her considerations of the masochistic nature of film reception in her later studies on Chaney's masochistic films. The masochism represented in *The Unknown*, for instance, which Chaney made with Browning, can be regarded as a reflection of the masochism inherent in their own reception, in the reception of horror films and melodramas (the two genres which were characterized as more masochistic than others, and which Browning's films are generally subsumed in), and in film reception in general.[19]

There are two reasons for this. First, when pointing out the revelation of masochism's theatrical nature in Browning's films, I suggested that both partners of the masochistic couple behaved like actors. However, in *The Unknown*, as well as in *The Show*, the position of the masochistic subject is not really taken by an intradiegetic actor, since in these films the masquerading generally characteristic of masochism also includes the masochist's suffering. Instead, the real masochistic subject is an intradiegetic *spectator*, who suffers from watching the actor's staged suffering and yet does not stop looking and thus obviously takes some pleasure in it. In *The Show*, Cock Robin does not really suffer because, as indicated above, his beheading as John the Baptist is only staged. But the patrons of the freak show who watch this execution do so with actual terror. Likewise, in *The Unknown*, Malabar is not really tormented during the variety act and its rehearsal as long as the horses only *seem* to pull at his arms. However, Alonzo, who is placed at the edge of the stage but remains invisible to the visitors of the variety theater, and who, like they, only watches Malabar and Nanon's act, is almost killed by his jealousy of the rival. Second, the masochistic stage performances make use of mechanical apparatuses. Since these apparatuses help to evoke the masochistic mixture of pain and pleasure in the intradiegetic spectators, they serve as torture machines turned into desiring-machines, while at the same time contributing to the production of the performances' illusions and therefore corresponding to the machines of cinema, the camera and the projector. In *The Show*, the staging of the decapitation is achieved by lowering the execution block with the help of a pedal that allows Cock Robin to avoid contact with the sword. The variety act in *The Unknown* is already a mechanical concatenation in itself, because the masochistic couple consisting of Nanon and Malabar is supplemented by three additional elements: the two horses, Alonzo, and a drummer who controls the rhythm of Nanon's whip lashes. Apart from these five living parts, the variety act also includes an actual machine, in that the horses are not actually tugging at Malabar's arms because they are placed on conveyer belts whose motions neutralize their own. This "S&M machinery," as Hans Schmid has called this structure (96), has been compared by Skal and Savada to *The Unknown* itself: "Like the stage contraption that kills Chaney at the film's conclusion, *The Unknown* itself is a perfectly constructed torture machine" (112). However, since the mechanism in question produces an illusion of motion by way of an actual revolution which drives two belts, just as a film camera and a film projector effect such an illusion by moving a film strip with the help of a few revolving parts, it could also be compared to the cinematic apparatus, as such. Correspondingly, the man at the control lever of the belts is an analogue to the cameraman and the projectionist.[20] Thus, Browning's films do not only depict masochism's phenomenological surface and illuminate its deeper structure, but also reveal the masochistic nature of cinematic spectatorship itself. And they did so more than half a century before Studlar would point to this cinematic masochism by means of theoretical discourse.

Notes

1. Chaney's ambiguous miming can be regarded as an intensive series, which is one of the three signs of the affection-image, a concept Gilles Deleuze developed in his film theory (*Cinema 1* 87–122).
2. Apart from Chaney's characters, the actor himself has been considered a masochist because he specialized in creating painful make-ups to depict his physically deformed characters (Stein 158, 161; Studlar, *Mad Masquerade* 204, 245–246; Morris). As the "mentor" of Chaney's own masochism, Gary Morris has identified nobody other than Browning.
3. Since my space is limited here I will restrict the following analysis to *The Unknown*, *West of Zanzibar*, *The Show*, *Dracula*, and *Mark of the Vampire*.
4. The quotes are taken from intertitles in *West of Zanzibar*. In the remainder of this text, all unidentified citations are from the film currently discussed.
5. Though this beheading is only staged, and the Greek's attempt to transform it into a real one fails, it is mirrored in the actual hanging of the brother of the actress who plays Salome (and who also shares her name).
6. In the two last-mentioned films, the clown is again played by Chaney.
7. To the phenomenological aspects already discussed, another one could be added. Jean-Marie Sabatier has noted that Browning's films are characterized by an unnatural slowness (86). This applies to many of their elements. Browning's characters only move very slowly or are frozen in a pose. The camera remains static for most of the time. The narration is slow, repetitive and circular. The flow of action-images is frequently interrupted by the affection-images mentioned at the beginning of this article. In *The Unknown*, which, according to Sabatier, is a particularly good example for this tendency of Browning's films (86), both men subordinated by Nanon are limited in their freedom of movement. Alonzo is constricted by his corset, while Malabar is tied up to the horses that Alonzo will use for his revenge. In *The Show*, John the Baptist's beheading is not only presented four times, but also frozen in a photograph. Reik has argued that masochism, too, is characterized by delay, freezing, suspense, and repetition (59–71, 67, 69, 115–118, 335–342). Deleuze adopted this view in his early theory on masochism (*Coldness and Cruelty* 33–34), and still adhered to it in his later remarks on this perversion (Deleuze and Guattari, *Thousand Plateaus* 155), though he gave up most of the other elements of his first approach. Masochism's close relation to immobility is already indicated by the masochist's fondness for being tied up. In Leopold von Sacher-Masoch's writings, movement is even stopped in a very similar way as in *The Show*—namely, by its being captured in sculptures and paintings.
8. Auto-aggression can be considered the origin of masochism, as it has been, in various ways, by Freud ("Instincts" 127–128), Reik (171–186) and Jean Laplanche (145–173); but it is not exactly the same.
9. On the masochistic contract, see Deleuze, *Coldness and Cruelty* 18–19, 20–21, 65–66, 75, 91–102; Smirnoff.
10. It can be added that this subversion of the law is already anticipated by the surgeon himself, who can be blackmailed due to his own conflict with the law. Thus, the transgression of the law by the law itself, which the masochist, like any pervert, wants to provoke (Juranville 261), seems to have already taken place here.
11. To be more precise, Deleuze distinguishes between three kinds of the mother, granting the oral one the greatest importance. In this he agrees with Reik, who already traced the masochistic mistress back to the oral mother (207, 209–210, 226–229).
12. Likewise, the Greek in *The Show* and Crane in *West of Zanzibar* are sadists who enjoy inflicting pain on others (and who, by the way, are both played by Lionel Barrymore, just as the masochists are often played by Chaney). The Greek, who even shares his name with the sadist in Sacher-Masoch's novel *Venus in Furs* (the most important literary source for the logic of masochism), does not only try to transform Cock Robin's staged beheading into a real one, but also anticipates this transformation in a daydream in which a photograph of the beheading is set in motion. This underlines his sadistic nature because, just as masochism is characterized by slowness and immobility, mobility and rapidity are prominent features of sadism (Deleuze, *Coldness and Cruelty* 73). However, though Browning's sadists are the suffering char-

acters' rivals, they are relegated to a marginal position — namely, a position subordinate to the masochistic mistress. In *The Show*, this subordination is expressed by the fact that the Greek's attempt to kill Cock Robin is prevented by Salome. Deleuze has demonstrated on a general level that there is no such thing as "sadomasochism" that would unite sadism and masochism and allow an easy transformation between both perversions (*Coldness and Cruelty* 37–46).

13. The masochistic nature of this variety act is also alluded to by the fact that the raised chair upon which Nanon is placed here bears the letter "M," which is not only the first letter of the name "Malabar" but also of the term "masochism."

14. The oral aspect is not completely absent from the earlier films. *West of Zanzibar* confronts the viewer with an even more intense form of oral aggression, since the members of Dead Legs' gang call the Africans living nearby "cannibals." However, this alleged cannibalism is not directly related to any of the sufferings presented in this film.

15. The crucifixes and the sculpture of the Virgin Mary do not only link Browning's masochists to Christianity, but, like the photograph of John the Baptist's beheading in *The Show*, they are also static representations that effect a masochistic immobilization.

16. Often the masochist is degraded by putting himself into a position of minority, such as that of a child or an animal. On becoming minoritarian in Browning's films, compare my essay "Different wiederholte Differenzen."

17. Whenever in the following paragraphs male pronouns are used to refer to the film spectator, both sexes are implied.

18. Since this manipulation of the mistress by the male masochist still serves the latter's subjugation to the former, it does not contradict masochism's anti-patriarchal nature. Furthermore, except for the fetishization, a female masochist creates her master as well.

19. While in earlier times Browning's films were usually identified as horror films (Seguin 45–46, 49, 51, 94; Sabatier 81–87), they are now often classified as melodramas (Viviani 46; Lenne; Delorme)

20. A third apparatus appears in *West of Zanzibar*. Here, the illusory transformations between living women and skeletons are effected with the help of a magic coffin that corresponds to the cinematic machines for two reasons. Just as the apparatus in *The Unknown*, it includes a revolving mechanism that allows its inner part to be turned. And like the cinematic substitution trick, it produces the illusion of transformation by way of a substitution. However, watching the coffin trick is not really a masochistic experience.

Works Cited

Berenstein, Rhona J. "Spectatorship-as-Drag: The Act of Viewing and Classic Horror Cinema." (Williams *Viewing Positions* 231–269).
Bergstrom, Janet. "Alternation, Segmentation, Hypnosis: Interview with Raymond Bellour." *Camera Obscura* 3–4 (Summer 1979). 70–103.
Clover, Carol J. *Men, Women, and Chain Saws: Gender in the Modern Horror Film*. Princeton: Princeton University Press, 1992.
Cohan, Steven, and Ina Rae Hark (eds.). *Screening the Male: Exploring Masculinities in Hollywood Cinema*. London/New York: Routledge, 1993.
Creed, Barbara. "Dark Desires: Male Masochism in the Horror Film." (Cohan and Hark 118–33).
Dadoun, Roger. "Fetishism in the Horror Film." (Donald 39–61).
Deleuze, Gilles. *Cinema 1: The Movement Image*. Trans. Hugh Tomlinson and B. Habberjam. Minneapolis: University of Minnesota Press, 1986.
Deleuze, Gilles, and Leopold von Sacher-Masoch. *Masochism: Coldness and Cruelty — Venus in Furs*. Trans. Jean McNeil. New York: Zone, 1991.
Deleuze, Gilles, and Félix Guattari. *A Thousand Plateaus: Capitalism and Schizophrenia*. Trans. B. Massumi. Minneapolis and London: University of Minnesota Press, 1993.
Delorme, Stéphane. "Corps et Mélodrame." *Cahiers du Cinéma* 550 (October 2000), 78–81.

Doane, Mary Ann. "Film and the Masquerade: Theorizing the Female Spectator." *Screen* vol. 23, no. 3–4 (September–October 1982), 74–87.
Doane, Mary Ann, Linda Williams and Patricia Mellencamp (eds.). *Re-Vision: Essays in Feminist Film Criticism*. Los Angeles: AFI/University Publications of America, 1984.
_____. "The 'Woman's Film': Possession and Address." (Doane, Williams and Mellencamp 67–82).
Donald, James (ed.). *Fantasy and the Cinema*. London: BFI, 1989.
Freud, Sigmund. "The Economic Problem of Masochism." *The Standard Edition of the Complete Psychological Works of Sigmund Freud*, vol. 19. London: Hogarth Press/Institute of Psycho-Analysis, 1961, 157–70.
_____. "Instincts and their Vicissitudes." *The Standard Edition of the Complete Psychological Works of Sigmund Freud*, vol. 14. London: Hogarth Press/Institute of Psycho-Analysis, 1963, 111–40.
Garsault, Alain. "Tod Browning: à la Recherche de la Réalité." *Positif* 208–209 (July–August 1978), 41–45.
Giles, Dennis. "Conditions of Pleasure in Horror Cinema." (Grant 38–52).
Grant, Barry Keith (ed.). *Planks of Reason: Essays on the Horror Film*. Metuchen/London: Scarecrow, 1984.
Hansen, Miriam. "Pleasure, Ambivalence, Identification: Valentino and Female Spectatorship." *Cinema Journal* 25.4 (Summer 1986), 6–32.
_____. *Babel and Babylon: Spectatorship in American Silent Film*. Cambridge/London: Harvard University Press, 1991.
Juranville, Alain. *Lacan et la Philosophie*. Paris: PUF, 1988.
Kaplan, E. Ann. *Woman and Film: Both Sides of the Camera*. New York/London: Methuen, 1983.
Koch, Gertrud. "Between Two Worlds: Von Sternberg's *The Blue Angel*." (Rentschler 60–72).
Kracauer, Siegfried. *From Caligari to Hitler: A Psychological History of the German Film*. Princeton: Princeton University Press, 1974.
Lacan, Jacques. *The Four Fundamental Concepts of Psychoanalysis*. New York: Norton, 1988.
Laplanche, Jean. *Vie et Mort en Psychanalyse*. Paris: Flammarion, 1970.
Lenne, Gerard. "Mélodrame et Illusion chez Tod Browning." *Positif* 476 (October 2000), 86–94.
Nowak, Lars. "Different wiederholte Differenzen: Zur filmischen Praxis von Tod Browning." *Wenn sonst nichts klappt: Wiederholung wiederholen*. Eds. Sabeth Buchmann et al. Hamburg/Berlin: Material-Verlag/b-books, 2005, 258–72.
Reik, Theodor. *Masochism in Modern Man*. New York: Grove, 1957.
Rentschler, Eric (ed.). *German Film and Literature: Adaptations and Transformations*. New York/London: Methuen, 1986.
Rodowick, David Norman. "The Difficulty of Difference." *Wide Angle* 5.1 (1982), 4–15.
Rosenthal, Stuart. "Tod Browning." *The Hollywood Professionals*, vol. 4. Ed. Peter Cowie. New York: Barnes, 1975.
Roud, Richard (ed.). *Cinema: A Critical Dictionary, Vol. 1—Aldrich to King*. London: Secker & Warburg, 1980.
Sabatier, Jean-Marie. *Les Classiques du Cinéma Fantastique*. Paris: Balland, 1973.
Schlüpmann, Heide. "Queen Kelly." *Frauen und Film* 39 (December 1985), 40–48.
Schmid, Hans. "Children of the Night: Das Kino des Tod Browning." (Stevenson 84–104).
Seguin, Louis. "Pour un Catalogue du Fantastique." *Cinéma 56* 2.7 (November 1955), 45–51, 94–95.
Silverman, Kaja. *Male Subjectivity at the Margins*. New York: Routledge, 1992.
Skal, David J., and Elias Savada. *Dark Carnival: The Secret World of Tod Browning, Hollywood's Master of the Macabre*. New York: Anchor Books/Doubleday, 1995.
Smirnoff, Victor. "The Masochistic Contract." *International Journal of Psycho-Analysis* 50 (1969), 665–71.
Stein, Elliott. "Tod Browning." (Roud 155–66).
Stevenson, Jack (ed.). *Tod Browning's Freaks*. Munich: Belleville, 1997.

Studlar, Gaylyn. *In the Realm of Pleasure: Von Sternberg, Dietrich, and the Masochistic Aesthetic.* Urbana/Chicago: University of Illinois Press, 1988.

_____. *This Mad Masquerade: Stardom and Masculinity in the Jazz Age.* New York: Columbia University Press, 1996.

Tesson, Charles. "Le Monstrueux Sentiment de l'Espèce Humaine." *Trafic* 8 (Autumn 1993), 39–63.

Viviani, Christian. "Lon Chaney ou la Politique de l'Acteur." *Positif* 208–209 (July–August 1978), 46–53.

Williams, Linda. "When the Woman Looks." *Re-Vision: Essays in Feminist Film Criticism.* Eds. Linda Williams, Mary Ann Doane and Patricia Mellencamp. Los Angeles: AFI/University Publications of America, 1984, 83–99.

_____. "'Something Else Besides a Mother': *Stella Dallas* and the Maternal Melodrama." *Home Is Where the Heart Is: Studies in Melodrama and the Woman's Film.* Ed. Christine Gledhill. London: BFI, 1987, 299–325.

_____. "Film Bodies: Gender, Genre and Excess." *Film Quarterly* 44.4 (Summer 1991), 2–13.

_____ (ed.). *Viewing Positions: Ways of Seeing Film.* New Brunswick, New Jersey: Rutgers University Press, 1995.

Žižek, Slavoj. *The Metastases of Enjoyment: Six Essays on Woman and Causality.* London: Verso, 1994.

Shaking an Elephant
Sound, Space and Suspense
in The Unholy Three

MICHAEL LAWRENCE

The Unholy Three, Tod Browning's "comeback" picture of 1925, his first film for MGM, his first collaboration with Lon Chaney, and the first of his works to focus on circus or sideshow performers, was based on the best-selling novel from 1917 by Clarence Aaron "Tod" Robbins (the author of "Spurs," the short story on which Browning based his 1932 film *Freaks*), which had been languishing in Hollywood for several years. Browning's film is both grotesquely sinister and strangely sentimental, concerned as it is with the eventual redemption of the central character, played by Chaney, which leads to the kind of climactic and masochistic renunciation Gaylyn Studlar has argued characterizes the majority of Chaney's most celebrated roles (214). Vivian Sobchack suggests that Browning's film combines aspects of his "crime melodramas" with those of the "bizarre melodramas" for which he is more often remembered (25). Indeed, Georges Sadoul called *The Unholy Three* "one of the most bizarre films in the history of the cinema" (375). *The Unholy Three*, then, is one of the earlier works of Browning's to demonstrate how, as his biographers David J. Skal and Elias Savada put it, he "almost single-handedly ... would push the envelope of the weirdly impossible to its acceptable outer limits in the commercial studio system of the 1920s" (96–97).

The film focuses on the nefarious exploits of a triumvirate of sideshow perfomers: Professor Echo, a ventriloquist (Lon Chaney); Hercules, a strongman (Victor McGlaglen); and Tweedledee, a midget "twenty years old and twenty inches tall" (Harry Earles). After the sideshow is closed by the police (following Tweedledee's violent assault of a child), they set themselves up as "the Unholy Three," disguising themselves as, respectively, Mrs. O'Grady, an elderly pet-store proprietress, her son-in-law, and her baby grandson, Little Willie. Echo, masquerading as Mother O'Grady, uses his voice-throwing skills to sell customers "talking" parrots, and then, with "Little Willie" in tow, visits the birds in their new homes when their owners complain that the parrots have refused to talk. Having cased the properties, the Unholy Three then return in the middle of the night to rob them. The success of their operation is jeopardized only by the growing discord between the three thieves, and from Echo's suspicions concerning the relationship between his pickpocket girlfriend Rosie (Mae Busch), who knows all about the racket, and the pet store clerk (and the gang's "boob") Hector (Matt Moore), who knows nothing. After Tweedledee and Hercules murder a rich gentleman who surprises them during a burglary, and Echo discovers Rosie has agreed to marry Hector, the Unholy Three decide to plant some stolen rubies in Hector's rooms to incriminate him for the murder, and then leave the city, taking with them (and against her will) Rosie, as well as a giant gorilla (actually a chimpanzee.) Rosie eventually persuades Echo to return to the city to save Hector, whose death by electric chair is imminent. Hercules, meanwhile, tries to persuade Rosie to run away with him, but is overheard by Tweedledee. In the struggle that ensues, Hercules strangles Tweedledee and then is himself killed by the gorilla. Echo confesses all in court, and both he and Hector are released. Echo then sends Rosie, who had promised to stay with him if he saved Hector, to be with her true love, and returns to performing with his dummy, Nemo.

The Unholy Three was immediately, and perhaps unexpectedly, popular, so that MGM made this low-budget crime melodrama a high-profile release for the Summer of 1925. The film's worldwide gross reached $704,000, and its success led MGM to put Browning under contract. Contemporary responses to the film, however strange it may seem now, praised its realism: the review in the *New York Times* stated that "(there) is nothing ludicrous or slap-stick about a single scene. It all seems plausible, and the way in which the story is worked out, with the possible exception of the introducing of a giant gorilla, is a credit to the director." The film's impression of plausibility no doubt contributed to the effect most commonly noted in the reviews of the time, that of the film's achievements in generating suspense. The *New York Herald Tribune* called *The Unholy Three* "the most exciting and terrifying of all screen thrillers." *Moving Picture World* thought it "one of the most unusual and powerfully gripping stories ever unfolded on the screen." *Motion Picture Magazine* praised its "vivid surprises and overpowering suspense." The *New York Times*, which included it in its Ten Best Films of the Year, thought it "a picture that teems with surprises and one in which the suspense is kept as taut as the string of a bow." Stuart Rosenthal and Judith M. Kass, in their 1975 study of the director, suggest that *The Unholy Three* is one of only two films in which Browning sought to develop suspense (50–51). It is this aspect of the film which interests me here. In 1925 the reviewer for *Picture Play* claimed never to have seen "suspense so deliberate and terrifying," adding, "Usually even the best pictures will have dull moments when the man three rows back of you with a cough suddenly becomes an annoyance, but in this picture a school of whooping cough patients could scarcely be noticed."

It is significant that the critic describes the film's achievement in suspense by referring to the sounds typically heard in the space of the movie theater, since *The Unholy Three* is, above all, concerned with characters hearing, listening to, and noticing noises; with, in other words, characters' aural and audible behavior, and, specifically, their auditory experience of space. Indeed, while *The Unholy Three* repeatedly presents scenes in which characters eavesdrop on one another's private conversations, narrative suspense in the film also depends to an unusually high degree upon characters hearing and listening to, and interpreting and responding to, various non-vocal noises made by things (for example, a bird cage falling to the floor, or a doll being knocked off its shelf, or, in a sequence of exquisite suspense, the peculiar rattling noise made by Tweedledee's — or, rather, Little Willie's — toy elephant).

In this article I consider the representation of sound and space in Browning's *The Unholy Three*, the relation between scenes of listening (or hearing) and suspense, and audiences' auditory experiences in movie theaters in 1925, before the transition to synchronized sound film. I then look at (or rather listen to) the "all-talking" remake of *The Unholy Three* directed by Jack Conway in 1930, released towards the end of the period of transition. Robin Blyn has previously examined the significance of ventriloquism in Browning's film in relation to popular cinema's response to the emergent technology of recorded sound, specifically the human voice. She argues that *The Unholy Three*, concerned as much with "*trompe l'oreille*" (trick of the ear) as with visual deception, exemplifies the "cinema of sound attractions" of the years immediately before and during the transition to sound (119). The present essay addresses how non-vocal sound effects contribute to the tricking of the spectator-listeners' ears during the same period by comparing Browning's film with its sound remake (which Blyn does only briefly).

As noted by *Film Daily* (reviewing the remake in 1930), "many of the dramatic incidents depend on audible effects" (cited in Crafton, 325). The two versions of *The Unholy Three* will here be examined in order to think about the representation of narrative sound, of listening to and hearing sound in specific spaces, *before* and *after* the arrival of the pre-recorded soundtrack, or before what Steve Neale calls "the standardization, through mechanical and electronic recording and reproduction, of the aural address of mainstream film" (91). I address, then, the different ways that auditory experience (hearing, listening to, understanding, and responding to various non-vocal sounds and noises) functions in the two versions of *The Unholy Three* in relation to space, both the space presented in the narrative itself, and the space of the theater in which the screenings took place. The differences between Browning's "silent" film and Conway's "all-talking" remake encourage a consideration of the relationship between listening, hearing and spectatorship, and spectators' experience of "dramatic incidents" (which) depend on audible effects" in cinemas before and during the transition to sound.

The following analysis, then, considers what Gianluca Sergi has called "the virtually unknown figure of the spectator as listener" (121). Elisabeth Weis has suggested that listening is "a neglected aspect of the compelling connection between audiences and films," and, moreover, that "the narrative foregrounding of scenes of listening raises in a reflexive manner issues to do with the nature of the medium itself and with our experience of it" (79). Many times during *The Unholy Three* we are presented with examples of the eavesdropping scenarios Weis describes as "conversations overheard in adjacent rooms or spaces, particularly by jealous or paranoid characters" (84). I am more interested, however, in those scenes in which characters gain (or attempt to gain) knowledge (and, with it, power) in a similar way — but in relation to noises rather than voices — and how such scenes raise issues to do with the nature of the medium during the transition, and after the arrival of the prerecorded "sound effect."

Many film historians have examined the role of sound in early and "silent" cinema. As James M. Scott reminds us, "... though the screen was silent the theater was not" (124). Miriam Hansen has counselled that when considering "silent" cinema we must address "the mediation of the image on the screen by exhibitors or by personnel present in the theatre — lecturers, musicians, or sound-effect specialists," how, in other words, "(early) exhibition still claimed the singularity of a live performance" (42–43). Similarly, Andre Gaudreault has described how sound was thus "actualized anew for each performance" (275). James Lastra, going further, suggests that "live" sound produced in the theater "functioned as a mediating device between the impersonality of the mass-produced film and the particular screening situation" (106). It is the "actualization" of a film narrative's non-verbal and non-musical noises that interests me here, particularly given the presence of so many "dramatic incidents (which) depend on audible effects" in both versions of *The Unholy Three*.

James M. Scott has noted how "effects panels on some of the picture-palace organs could generate a repertoire of sounds almost as elaborate as the studio noise of the 1930s" (124). Raymond Fielding has provided a vivid description of the available sound effects during this time:

> Sound effects of a variety of sorts also were introduced regularly into early motion picture exhibition. Some of these were generated by elaborate organs or special effects machines such as the Noiseograph, the Dramagraph, the Kinematophone, the Soundograph, and the Excelsior Sound Effect Cabinet, and from whose keyboards and associated equipment came galloping horses ... mockingbird calls, tugboat whistles, auto horns ... marching feet, gun shots, tom-toms, thunder ... castanets, frog croaks ... tambourines, telephone bells, glass crashes, auto chugs, water splashes, and the blowing of noses" [4].

The two versions of *The Unholy Three* invite consideration of the production, and the work — the effects — of sound effects in 1925 and in 1930. The many scenes in the films in which characters hear noises encourage us to think about how the films dramatize modes of listening, and types of listeners, during the last years of "silent" cinema and the first years of "sound" cinema.

Film sound theorist Michel Chion has suggested that noises, which he calls "those humble footsoldiers," have remained "the outcasts of theory, having been assigned a purely utilitarian and figurative value and consequently neglected " (145). "For much traditional cinema," Chion continues, "this neglect is proportional to the scanty presence of noises in the films themselves." In *The Unholy Three*, as will be shown, noises occupy an over determined status in the narrative and in the films' achievement in suspense. The deceptive aspects of the film soundtrack have been most incisively examined by Rick Altman, who focuses on what he calls cinema's "ventral apparatus," its "ventriloquial illusion." His discussion raises issues that apply as much to noises on the soundtrack as to dialogue. Altman writes:

> The sound track is a ventriloquist who by moving his dummy (the image) in time with the words he secretly speaks, creates the illusion that the words are produced by the dummy/image whereas in fact the dummy/image is actually created in order to disguise the source of the sound [67].

Rick Altman's description of our relation with the film soundtrack seems particularly pertinent.

> [The] ventriloquist's art depends on the very fact which we have found at the heart of sound film: we are so disconcerted by a sourceless sound that we would rather attribute the sound to a dummy or a shadow than face the mystery of its sourcelessness or the scandal of its production by a non-vocal (technological or "ventral") apparatus [76–77].

Significantly, Steven Connor has suggested that "(given) the ventriloquial nature of cinema as such, the preoccupation with ventriloquism which is a minor thread in the history of the cinematic Gothic" may be seen in relation to cinema's "uncanny powers" (411).

This essay, then, addresses the different functions of various noises in the two films, and thinks through the second film's auditorily augmented versions of the earlier film's "dramatic incidents (which) depend on audible effects." I wish to think about the films' concerns with illusion and deception (and with, therefore, knowledge and its manipulation) in relation to the transformation of spectatorial relations by the arrival of the "all-talking" film, namely the need for attentive listening, and the desire that the pre-recorded soundtrack's augmentation of the moving image, its structural illusory or deceptive qualities, *not* derail the suspension of disbelief so important for the absorption preferred by commercial narrative cinema.

I will consider the films' presentation of scenes in which characters respond to noises, and, in particular, a key scene of suspense in which a detective looks for the source of a toy elephant's unexpected rattling noise. This scene, in Browning's film, perhaps more than any other presented scene of listening, requires we consider the auditory experience of the spectator before the arrival of sound cinema. And Conway's augmented version of this scene, I will suggest, provides a reflexive consideration of the deceptive nature, the uncannily persuasive power, of the pre-recorded sound effect.

In the opening sequences of Browning's film, after the fight has broken out in the sideshow tent, someone blows a whistle to raise the alarm, and several policemen soon arrive on the scene. During the trial scenes which conclude the film, the judge repeatedly bangs his gavel down to call the courtroom to order. In both instances, then, the human action presented by the image (whistle-blowing, gavel-banging) produces a noise with a specific meaning, an intelligible (though purely conventional) message, and a particular result, or effect. These two instances demonstrate how noises can function in unambiguous ways. Other sounds, however, may not be so clearly understood by those who hear them. Other kinds of sound, moreover, may provoke, above all, curiosity concerning either their source, their meaning, or both.

Suspense in *The Unholy Three* is generated by the fact that the criminals' operation takes place behind an elaborate front, in which Echo and Tweedledee disguise themselves for public view as an elderly woman and her grandson. Mrs. O'Grady's pet store is divided into two spaces, the front of store and the parlor, divided by a single door; their adopted personas must be performed whenever they are in the store, or whenever someone enters their private parlor from the store area. The physical proximity of the two spaces, and the fact that the three must switch between their public/false and private/true selves as they or others move between these two spaces, adds to the narrative suspense since their maintaining their operation in secret so close to public space seems unlikely, and their discovery seems imminent.

That only one door separates the public front and the private or secret truth of their actions is emphasized when, on three separate occasions, Hector knocks on the parlor door, and the criminals must quickly adopt their false personae. These spaces, however, are porous in ways beyond the door which links the two rooms; what occurs unseen in one room can nevertheless be heard (or listened to) in the other room. The first appearance of Tweedledee as Little Willie occurs after Rosie returns to the shop; Echo, as Mrs. O'Grady, explains that her grandson must have heard Rosie's voice from the parlor and wants her to "take him bye-bye." When, a little later, Hercules and Echo are arguing in their quarters, Rosie warns them that Hector might hear them from the adjacent room.

Listening is in the first instance foregrounded in the film by the many scenes involving characters hearing or listening to others; suspense is generated by the characters' vulnerability (as speaking subjects) to being overheard by other listening subjects. Scenes of deliberate eavesdropping punctuate the film; the Unholy Three listen at the parlor door to the detective investigating Arlington's murder talking with Hector in the store; Echo hides in Rosie's closet to listen to her and Hector's conversation; Rosie listens from the other side of the door to the Unholy Three arguing about the plan to frame Hector for Arlington's murder; and Tweedledee skulkingly eavesdrops on Hercules' and Rosie's conversation in the forest cabin when the strongman asks Rosie to run away with him.

The film consistently presents scenes in which people are heard or overheard by characters in adjoining rooms, or adjacent hallways, or even closets — every space or room in the house seems to allow others, separated by walls or behind doors, to hear what takes place therein. The domestic spaces are therefore linked together by a sonic porousness which works independently of the limitation of vision produced by walls, allowing characters to listen without being seen. However, as we shall see, to hear without seeing is not always to enjoy a position of power. Just as important as overheard conversations are the scenes in which characters hear or listen to non-vocal noises. When Hector knocks over the birdcage upon his return to the pet store with Rosie, the sound is heard by Echo and the others, which results in Echo, paralyzed by jealousy and paranoia, being left behind by Hercules and Tweedledee, who tire of waiting for him. Without Echo to stop them, the strongman and the midget kill the owner of the house, Arlington. That Echo's distrust of Rosie directly causes the split between the three (and, therefore, Arlington's death) is emphasized when Echo hears the truck start up while he is in the parlor with Rosie and Hector, only to discover that Hercules and Tweedledee have already gone by the time he has run outside.

Later, after Rosie has told Hector her affection has only been in jest, and Hector has left her, her frustration and anger at her having denied her true feelings for him leads her to hurl a missile of some sort (we do not see exactly what it is) across her room at a doll that sits on a shelf. Upon hearing the sound from the hallway, Hector suddenly decides to re-enter the room and, without knocking first this time, finds Rosie, overcome with sorrow, who admits that she had just then lied to him, and that she would willingly accept his proposal (unaware, as we are, that Echo is eavesdropping on their conversation in her closet). On such occasions, then, Browning's film presents scenes in which characters' fortunes are shaped by their reactions to sounds made by others, and in which important moments in the narrative (Echo's hesitation, Hector's return to Rosie) pivot upon the audible actions of others — the aforementioned "dramatic incidents (which) depend upon audible effects."

Given the narrative foregrounding of noises, the repeated scenes of listening to and hearing noises made by others in adjacent spaces, Browning's film, if accompanied by sound effects produced by theatrical personnel in the way described above, repeatedly emphasizes the split between (or, rather, the synchronization of) the recorded image and the actualization of an appropriate audible augmentation of that image during the screening itself, and, if not accompanied by sound effects produced in this way, repeatedly emphasizes the lack (of sound) in the world presented by film. Either way, the film seems to insist that either the presence of sound (in the theater) or the absence of sound (in the film) be experienced most intensely during those moments on which the narrative twists and turns hinge. In other words, Browning's film repeatedly presents scenes of listening in which spectators would be intensely aware of either the lack of or the provision of the appropriate sound (effect). Furthermore, the provision in the theater of sound effects "for" the film would emphasize all the more the lack of sound effects "in" the film being screened.

The most suspense-filled moment in the film occurs when Regan, the detective investigating Arlington's murder, visits Mrs. O'Grady and her "family" at the pet store after learning that she had visited Arlington (and his parrot) at his home the day he was murdered, and had, furthermore, seen the rubies being delivered. Hector knocks on the door of the parlor and announces that the detective wishes to talk to Mrs. O'Grady; Tweedledee, who has the stolen ruby necklace, hides the jewels in a toy elephant which is on the floor among other toys and various Christmas presents. During his talk with Mrs. O'Grady, Regan accidentally knocks the toy elephant with his foot, is amused to notice the elephant's nodding head, and reaches down to pick it up and take a closer look. Tweedledee and Echo freeze in terror, while Regan handles the toy elephant in such a way that he hears something rattling or jangling around inside, and then begins to shake the toy elephant beside his ear and inspect the toy more closely in order to satisfy his curiosity concerning the mechanism or source responsible for the sound he hears. At this point, then, the fate of the criminal gang seems to hang in the balance; this is perhaps the most important of those "dramatic incidents (which) depend upon audible effects."

The rubies secretly concealed inside the toy elephant, which might so easily be found by Regan, reminds us of the vulnerability of the Unholy Three's entire operation, since their disguises, and even their use of the shop as a front, seem rather to invite curiosity more than anything else. In the same way that the charming toy conceals the murdered man's rubies, Tweedledee's nursery dresses conceal a cold-blooded murderer, and Mrs. O'Grady's pinafore and wig conceal Professor Echo. Regan cannot see Echo inside Mrs. O'Grady, or Tweedledee inside Little Willie, but their criminal identities and actions would soon be uncovered if the stolen rubies were discovered in their household.

The film, as I have suggested, hinges on scenes of hearing, and repeatedly shows how acts of listening provide the listener with knowledge, and therefore power. This scene shows instead how Regan is unable to fully understand how the sound is made, or what the sound means (or what is inside the elephant), and how he is then prevented from discovering for himself (with further inspection) the source of the sound he has heard. The scene in which Regan shakes Tweedledee's toy elephant, then, represents a subject's desire to discover the true source of the sound, to find the hidden device, the secret truth, of a sound. Such a scene, given a central place in the narrative, demonstrates how Browning's film, in a highly self-conscious fashion, reflects on the spectators' experience of the film's mute images presented in (and usually augmented by) theaters in 1925, whereby Regan's inability to discover the source of the sound (which allows the narrative to continue, at least for a while) can be compared with the spectators' collusion with the conventions with which the "silent" film proceeds, whether or not sound effects were added by theatrical personnel. That such a moment of sustained and curious listening is so central to the film's achievements in suspense demonstrates, I would suggest, Browning's recognition of the fact that, during this period, hearing sounds while watching films only served to expose all the more clearly the strange and sinister silence of the worlds these films revealed, and to emphasize the illusory and deceptive nature of the cinematic experience theaters produced. The arrival of pre-recorded soundtracks a few years later meant that by the time Conway's version of the film was released, theaters no longer needed to serve, or to give sound to, the film image in this way.

Ron Mottram has noted that most of the major Hollywood studios released their first "all-talking" films in 1929 (231n1). According to Donald Crafton, the "transition to sound" lasted until the Spring of 1931 (323–24). Thus Conway's *The Unholy Three* came midway during the arrival of "all-talking" films and at the end of the transition. Furthermore, as a crime melodrama, albeit a bizarre one, the second version of *The Unholy Three* reflects the invigoration of this genre during (and after) the transition to sound. Harry M. Geldud has argued that crime pictures increased in popularity compared with other genres after synchronized sound permitted a new vocal "realism," and as the public acquired a taste for the "tough vernacular speech" of gangsters, as well as for wordy scenes of police interrogation or courtroom proceedings (266). Conway's *The Unholy Three* indeed presents plenty of tough-guy dialogue (for example, when Echo and Hercules argue), as well as a much longer courtroom sequence than the original (dominated, unusually for a transitional film, by the off-screen voice of the prosecuting attorney summing up the case against Hector).

The remake was the idea of producer Irving Thalberg, who had personally persuaded the reluctant Lon Chaney to commit to make several "all-talking" versions of his "silent" hits as part of Chaney's own attempts to negotiate a new contract. The "all-talking" remake of *The Unholy Three* would present Lon Chaney in a speaking starring role for the very first time; the "Man of a Thousand Faces," re-creating the role of Echo, would now demonstrate vocal talents equal to his celebrated physical transformations. When the ballyhooer introduces "Professor Echo" in the 1930 version of the film, he calls him "the man of a hundred golden voices" (as opposed to the "velvet-voiced ventriloquist," as he is labelled in the original); the "all-talking" version acknowledges its own promotional campaign, which was based on foregrounding Chaney's vocal skills and updating its star's established mercurial persona for the "talkie" era. Adverts for the film emphasized how Chaney's character (and, therefore, Chaney) used five distinct voices in the film. Lon Chaney's first speaking (and triumphantly polyvocal) role was publicized further with reference to the affidavits which guaranteed that Chaney had indeed performed all of his character's vocal and ventriloquial deceptions.

As Chion has noted, in the years immediately following the arrival of synch-sound dialogue, non-diegetic music became a much less popular component of the film soundtrack; and because of the temporary banishment of music, early sound films contained "no shortage of courageous experiments in admitting noise into the audiovisual symphony" (146). Conway's film indeed contains no non-diegetic music after the opening credits; the only music in the film occurs in the opening sequences at the sideshow (and is shown to be produced by the sideshow band) and, much later, when Rosie *turns off* the music she is playing (the better to listen to Hector talk). It was more customary in the early years of sound cinema that characters would *turn on* radios so that diegetic music accompanied conversations, as seen in, for example, Roy Del Ruth's *The Maltese Falcon* (1931). The "audiovisual symphony" provided by Conway's film is one of voices and noises, rather than music.

Critical response to the sound version was ambivalent, and hinged, as did so many reviews of "all-talking" remakes of silent films, on whether the addition of sound was an improvement or no. The review in *Film Daily* (referred to above) described Conway's film as "a bigger draw in sound, for so many of the dramatic incidents depend on audible effects" (cited in Crafton, 325). *Bioscope* wrote that "(the) introduction of sound effects enormously enhances the value of the picture" (25). *Time Magazine*, finding the remake inferior to the original, suggested that the "macabre horror" of the earlier version "was largely dependent on the fact that none of the participants in its gruesome goings-on was able to make himself heard" and concluded that, as a talkie, *The Unholy Three* "is less hair-raising because its sounds have become explicit." The reviewer for *The Film Spectator* claimed that the film "could not stand translation into a talkie without all its glaring absurdities being brought out in bold relief" (9). More recently, Jeanine Basinger has suggested that "(with) sound added, *The Unholy Three* takes on a new quality that can only be described as screwball" (363). The second film was, however, a success, though perhaps mainly due to the novelty value of hearing Chaney speak.

Robert Spadoni has suggested that the arrival of synchronized sound emphasized the "mechanical contrivance" of cinema, and the fact that the audible spoken dialogue clearly did not issue from the lips moving on the cinema screen foregrounded for many the "uncanny" aspects of the cinematic image (6). The arrival of "all-talking" movies, Spadoni argues, "triggered the first major return of medium sensitivity to ordinary viewing in thirty years" (6). Although, as Spadoni notes, audiences very quickly got used to sound cinema, during the transitional period the "state of narrative absorption ... intrinsic to the Hollywood film-viewing experience was partially disrupted as the augmented medium began to exhibit its materiality and the unsteadied practice to flaunt its techniques" (7).

It seems, then, that Conway's *The Unholy Three* was perceived by some to be less successful at maintaining suspense because a sense of realism (and a suspension of disbelief) was derailed by the newly apparent "materiality" of the "augmented medium" for the "medium sensitive" spectator. In his "all-talking" remake of *The Unholy Three*, Conway retains most of the scenarios from the original film. Several new lines of (spoken) dialogue refer to the possibility or danger of being overheard by others in adjacent rooms, such as when Rosie, fearing Echo, asks Hector not to talk so loudly in case "Mrs. O'Grady" hears them. Scenes in which characters react to noises are presented in much the same way: we see (and hear) the sound being made (by the cage or the doll falling to the floor) and then see Echo or Hector hear and react accordingly. Just once does Conway show a character hear something without first showing the sound being produced, when Echo hears Hercules and

Tweedledee drive away, and the sound of the truck starting accompanies the shot of Echo in the parlor with Rosie and Hector. Conway's film also presents several effective instances of ambient sound, such as the squawking parrots in O'Grady's store (parrots which we also see) and the chuffing trains at the station in the film's penultimate scene (trains which we do not see). The presence of the trains suggested by the chuffing sounds remind us of the illusory nature of the soundtrack, and we may speculate that the film has supplied the sound of squawking parrots in much the same way that Echo provides the spoken dialogue for the parrots.

A sound remake of a "silent" film inevitably provides interesting material for a consideration of sound and narrative film. There are two scenes in Conway's version which demonstrate the film's self-reflexive interest in the act of listening, seeing and believing. In both instances Conway's film builds on Browning's by showing how seeing and hearing contribute to certain convictions concerning a situation's truthfulness. When the strongman's ballyhooer knocks together two steel horseshoes to prove they are "real" before handing them to Hercules to bend, the sound the horseshoes make is clearly meant to demonstrate (to the sideshow crowds) that Hercules' act requires no deception or illusion. However, a sceptical, bespectacled, purse-lipped pantywaist standing in the crowd remains unconvinced, and shouts out that he thinks it is an illusion, despite the evidence that has been put before his eyes (and ears). He has a notion that he is being tricked or manipulated, that the sound apparently made by the horseshoes by no means guarantees that they are really steel. This spectator-listener's suspicions concerning the truthfulness of the act he is watching are, however, mocked by the others; he is publicly ridiculed and silenced. In this scene, then, Conway's film presents as a fool the spectator-listener who refuses to believe in or trust the audiovisual evidence or spectacle put before him, who refuses to believe in what is presented to his eyes (and ears)— the kind of spectator-listener (which Spadoni discusses) for whom the suspension of disbelief was derailed by the audible component of visual spectacle.

The scene in which Regan shakes the toy elephant is also different from Browning's, in a way comparable with the sensational de-wigging by Hector's lawyer of Mrs. O'Grady/Professor Echo in court (with which spectacle the remake's trial scenes conclude). The elephant scene in Conway's film, like the courtroom climax, concerns revealing. In the same way that the attorney rips off Echo's wig to reveal the man "inside" the old lady, Tweedledee, once the elephant has been returned to him by Hercules, reaches inside and takes out some candy, revealing (as far as Regan is concerned) the source of the rattling sound that had so intrigued him moments earlier. Regan accepts that the noise inside the elephant must have been produced by the candy which Tweedledee has removed from inside the toy. (Incidentally, when Tweedledee first grabs the rubies at Arlington's, he proceeds in Conway's version to hide one of the jewels in his mouth, as if it were a sweet.) Regan's curiosity concerning the sound made by the elephant is satisfied once he has seen the candy. His satisfaction, moreover, can, like the suspicion of the onlooker in the earlier scene, be linked to attitudes and experiences of spectator-listeners attending the movies during the transition to sound. While the real source of the sound (the rubies) remains hidden, the candy, presented to Regan as the source of the sound, satisfies his need to trace a sound to a source, to know the true cause of what he hears.

While in Browning's film Regan fails to discover the source of the sound, in Conway's version he is fooled into thinking he has discovered, or has been shown, the source. In this way the dialogue in the second film revises this scene in a way peculiarly appropriate for the developments in synchronized sound that had transformed the medium by 1930. Since sound effects are added to the film image in a way that only seems less deceptive than the convention by which theatrical personnel provided sound effects in theaters, the addition of the explicit and audible reference to the candy to the scene in which Regan shakes the elephant means that this "dramatic incident (which) depends upon (an) audible effect" functions in Conway's film in a highly self-reflexive manner, revealing the illusory nature of film sound.

For Browning, and for Conway after him, *The Unholy Three*, while outwardly a bizarre crime melodrama, functioned, much like Tweedledee's elephant, as an unlikely container within which they reflected, and dramatized, the various ways in which spectators watch/ed and listen/ed to film before and after the arrival of synchronized sound.

Works Cited

Contemporary reviews of *The Unholy Three* from *Motion Picture Magazine, Moving Picture World, New York Herald Tribune, New York Times, Picture Play* and *Time Magazine* are available at *www.tcm.com/underground/movies/index.jsp?cid=152311* and *http://www.silentsaregolden.com/unholythreereview.html*
Review of *The Unholy Three. Bioscope* 1244.84 (August 6, 1930).
Review of *The Unholy Three. The Film Spectator* 10.6 (August 30, 1930).
Altman, Rick. "Moving Lips: Cinema as Ventriloquism." *Yale French Studies* 60 (1980), 67–79.
Basinger, Jeanine. *Silent Stars*. Hanover and London: Wesleyan University Press, 1999.
Blyn, Robin. "Between Silence and Sound: Ventriloquism and the Advent of the Voice in *The Unholy Three*." (Herzogenrath 117–27).
Brophy, Philip (ed.). *Cinesonic: The World of Sound in Film*. New South Wales: Australian Film, Television and Radio School, 1999.
Cameron, Evan William (ed.). *Sound and the Cinema: The Coming of Sound to American Film*. New York: Redgrave Publishing Company, 1980.
Chion, Michel. *Audio-Vision: Sound on Screen*. Trans. Claudia Gorbman. New York: Columbia University Press, 1994.

Connor, Steven. *Dumbstruck: A Cultural History of Ventriloquism.* Oxford: Oxford University Press, 2000.
Crafton, Donald. *The Talkies: American Cinema's Transition to Sound, 1926–1931.* New York: Charles Scribner's Sons, 1997.
Elsaesser, Thomas, with Adam Barker (eds.). *Early Cinema: Space, Frame, Narrative.* London: BFI, 1990, pp. 274–81.
Fielding, Raymond. "The Technological Antecedents of the Coming of Sound." (Cameron 2–23).
Gaudreault, André. "Showing and Telling: Image and Word in Early Cinema." (Elsaesser 274–81).
Geldud, Harry M. *The Birth of the Talkies: From Edison to Jolson.* Bloomington and London: Indiana University Press, 1975.
Hansen, Miriam. *Babel and Babylon: Spectatorship in American Silent Film.* Cambridge, MA, and London: Harvard University Press, 1991.
Herzogenrath, Bernd (ed.). *The Films of Tod Browning.* London: Black Dog Publishing, 2006.
Lastra, James. *Sound Technology and the American Cinema: Perception, Representation, Modernity.* New York: Columbia University Press, 2000.
Mottram, Ron. "American Sound Films, 1926–1930." *Film Sound: Theory and Practice.* Eds. Elisabeth Weis and John Belton. New York: Columbia Univeristy Press, 1985, pp. 221–31.
Neale, Steve. *Cinema and Technology: Image, Sound, Colour.* London: BFI, 1985.
Rosenthal, Stuart, and Judith M. Kass. *Tod Browning and Don Siegel.* London: Tantivy Press, 1975.
Sadoul, Georges. *Dictionary of Film Makers.* Trans. Peter Norris. Berkeley: University of California Press, 1972.
Scott, James M. *Film: The Medium and the Maker.* New York: Holt, Rinehart and Winston, Inc., 1975.
Sergi, Gianluca. "The Sonic Playground: Hollywood Cinema and its Listeners." *Hollywood Spectatorship: Changing Perceptions.* Eds. Melvyn Stokes and Richard Maltby. London: BFI, 2001, pp. 121–131.
Skal, David J., and Elias Savada. *Dark Carnival: The Secret World of Tod Browning, Hollywood's Master of the Macabre.* New York and London: Anchor Books, 1995.
Sobchack, Vivian. "The Films of Tod Browning: An Overview Long Past." (Herzogenrath 21–39).
Spadoni, Robert. "The Uncanny Body of Early Sound Film." *The Velvet Light Trap* 51 (2003), 4–16.
_____. *Uncanny Bodies: The Coming of Sound Film and the Origins of Horror.* Berkeley, Los Angeles and London: California University Press, 2007.
Studlar, Gaylyn. *This Mad Masquerade: Stardom and Masculinity in the Jazz Age.* New York: Columbia University Press, 1996.
Walker, Alexander. *The Shattered Silents: How the Talkies Came to Stay.* London: Elm Tree Books, 1978.
Weis, Elisabeth. "Eavesdropping: An Aural Analogue of Voyeurism?" (Brophy 79–107).

The Black Bird
Mocking Duality

F. Gwynplaine MacIntyre

Although Tod Browning received a story credit on most of his later films, extensive searching (in the script libraries of MGM and Universal, and elsewhere) has failed to discover any manuscript or typescript that is indisputably Browning's handiwork. One possible explanation for this may be that Browning assigned himself a "vanity" credit on films which he directed but did not write. A more likely explanation is that Browning worked in tandem with a "word man" such as Waldemar Young or Garrett Fort. Browning would describe an original premise to his co-author, who then fleshed out this skeleton with his own ideas in the process of crafting a screenplay or scenario. (The terms "screenplay" and "scenario" are not interchangeable, as we will see.)

For Tod Browning's film *The Black Bird* (produced in 1925, released in January 1926), we have more knowledge than usual concerning its gestation. The film's credits identify Waldemar Young as author of the scenario, based on a story by Browning. This particular film's story can be traced through its development because we have a version independent of the film: a 1925 paperback novelization, which deviates from the film in several crucial elements. Throughout the 1920s, the Jacobsen-Hodgkinson Corporation in New York City published a series of paperback novels collectively named *Popular Plays and Screen Library*. These books, each just under 140 pages long, were crude novelizations of movies, issued at the rate of one volume each week to coincide with the release of the respective film. Some of the volumes in this series are very faithful adaptations of their cinema sources. For example, Jacobsen-Hodgkinson's 1920 paperback novel of Tod Browning's film *Outside the Law* closely follows the plot of that movie, with new material padding the story to a novel's length. However, Jacobsen-Hodgkinson's 1925 novelization of *The Black Bird* is significantly different from its source film.

The most noticeable difference is that the novel is titled *The Mocking Bird*, and the central character is named Dan Glover, alias "the Mocking

Bird." (In the film, Lon Chaney plays Dan Tate, alias "the Black Bird.") In the movie, the Black Bird's henchman is called the Shadow; the novel has the Mocking Bird's henchman named the Ghost, alias Hal Dixon. Dan's criminal rival in the film (played by Owen Moore) is nicknamed West End Bertie. In the novel's text, he is called Edward Glayde, alias West End Eddy. But the novel contains a photo plate of Moore in costume for this film, with a caption identifying his character as "West End Algernon"! These contradictions are explained by the fact that most silent films were made from scenarios rather than screenplays. A scenario is merely a detailed synopsis describing the situations and action of the story. A scenario would indicate the characters' physical actions and emotional reactions (in phrases such as "she takes it big"), but would almost never offer specific dialogue for the actors to speak. Scenarists often identified characters generically — "the Girl," "the Villain" — and it was very often not until after the film was shot and edited that the characters were given names and dialogue by the title-writer, who wrote the text for intertitles.

Although the novel *The Mocking Bird* credits Tod Browning as its author, this volume (like all of the Popular Plays series) is actually the work of an anonymous ghost-writer. (*The Mocking Bird* is very crudely written by someone who clearly had no knowledge of London nor of Londoners' speech patterns.) It is evident that the film, the novel, and the photo plates illustrating the novel were all in production concurrently, all rushed forward so that no department had time to consult any other. The novel's ending is slightly different from the movie's ending, raising the possibility that Browning may have changed the film's conclusion during production. The front cover of the paperback novel *The Mocking Bird* is illustrated with a portrait of Lon Chaney, but *not* in character make-up as he appears in the movie *The Black Bird*; rather, it is an ordinary head shot of Chaney wearing a necktie and cloth cap that were part of his own usual attire. Some studio artist has added a hand clutching a lighted cigarette — an ironic touch, since Chaney would ultimately die of throat cancer. Behind Chaney's head is a drawing of a mockingbird, which has absolutely nothing to do with the plot of this novel or the movie *The Black Bird*.

Whether this story's protagonist is the Black Bird or the Mocking Bird, his avian nickname is irrelevant. He is a London thief living a double life. But he does not fly, does not swoop down on his prey, does not do anything emulating a bird. There really is no clear reason why this character cloaks his crimes in a bird's name. Here, too, we have a clue to the story's development. It is virtually certain that the main character's nickname, in both versions of the story, was created not by Browning but rather his scenarist Waldemar Young. Young (1878–1938) was a grandson of Brigham Young, one of the founders of the Mormon Church. Over the course of his writing career, Waldemar Young showed a strong penchant for avian story titles. Although residing in Los Angeles throughout his screenwriting career, Young was a long-time member of a San Francisco fraternal society called the Bohemian Club, and he wrote plays for its members to perform. A few of these plays' titles reveal Young's avian predilection: *At the Sign of the Stork* (1927), *Birds of Rhiannon* (1930), *The Golden Feathers* (performed in 1939, after Young's death).

It was evidently Young's idea, rather than Browning's, to nickname Lon Chaney's character in this 1925 film "the Mocking Bird"—and then to rename him "the Black Bird," probably when someone realized that mockingbirds are not native to London. Blackbirds occasionally visit London, but this nickname is still arbitrary; there is nothing black about Dan Tate's appearance, except in the symbolic sense of villainy. In fact, it is Dan's brother—nicknamed "the Bishop of Limehouse" because he runs a salvation mission—who wears black clothing. In the novel *The Mocking Bird*, Dan's brother is named Simon Glover (alias the Bishop), and his mission house—rather improbably illuminated with a flashing electric sign—is called "Safe Harbor." In the film, this character is identified merely as "the Bishop." Here is how the very badly-written novel compares the two brothers (it should be noted that none of the purple prose in *The Mocking Bird* should be blamed on either Tod Browning or Waldemar Young, even though Browning is named as author):

> "The Bishop" was everything that The Mocking Bird was not. Strange, sinister, evil, a creature without a soul, with the lithe body of a panther, the cunning of a serpent, the cruelty of a demon, the Mocking Bird was feared as the "Bishop" was loved. The Bishop was a gnarled, twisted pathetic cripple, who hobbled on a crutch. In his eyes shone an ineffable sweetness which indicated his charitable heart.

The above paragraph is typical of the entire novel. Notice the wretched standards of the copy-editing: in this one paragraph, a major character is identified as "The Bishop" (with both words in quotation marks), then as the "Bishop" (with only one word in quotes), and lastly as the Bishop, with no quotation marks at all. As both a novel and a film, *The Black Bird* offers one of melodrama's standard plots: the rivalry between brothers, one evil, one good. Dan Tate is the evil sibling; his brother is virtuous. But Tod Browning's film is not so much Cain and Abel as Jekyll and Hyde, because—in a typically Browning twist—both brothers are the same man, employing a ruse which might indicate a split personality.

As in another Browning-Chaney collaboration, *The Unknown*, Chaney's protagonist in *The Black Bird* conceals a physical secret which is revealed to the audience (but not to the other characters) early in the film. The police and the underworld believe Dan Tate and the Bishop to be brothers, which explains their physical resemblance. Only Dan's lover, Limehouse Polly, knows that they are the same man. While the police seek Dan, he hides in plain sight as his invented brother. As Dan Tate, Chaney wears the traditional garb of a London costermonger (street peddler): flat cap, short tight jacket, kerchief at the throat. The Bishop's guise is more elaborate: his right arm and right leg are paralyzed, and permanently bent. (Nobody in this film ever wonders how the Bishop gets dressed and undressed.) Lon Chaney's costume for the Bishop was a simple black suit, but with the right side slightly longer than the left side. This created the subtle effect of making his "crippled" limbs seem slightly withered. (Lon Chaney is remembered for using elaborate harnesses to distort his body, and complicated facial make-ups; but whenever possible he took a more subtle approach.) In his sequences as the Bishop, Chaney propels himself with his left leg and a crutch beneath his arm. More than once in this film we witness the process by which Dan Tate transforms himself into his crippled brother. Chaney stands erect, takes a breath, and then — with a dramatic flourish — he throws his shoulder and hip into their disjointed postures.

Many false rumors have been spread about Lon Chaney's craft: among them, that he was a trained contortionist (he was not) who dislocated his limbs to portray cripples. It has also been reported (incorrectly) that Chaney was "double-jointed," or that he had some natural ability to distort himself. For his transformations in *The Black Bird*, Chaney's elaborate gestures may be intended to persuade the audience that he is literally throwing his limbs out of joint. Careful study of Chaney's scenes as the Bishop reveal that he is merely keeping his right elbow and right knee bent at roughly 90-degree angles; the limbs are not dislocated.

Although the Black Bird and the Bishop are the same man, there is another difference between these two *personae* which enables them to qualify as two separate masks in Lon Chaney's gallery of a thousand faces. In his scenes as the Black Bird, Chaney wears a harsh make-up that makes Dan Tate's face appear harder and younger than Chaney's own features. In his scenes as the crippled Bishop, Chaney wears a softer make-up with a touch of gray in his hair, making the Bishop appear several years older and more kindly than the Black Bird. They share a family resemblance, yet we absolutely accept that the police of Limehouse would be convinced that these are two different men. The parallel between Black Bird/Bishop and Jekyll/Hyde becomes stronger when we realize that the fictional Doctor Jekyll and Mister Hyde were inspired by a real person very similar to the fictional Dan Tate. Deacon William Brodie (1741–1788) was by day a cabinet-maker of Edinburgh, active in the local Presbyterian church and well-known for his charitable deeds; by night, he was the leader of a gang of burglars who looted the homes containing Brodie's cabinets. (Like the criminal trio in Tod Browning's film *The Unholy Three*, Brodie visited his customers' homes on legitimate business by day, then returned to burgle them at night.) When William Brodie's double life was discovered, he was arrested and sentenced to death. In an irony which Browning would have savored, William Brodie the criminal was hanged on a gibbet which had been built by William Brodie the cabinet-maker, and which had been donated to the city of Edinburgh by William Brodie the philanthropist: all the same man!

Deacon Brodie may have been a genuine split personality: while awaiting the hangman in his death cell, Brodie played "draughts" (checkers) against himself, his right hand versus his left. Although neither Browning nor Chaney calls attention to this in the film, when Chaney switches personalities he also changes his tropism: the Black Bird is (like Chaney himself) right-handed, but the Bishop's paralysis renders him left-handed. In the film *The Black Bird*, the Bishop exists solely to give Dan Tate a cover identity. Yet the novel *The Mocking Bird* goes into greater detail about the Bishop's good works. He has genuinely helped the poor and afflicted of Limehouse. In the novel, unlike the film, we enter the protagonist's mind during his transformations. Dan Glover (as he is named in the novel) does not perceive himself to be two different people; he knows that the Bishop is merely a disguise. (Several times, the novel's narration identifies him as "the Mocking Bird–Bishop," stressing that they are the same man.) Apparently, neither Browning nor his writing partner Waldemar Young envisioned this story's protagonist as a truly schizoid personality.

Although most of the novel *The Mocking Bird* is laughably inept, one of its very few decently written passages conveys the inner nature of Dan Glover's criminal mind during the moments when he is impersonating his nonexistent benevolent brother (I have retained here the grammatical errors and peculiar punctuation — and lack of it — from the original novel):

> During the dark days when hate swelled in his heart and jealousy gave rise to plans of murder and revenge, the only relief that came to the Mocking Bird was in those hours when he played the part of the good "Bishop" of the Safe Harbor Mission. When he jerked his arm and leg out of joint and twisted his neck awry, it was, each day, with a cynical sneer. But once he had contorted his face and body, and donned the "Bishop's" semi-clerical garb, he took pride in his impersonation. It was queer he thought how playing at good deeds made him feel really good. One could not smile and do good deeds he found without being influenced by them. Playing at love of his fellow men, he came actually to feel a sympathy which was utterly foreign to his other attitude of looking upon them all as possible victims. When he was advising and assisting poor mothers with sick children, old men out of work, convalescents

needed care and rest, even repentant Magdalens home-sick for the loved ones they had disgraced, he actually felt benevolence in his heart.

Regrettably, the film *The Black Bird* makes no attempt to convey the inner mind of the double character that Lon Chaney portrays. In the film, the Bishop exists only as a hiding place for the Black Bird while eluding the police. We never get any indication that Dan Tate actually obtains pleasure by becoming his crippled sibling.

The dichotomy of the two brothers — one evil, one virtuous — has been used in so many stories and films that it was already a cliché long before *The Black Bird* was made. Browning and his scenarist Young have rescued the premise from cliché by giving it two clever twists: one of them being that the two "brothers" in this film are actually the same man. The other twist is a visual one: the cliché of "good brother/bad brother" requires that the good brother be pure and whole of body, while the bad brother is twisted and stunted. Avoiding the obvious path, Browning and Young have chosen to give the evil brother Dan Tate an athletic body, while placing his virtuous brother the Bishop in a crippled and paralyzed body. Browning may have intended this to symbolize the impotence of virtue in the presence of evil. Or perhaps not, since *The Black Bird* (like most Browning films) ends with virtue triumphant and evil renounced or punished.

Watching *The Black Bird* again, I am reminded of a later film with a similar title: *The Black Room* (1935). This is a moody character study, a borderline horror film starring Boris Karloff as twin brothers. Conveniently, one twin is good, the other evil. As in *The Black Bird*, the evil brother is virile and athletic, while the virtuous brother has a paralyzed arm. In his performance as the good twin (and, later, as the evil twin impersonating the good twin), Karloff keeps his right arm bent at a grotesque angle; as in Lon Chaney's portrayal of the paralytic Bishop, nobody seems to wonder how this unfortunate man gets his clothes on and off.

A serious flaw in both the film *The Black Bird* and its source novel *The Mocking Bird* is the unconvincing depiction of Limehouse. This district in London's East End received its name from the local warehouses storing the large quantities of citrus fruit that were victualled to Royal Navy ships to protect sailors from scurvy. (Unlike the ships of other nations, vessels of the Royal Navy routinely put to sea with large supplies of citrus fruit for their crew, which is why British sailors became known as "limeys.")

But there is very little genuine sense of place in *The Black Bird*, and even less in the novel *The Mocking Bird*. Some of the novel's action occurs at "the corner of Plum Alley and Queen's Lane," as the novel's uncredited author (surely an American) describes it. There are no such streets in the real Limehouse, and a Londoner of this period would have been more likely to describe the street intersection as a "crossroads" or a "crossing," not a corner. There are similar inaccuracies and howlers (such as "harbor" instead of the British spelling "harbour") all through the text of *The Mocking Bird*. Worst of all is the dialogue for the character Fifi Lorraine (played in the film by French actress Renée Adorée), which is written in a *"wee wee, monsewer"* dialect.

It is instructive to compare Browning's movie *The Black Bird* with D.W. Griffith's 1919 film *Broken Blossoms*. Both movies take place in London's Limehouse district but were filmed in Hollywood. *Broken Blossoms* is based on a story by Thomas Burke (1886–1945), an English author who knew London's East End intimately. Although Burke had no direct input into Griffith's film, the authenticity of his story survives in the movie version, while Browning's film suffers from a lack of accurate detail. Among the details which Browning gets wrong: Dan Tate and the other London criminals have easy access to firearms. This is simply not an accurate depiction of Britain's underworld in the 1920s. Browning and Young may have been aware of a notorious London gun-battle of a few years earlier: the siege of Sidney Street, in 1911, in which the Metropolitan Police were forced to shoot it out against well-armed criminals. But this was not part of London's normal underworld activity; the Sidney Street gang were political radicals who had smuggled their weaponry into Britain from Latvia.

In keeping with its title, *The Black Bird* is probably the blackest, darkest and most claustrophobic of Tod Browning's films; certainly it is the darkest and most claustrophobic of the Browning-Chaney collaborations. Even *London After Midnight* (with its cobwebbed crypts) and *West of Zanzibar* (with its nocturnal jungles) feature more scenes of brightly-lit interiors, daylight and open space than *The Black Bird*. Much of the action of *The Black Bird* takes place in small, squalid rooms — either in the cramped upstairs bedsit of Dan Tate, or in the slum mission of the Bishop. The pub where the Black Bird meets his cronies, the music hall where Fifi Lorraine performs — these are packed with grimy lower-class patrons. When Chaney's Black Bird does go outdoors, the exterior sequences in this film are still dark, constricted and oppressive. It is clear that these "exteriors" have been filmed indoors on one of MGM's sound stages. After repeated screenings of *The Black Bird*, I have been unable to find a single shot in this film which I would confidently state was actually filmed outdoors. *The Black Bird* is not only Browning's blackest movie, it is also his movie which most nearly approaches the genre of *film noir*, with its doomed souls and twisted destinies.

The London streets in this film are dark, crowded with paupers, and choking with smoke and decay. In this single detail the film is accurate. We have heard the clichés about "London fog." For more than a century (up until the blackouts of the Second World War), the poorer districts of London were cloaked in thick clouds of low-hanging vapor that resembled fog, but which was actually smoke produced by the burning of peat, which the lower-class denizens of London put into their stoves because it cooked their food and warmed their rooms more cheaply than coal. The foggy darkness of the exterior sequences in *The Black Bird* brings a welcome touch of authenticity to the film. However, I cannot help speculating that the fog serves another purpose as well: it prevents us from getting a good look at the exterior sets in this movie, and discovering how very badly they resemble any aspects of the actual London. Surviving Metro-Goldwyn-Mayer production logs show that *The Black Bird* was shot in only 26 days, on a total budget of $166,000. This is an astonishingly low figure for an MGM film starring an actor of Lon Chaney's stature. Metro-Goldwyn-Mayer was Hollywood's most opulent studio, famed for producing the most glamorous and elaborate movies of the silent era. Yet there is a cheapness, a dirty appearance to *The Black Bird* that transcends its ugly subject matter and its underworld settings. Three years later at MGM, Browning's film *The Big City* glamorized New York City's criminal life, yet *The Black Bird*—telling a story of comparable people in London—deals with cheapness and crudity.

The Black Bird is the nearest that Tod Browning ever came—and it is not very near—to filming the story of Jack the Ripper, the notorious sex-murderer who stalked London's lower-class Whitechapel district in 1888. It is not clear precisely when *The Black Bird* takes place: nothing in this movie looks up-to-date and modern for the year 1925, with the possible exception of the fashionable clothes worn by Renée Adorée when Fifi and Bertie ask the Bishop to perform their marriage ceremony. Throughout the film we see clothes and architecture that could easily date from the late Victorian era rather than 1925. The Black Bird stalks the alleys of Limehouse, while Jack the Ripper terrorizes the streets of Whitechapel—but the two districts could be nearly interchangeable. Both were slums in London's East End: Whitechapel is full of immigrants from East Europe, many of them Jewish, while Limehouse contains many Chinese immigrants. Nothing in the plot of *The Black Bird* would change significantly if the action were moved to Whitechapel. This offers a possible explanation for why the real Jack the Ripper was never caught. Perhaps he was two people sharing one body, as the Black Bird and the Bishop seem to be—or as Deacon William Brodie was, precisely one century before Jack the Ripper. Perhaps the good half of Jack the Ripper's divided soul was unaware of the existence of the evil half of his soul. Perhaps, after committing his last murder in 1888, Jack the Ripper never felt remorse for his crimes because his virtuous half had no memory of his evil half's dark perversions.

The only real sunlight in the movie *The Black Bird* is glimpsed through the window of the only large and spacious room in this film: the bachelor flat that is the residence of West End Bertie. During the movie's development from scenario to screen, this character went through at least three different name changes — Bertie, Eddy and Algernon — so it's significant that, throughout the project's gestation, Browning and Waldemar Young invariably attached the nickname "West End" to this character. Londoners of every social class speak of going "up west" when they visit the West End, as if this portion of their city is somehow higher or greater than the other boroughs. In fact, the West End of London is the posh district, where the wealthy and influential live — the diametric opposite of the East End, with its slums. Was Browning perhaps attracted to the duality of London's two unequal halves? West End Bertie is a gentleman crook in the tradition of Raffles the Cracksman (an immensely popular character in the fiction of Victorian England). Bertie's rival, the Black Bird, however, is merely a crook. Bertie is cultured, well-spoken, polite — everything that Dan Tate is not. From a realistic viewpoint, both men make their livings as thieves, and therefore both are equally bad. But Browning is not interested in a realistic viewpoint. He consistently contrasts the elegance of Bertie with the coarseness of Dan Tate. Both men are rivals, not only competing for the same stolen goods, but also competing for the love of Fifi Lorraine. At the film's end, Bertie has reformed his criminal ways and won Fifi, while Dan Tate dies in agony. Browning strongly implies that Bertie is innately *better* than Dan, that Bertie deserves happiness but Dan does not.

A running theme through many of Browning's films is the "good crook/bad crook" rivalry: two criminals compete to steal the same loot, yet we sympathize with one of them because he is good-looking, well-dressed, witty, and charming, while the other crook is merely a thug. *The Black Bird* and Browning's later film *The Big City* both employ this contrast. Interestingly, in *The Black Bird* Lon Chaney plays the "bad" crook, while in *The Big City* Chaney plays the so-called "good" crook. In the first film Browning juxtaposes the coarse-featured Chaney against the taller, better-looking Owen Moore. To make sure we understand that Moore is the "better" thief, Browning has Moore attired in impeccable evening clothes. In *The Big City*, Browning had the more difficult job of presenting the unattractive Chaney as the "good" crook; he achieved this by costuming Lon Chaney in expensive, flashy clothes and giving him witty dialogue, while contrasting Chaney with a rival "bad" crook in the form of Matthew Betz, an actor who was shorter and uglier than Lon Chaney, dressed unattractively and given thick-ear dialogue to make his character clearly less sympathetic than Chaney's. Browning also consistently elicits the audience's sympathy for his "good" crook by the contrived device of having the "good" crook only steal from other crooks, never from innocent victims. In *The Big City*, sympathetic criminal Chaney is only shown robbing unsympathetic criminal Betz. In *The Black Bird*, when a high-society woman (played by actress Louise Emmons) visits the Limehouse music hall wearing an expensive diamond collar, sympathetic crook Bertie and unsympathetic crook Dan both decide to steal the collar for the same reason — each thief wants to give the jewels to Fifi Lorraine. What happens next is significant, and it reveals Browning's skill in manipulating his audience's sympathies. Since Bertie is the "good" crook who must win the rivalry, it must be Bertie (not Dan) who succeeds in stealing the diamonds. But the diamond collar belongs to an innocent woman who doesn't deserve to be robbed; if Bertie robs her, he loses the audience's sympathy. Cleverly, Browning's script manages to have it both ways: it is the Black Bird's henchman, the Shadow, who steals the collar from the society woman, and then the Shadow in turn is robbed by Bertie's henchmen. This contrivance allows Bertie to get the diamonds (and win the rivalry) without getting his hands dirty by robbing an innocent victim (the society woman): the "good" crook has only actually robbed a member of the "bad" crook's gang.

Chaney's character Dan Tate is a clear-cut villain, with no redeeming characteristics at all. This is because anything virtuous that might exist in Dan Tate's nature has been transferred to his other self, the Bishop. And yet Browning attempts to create some sympathy for Dan Tate through an unusual method. During an early scene we see the Black Bird prowling through his criminal terrain. Suddenly he spots an adolescent girl, played by young actress Peggy Best; she is wearing elaborate make-up and going out for the night with an older man. Sternly, the Black Bird orders her to go home and wash off the make-up. We understand that he has only her best interests at heart. (Scenarist Young later wrote an almost identical sequence for Chaney in Browning's *The Big City*.) Yet there is an odd detail here: the girl's older companion is a Chinese man. (In real life, a sizeable percentage of Limehouse's population at this time were Chinese immigrants or their descendants.) Does Dan Tate have a legitimate reason for dissuading the girl from dating this man? Or does Dan object to the relationship only because it is interracial? In another Browning-Chaney collaboration, *The Road to Mandalay*, Chaney plays a criminal who constantly inflicts racial taunts and insults upon his Oriental partner, played by the Japanese actor Sojin Kamiyama. Before Browning arrived in Hollywood, he had toured vaudeville in a blackface act called "The Lizard and the Coon," which featured racist stereotypes directed against Negroes. Was Browning a racist? He appears to be seeking audience sympathy here, during the scene in which Dan Tate dissuades a white girl from dating an older Chinese man. What we cannot know is how much of Tate's (and Browning's) concern is premised on the racist belief that a white woman should never date a non-white man. Let us recall that all of Browning's films were made in an era when many American cinemas refused to admit black patrons, or required them to sit upstairs in a separate balcony (distressingly nicknamed "nigger heaven"). The racism in *The Black Bird* and in *The Road to Mandalay* may signify more about the time they were made rather than revealing anything about Browning's personal beliefs. Also, the brief appearance of an Oriental man in one scene of *The Black Bird* is one of this film's very few touches of authenticity, acknowledging that Limehouse (more so than any other of London's slums at this time) had a substantial Chinese population.

Another interesting decision made during the production of *The Black Bird* cannot be explained today, as there is no mention of it in MGM's surviving production logs. During the sequences in the Bishop's salvation mission we briefly glimpse an elderly man — one of the London unfortunates who has become dependent on the Bishop's charity. The role is short and undemanding, and there must have been many elderly actors in Hollywood's Central Casting Agency whom Browning could easily have chosen for this part. But the elderly man whom we see onscreen is actually played by a 38-year-old actor in heavy make-up: he is Cecil Holland, who would soon become the supervisor of the make-up department for all MGM films. While *The Black Bird* was in production, Cecil Holland was writing *The Art of Make-Up for Stage and Screen*; this book, published in 1927, is the first important reference work on the art of film make-up. The book's foreword is by Lon Chaney. Holland and Chaney remained friends until the latter's death in 1930. I have seen a photograph of Holland and actress Jean Harlow, taken six years after Chaney died: Harlow is seated in Holland's make-up chair while he applies her cosmetics; above the chair, clearly seen in this photo, is a portrait of Lon Chaney made up as Jesus Christ. Cecil Holland had acted small roles in several previous Hollywood films. *The Black Bird* would be his last acting job; his duties as a make-up artist would soon claim all of his time. To my knowledge, his portrayal in *The Black Bird* was Holland's only film role that required him to wear heavy make-up. I would dearly like to know whose idea it was — Browning's? Chaney's?— to cast Cecil Holland in this film, since his role could more easily have been played by an elderly actor without any special make-up. Holland's presence in *The Black Bird* constitutes a sort of inside joke in a film which is not otherwise light-hearted.

Tod Browning's fascination with freaks and cripples is legendary. In Browning's *The Unknown*, Lon Chaney plays a genuine freak (with a double thumb) who is a phony cripple (he goes to considerable trouble to appear to be armless). At the climax of the film he ceases to be a freak (losing his double thumb) by becoming a genuine cripple when his arms are amputated. A similar transformation occurs at the climax of *The Black Bird*. With the police closing in on Dan Tate, once more Chaney begins the elaborate ritual which alerts the audience that he is about to become the Bishop. But this time the police break in the door and knock him down—with the ironic result that Dan's spine is broken, paralyzing him in the contrived posture of the Bishop. We see Chaney's expressive face as Dan realizes that he is permanently trapped in the Bishop's body, the Bishop's identity. But rescue of a sort comes soon after, as he dies from this injury. While Browning's visual skill and Chaney's talents do much to help this ending, it is ultimately implausible. A trauma to the lower spine might render a man paraplegic, but it will not kill him unless there are other major injuries. Ultimately, Lon Chaney's fate in *The Black Bird* seems to be inspired by the urban legend about the boy who kept distorting his face into disgusting expressions until one day it froze like that.

The ending of the paperback novel *The Mocking Bird* is more ambiguous than the ending of the film. Dan Glover (unlike Dan Tate) does not die so quickly. The police have come looking for Dan, but, finding him in the Bishop's clothes, with his body trapped in the Bishop's contorted posture, they assume that Dan is his brother the Bishop, and the police leave without making any arrests. In the novel (unlike the film), Dan and Polly have time to contemplate his ironic situation, and they consider escaping to America, where surgeons may be able to reverse Dan's paralysis:

> "I have no pain now. I am at peace."
> A spiritual light shone in his eyes, as Polly caressed him gently. But over her face there was a veil of anxiety as she looked at the twisted limbs of her loved one. She shook her head sadly, like a mother hovering over a sick child.

Although Dan's paralysis is now genuine, the text of the novel implies that (unlike in the film) he does not die from his injuries. Instead, Dan now chooses to become the Bishop permanently, continuing to do good works for the poor of Limehouse. It is the Mocking Bird, not the Bishop, who has died.

And here we have perhaps the greatest irony in all of Tod Browning's world. Several of his films—*The Big City, The Unholy Three, The Devil Doll*—feature a shop which is a front for criminal activity. The Bishop is himself a false front, but his mission house is genuine. We are never told how the Bishop finances his poorhouse—from Dan's criminal gains? from donations?—but this is no phony charity; the Bishop gives genuine aid and comfort to sincerely afflicted people. Tod Browning's universe is filled with charlatans whose public good works are camouflage for their secret evils. So it is deeply ironic that one of Browning's few genuinely virtuous protagonists—the Bishop of Limehouse—is the ultimate fraud: a person who does not exist.

Seeing Through Seeing Through
The Trompe l'Oeil *Effect and Bodily Difference in the Cinema of Tod Browning**

HUGH S. MANON

> *Trompe-l'oeil is only apparently realistic. It is in fact linked to the self-evidence of the world, with such meticulous likeness that it becomes magical.*
> —Jean Baudrillard from *Photographies*
>
> *I show you my tricks. Would I have done that if I wanted to fool you? I would not. Well, then, why can't you give me credit for being honest?*
> —Madame LaGrange in *The Thirteenth Chair*
> (Tod Browning, 1929)

In advancing a critical appraisal of the cinema of Tod Browning, it is difficult to ignore the obvious biographical connection between the director's films and his youthful experience as a magician's assistant and showman on the American carnival sideshow circuit. Browning's films reference the dark interior of such traveling attractions not only in their subject matter (most notably in the director's 1932 film *Freaks*), but also in their unveiling of a "backstage view" as an implicitly interesting subject for viewers of Hollywood film.[1]

In films such as *The Unholy Three* (1925), *The Unknown* (1927), and *The Thirteenth Chair* (1929), Browning's characters engage in various deceptive schemes, but in each case the film reveals to the viewer precisely how the deception is accomplished. At such moments Browning's films can be understood as the very antithesis of the magician's code—*always* revealing the secret behind the deception. But while it is easy to connect the director's personal

---

*Originally published in *Framework: The Journal of Cinema and Media*, Volume 47, Number 1, Spring 2006, pp. 60–82; reprinted with the permission of Wayne State University Press.

history with his films' carnival milieu, very little has been done to theorize the structure and function of Browning's demystifying revelations.

In this essay I draw upon Jacques Lacan's discussion of *trompe l'oeil* in Seminar XI in order to identify a pervasive motif within the Browning *oeuvre*, a repetition in which the director gestures beyond the ostensible truth of cinema's costumed realism, confronting viewers with the limitations of his actors' own bodies — limitations that exist both inside and outside the story world of his films. Replicating the leisurely, self-directed pace necessary for a *trompe l'oeil* painting to have its effect, Browning allows his narratives to momentarily "stall out," calling attention to the one-to-one correspondence between his characters' size, shape and stature, and the undisguisable materiality of his actors' real bodies. The result is a visual paradox. The onscreen appearances of "master of disguise" Lon Chaney, for instance, or of little person Harry Earles (disguised as a two-year-old child in *The Unholy Three*), captivate audiences not because their costumes succeed in fooling us, but precisely because they immediately and manifestly fail to deceive the eye. In a series of game-like diversions comparable to the pleasures of *trompe l'oeil*— a hyperrealistic genre of painting, anchored not in the success of mimesis but its failure — the director invites a remarkably self-directed form of enjoyment, permitting viewers to re-deceive themselves in the context of a revealed deception.

Browning repeatedly invites his viewers to press beyond the passive acceptance of cinematic realism, instead ensnaring audiences in the convolutions of a "trick"— an inherently reflexive strategy that seduces audiences precisely by making them aware that they are being fooled.

In his 1964 Seminar entitled "What Is a Picture?" Jacques Lacan addresses the subject's pleasure in *trompe l'oeil*:

> What is it that attracts and satisfies us in *trompe l'oeil*? When is it that it captures our attention and delights us? At the moment when, by a mere shift of our gaze, we are able to realize that the representation does not move with the gaze and that it is merely a tricking of the eye. For it appears at that moment as something other than it seemed, or rather it now seems to be that something else [*Concepts* 112].

In encountering an instance of *trompe l'oeil*, the viewer pauses — in effect, mentally "toying" with the self-evident falsity of the image. But whereas such contemplation would seem to undermine a viewer's ability to suspend disbelief (and accept realism), I understand Browning's *trompes l'oeil* not as subverting, but as, in fact, stabilizing the viewer's relation to the director's frequently hyperbolic content. Browning's films permit us not only to see through to uncover hidden diegetic truths, but above all encourage viewers to *see through seeing through*, positioning the bodily object onscreen not as a hermeneutic puzzle, but as a self-evident answer. Lon Chaney, appearing as "Alonzo the Armless" in *The Unknown*, is manifestly not armless. Harry Earles, appearing in the guise of a two-year-old in *The Unholy Three*, is manifestly not a child. Yet by establishing, and just as quickly revealing to the viewer, a series of duplicitous bodies, Browning devalues the simple satisfaction of moving from deception to a resolved truth, and instead foists upon his audience a second, arguably more primal, form of pleasure — an endless oscillation between the truth and its deliberate denial.

Which Is Which: The Structure of the trompe

In order to understand the structural centrality of real material bodies in both *trompe l'oeil* and the Browning *oeuvre*, it will be useful to consider a proper example of *trompe l'oeil* from the realm of painting. The fact that this example takes the form of a personal anecdote underscores Lacan's presupposition that *trompe l'oeil* is not merely a representational style, but a particular form of subjective experience. On a trip to southeastern Pennsylvania, while visiting a museum known primarily for its Wyeth collection, I encountered amidst a series of much larger canvases a very small painting, no bigger than five by seven inches, depicting two life-sized one-cent postage stamps positioned side-by-side. Entitled *Which Is Which?*, the painting was composed by Delaware artist Jefferson David Chalfant around 1889 (Gorman 15). I had, of course, seen examples of *trompe l'oeil* before, both in galleries and elsewhere: a false Mediterranean window painted on the wall of a local bistro, a Victorian trade card printed to look like a handwritten love-note or like a broken picture frame, a carefully randomized cluster of fake bullet-hole stickers on the tailgate of a pickup truck at a stop light. In comparison to these more common examples, Chalfant's personal brand of *trompe l'oeil* can be understood as particularly advanced, employing a reflexive, multi-layered strategy to lure his viewers — a *trompe* within a *trompe*.

Encountering "Which Is Which?" for the first time, the viewer is confronted not just by the two centrally positioned stamps, but also by a marginal scrap of printed text — a newspaper clipping affixed to the lower left corner of the canvas publicly proclaiming that one of the two stamps is a forgery, in case we missed the point. The tiny clipping reads as follows: "Mr. Chalfant proposes to paste a real stamp on the canvas beside his painting, and the puzzling question will be 'Which is which?'" Chalfant's viewer is ostensibly positioned as an informed viewer — not deceived but generously "clued in" to the existence of the forgery as such.[2] In addition to this discursive clue, however, the modern viewer is hailed by a second, equally telling detail. At the center of the painting is a material body of sorts — a bit of decayed flesh that compounds the pleasure of the trick. In a most literal sense, time has not been kind to Chalfant's original product. A hundred years of oxidation (and, one imagines, the oil from a thousand curious fingertips) has severely deteriorated the real stamp — the one on the left — making it entirely obvious to any modern viewer "which" is, in fact, "which." The painted stamp has retained its original vibrant color, while the real stamp is faded and brown. Strangely, however, although one can only imagine the two stamps as ever having been perfect mirror images of one another, the captivating effect of Chalfant's painting is in no way diminished. Indeed, far from ruining the basic premise of his work, the deterioration of the real stamp calls our attention to a second order of trickery. Having momentarily considered the resiliency of oil paints in comparison to printed paper, the modern viewer instantly deduces the second forgery in Chalfant's composition. Like the fake stamp on the right, his roughly-torn newspaper clipping has itself failed to decompose. By connecting the bright and legible stamp with the bright and legible news clipping, the viewer draws the correct conclusion: that the newspaper write-up proclaiming the brilliance of Chalfant's *trompe l'oeil* is itself a microscopically detailed fake, painted on the canvas. A number of Chalfant's *trompes l'oeil* rely upon this same structure — including a painted news clipping as part of their composition — but, to my knowledge, only in "Which Is Which?" did the painter see fit to include a fragile and eminently damageable real object like a paper stamp. This decaying object, though it would appear to defy Chalfant's original intent, is instead the work's greatest asset. Through time, the disintegration of the real stamp has transformed the painted material from a hermetically sealed puzzle into what Lacan refers to as a subjective "lure" (*Concepts* 111). Though there is no way to verify that such textual decomposition is what Chalfant had in mind, in terms of the structuration of *trompe l'oeil* it would be a disastrous mistake to "restore" his painting, replacing the decaying old stamp with a better-preserved philatelic specimen. Unwittingly or on purpose, Chalfant has created not a simplistic or "too perfect" deception, with the whole of his subject unrealistically embalmed in oils for all time, but instead succeeds in *incorporating imperfection*— making mortality a part of the show. As director Tod Browning will do in a series of films some 35 years later, Chalfant trots out a real body in the midst of fakery, and in doing so produces a *trompe* which appears shockingly out of place at first glance, but which paradoxically withstands the test of time precisely by revealing the mechanism of its deception.[3]

To deceive is not the same as to "trick," since deception genuinely desires the viewing subject's obliviousness, whereas all trickery doubles back on itself, gesturing beyond representation to indicate the source of the trick — the fact that there is "something to it." For Lacan, the pleasurable effect of *trompe l'oeil*, despite (and ultimately because of) its manifest deceit, is proof of the human subject's operation on the order of the symbolic. Beyond imaginary representation, the human subject is most acutely ensnared by the symbolic structure of a truth that misleads because it is true — a double deception in which the deceiver lays "tracks whose deceptiveness lies in getting them to be taken as false, when in fact they are true — that is, tracks that indicate the right trail" (*Écrits* 293). In order to produce what I am calling the "*trompe l'oeil* effect," an object must present not only a plausible level of verisimilitude, but also a spatially or temporally proximate (if not always concurrent) *full disclosure* that a deception is being attempted. Moreover, because disclosure is so integral to the structure of *trompe l'oeil*, the order in which the beholder apprehends the trick ("disclosure first" or "deception first") should be largely irrelevant. An advertised, much-anticipated gallery exhibition of *trompe l'oeil* will ultimately produce the same effect as a *trompe* encountered by accident, or by surprise. Indeed, it could be argued that any representation that stakes its whole effect upon the sequence in which a deception is revealed cannot be *trompe l'oeil*, and is instead an attempt at simple, first-order deception.

But what exactly is the effect of *trompe l'oeil* on the spectator? What are all those gallery visitors doing when they stand in front of Chalfant's painting? They are pausing to re-trick themselves into believing that the painted stamp is real, so that they can again realize that it is a fake — on again, off again in a self-sustained alternation that James Cook aptly characterizes as a "dynamic of indeterminacy and forgetting" (225). At the risk of stating the obvious, then, we must add a third structural requirement for *trompe l'oeil*. Along with establishing convincing verisimilitude and disclosing the deception, the object of *trompe l'oeil* must by definition remain present and relatively static; the convincing forgery — in painting, cinema and elsewhere — must remain available to the senses. Any representation that can only be glimpsed in passing, or which cannot be inspected closely, cannot support the *trompe l'oeil* effect, since to remove the object (either temporally or spatially) obviates the crucial dynamic — the viewer's compulsion to playfully oscillate between true understanding and pretending naïveté.

Given this set of basic structural elements, it becomes clear that *trompe l'oeil* cannot be limited exclusively to the realm of painting, or to the visual arts more broadly. As an example of the *trompe l'oeil* effect outside the realm of static visuals, consider the American vocal harmony group the Mills Brothers, whose rise to fame in the early 1930s was due in part to their ability to vocally mimic the sound of various Dixieland instruments. On the vaudeville stage, the novelty of the group's performance was obvious, owing to the conspicuous absence of the trumpet, trombone and saxophone the audience was hearing. To be clear, however, the *trompe l'oeil* effect, in its function as a subject-controlled little game, would have been achieved by the beholder not in initially perceiving the contradiction between sight and sound, but instead at the moment of closing the eyes (or looking away) to imagine the presence of real instruments, only to open them again and behold four men standing alone, save for a single guitar. In recorded form — which is where the Mills Brothers found their greatest success — the *trompe l'oeil* effect became even more acute. When played on a phonograph, the requisite disclosure of the Mills Brothers' vocal impersonations would have been missing, disallowing the listener's pleasure in *trompe l'oreille*, and producing only a simple (i.e. single) deception. Wisely, however, Brunswick records saw fit to imprint the Mills Brothers' first singles with the following notice: "No musical instrument or mechanical devices used on this recording other than one guitar." Far from a legalistic disclaimer, this disclosure is the fulcrum supporting *trompe* enjoyment — a see-sawing alternation fueled by the subject's willful disbelief. Though we can assume that numerous individuals throughout history have misperceived various *trompe* artifacts as "the real thing," and moved on without remark, it should be clear that such an experience is the precise opposite of the captivating effect that *trompe l'oeil* intends.[4]

The early success of the Mills Brothers as a novelty act underscores the most basic premise of my argument about Tod Browning: that *trompe l'oeil* is fundamentally not a style, but a structure — available in various media, and appealing to various senses, but always playing content against context in order to enthrall the beholder with the subjective nature of their own perceptions (Cook 253). Regarding Browning, however, a crucial question remains: are there ways in which motion pictures — with their capacity for both indexical reproduction and temporal flux — exploit the *trompe* structure differently from other media? In the absence of any literal statement that reveals the mechanism of the deception ("No musical instruments used ..."), what *trompe l'oeil* wants is an empirical "control" object — a standard of reference which, like the wall and frame that surround a canvas, functions to "out" the slick deception as a trick. Because classical Hollywood cinema itself involves a highly complex, multi-layered set of deceptions (continuity editing, lighting techniques, set design, etc.), it becomes difficult to establish any absolute and fully reliable locus of authenticity onscreen. One striking opportunity, however, hinges on the viewer's ability to immediately discern implausibilities in the relative size, shape, weight, and mobility of human bodies. For instance, even in cinema, no one would mistake a man standing on five-foot stilts for a naturally tall man. Similarly, while it would be possible to disguise Jean Harlow in such a way that she might go unrecognized by viewers as Jean Harlow, it would be absurd, even with the most advanced makeup techniques, to attempt the reverse: to disguise another actor as Jean Harlow, filming the entire production with this false substitute. No one would buy it.

My point is that, where the human body is concerned, there exist absolute thresholds beyond which the viewer simply cannot persist in believing. The films of Tod Browning repeatedly tap into these *de facto* assumptions about corporeal limitation, undermining the realism of Hollywood costuming by playing it against the viewer's sense of an objective, plausible and "real" bodily standard. Whereas bodily deception in classical Hollywood often depends on a more-or-less convincing disguise or mask, Browning's deceptions are simultaneously more basic and more convoluted than simple disguise. Having established a context full of skepticism, deception and lies, Browning shows his audience the bald-faced truth, ensnaring viewers in an irresolvable loop. What results is the overturning of common first-order deception (e.g. "fooling," "duping," "faking") in favor of the "double deception" proper to trickery. As I go on to explain, like Chalfant's painting and the Mills Brothers' vocal performances, we need to conceive of the Browning *oeuvre* as a film-by-film reiteration of the director's desire to trick — and not deceive — his audience, especially where bodily difference is concerned.

Double Deception in The Unholy Three

To pinpoint the *trompe l'oeil* effect in the films of Tod Browning, it is helpful to identify those moments at which a certain residual "stillness" appears in the context of his moving pictures. That is, we need to locate those points at which the film pauses, like a docent in a gallery, allowing viewers to ponder an onscreen body in its obvious attempt to deceive. A paradigmatic example of Browning's approach appears in his 1925 film *The Unholy Three*, an unconventional anti-hermeneutic (and markedly proto-*noir*) crime story to which the director was immediately attracted for its cinematic potential (Skal and Savada 87). At numerous points in the film, ventriloquist Professor Echo (Lon Chaney) masquerades as an old woman — the proprietress of a store specializing in talking birds — as part of an elaborate front for a burglary ring. Serving as the fulcrum for the film's multiple instances of *trompe l'oeil* are the various onscreen appearances of little person Harry Earles, who dons the frilly uniform of a two-year-old and spends much of his time hiding out in a baby carriage. Positioned, as it were, "on the inside" with the criminals, the viewer watches as various peripheral characters fail to realize that the cute child they see, called "Little Willie," is actually an ill-tempered, child-hating, 23-year-old sideshow performer known as "Tweedledee." As the narrative of *The Unholy Three* unfolds, we are encouraged not only to see through this convincing deception, but are also provided with opportunities to re-deceive ourselves. Tweedledee's memorable first appearance as "Little Willie" is a long shot of the doorway that leads to the back room of the bird store. He is dressed in frilly white, and is lying on the floor (apparently having crawled there), beating his rattle. It is at this moment — in which we witness an adult, who we know to look more like a child than an adult, dressed as a child — that the *trompe l'oeil* object is first available.[5] There is no question that the child we see is Tweedledee — we do not for a moment think that this is some other child in the narrative — but it is nonetheless striking how easily we can convince ourselves that the adult actor is a real baby, producing an uncanny form of visual pleasure. The effect is only underscored when Chaney, dressed again as the elderly grandmother, wheels "Little Willie" out of the back room in a perambulator, all bundled up for a cold day. Compared to Chaney, whose hardened facial features betray him as a man in drag, Earles acts and publicly appears just like a child, yet we know better.

The *trompe l'oeil* effect is most pronounced, however, in the film's three "quick change" scenes, in which an unexpected knock on the door forces the unholy three to hastily resume their impersonations. Most notable is a scene late in the film when Police Detective Regan (Matthew Betz) shows up at the bird shop, surprising the three as they gloat about the success of a recent robbery and murder. It appears that everything is in order, and all disguises are in place, when mastermind Chaney notices that "Little Willie" still has Tweedledee's cigar in his mouth. Once it is removed, and placed more appropriately into the mouth of Hercules the strongman (the third of the unholies, played by Victor McLaglen), the detective is permitted entrance. What we see next, in a long shot, is a perfect little Christmas tableau — with "Little Willie," in a play fireman's helmet, running his toy train back and forth in front of a decorated tree. At such moments the visual track is structured not as a secret-revealing singular revelation, but instead positions the audience as always and already "in the know." Our only recourse is a loop-like alternation: at one moment we pretend that the illusion is reality, and at the next we "step back" to appreciate the artifice of the illusion.

Though it is tempting to dismiss such auto-deception as just another form of "suspension of disbelief," Browning's perverse trick is to force viewers to engage in a *suspension of belief*— in this case, a temporary moratorium on the un-skeptical certainty evoked by the body of Harry Earles. The key is that viewerly pleasure derives not simply from an advanced knowledge that this baby is not a "real" baby — that would be an unrepeatable and more intellectual form of pleasure, i.e. a satisfying answer as opposed to the endless flip-flopping circularity of *trompe l'oeil*. Instead, the eminently repeatable pleasure of Browning's *trompe l'oeil* appears in the instantaneous (moment-by-moment) splitting between the character disguised and the real physicality of the actor's body. Because we have known from the film's very first scene that Tweedledee is actually an adult man, for the remainder of the film's running time actor Earles always appears to us as simultaneously in and out of his cinematic clothes — at once real and false, adult and child. In other words, in a structural homology with the painted stamp that we may readily compare to the real thing next to it, actor Earles' real physical body becomes a standard of reference, a quasi-scientific control against which both the child "Little Willie" and the adult "Tweedledee" can be compared.

Following from Baudrillard, the body of Harry Earles is a necessary structural component of the film's *trompe l'oeil*, since it links the realm of representation concretely to "the self-evidence of the world"— directing viewers outside the realm of the story to consider the *hors-champ* of the film's production (142). Our pleasure derives from the fact that actor Earles' real diminutive physique may be either diegetic (i.e. the body of the character) or extra-diegetic (the body of the actor on the set), but as in *trompe l'oeil*, we can only visualize one of these possibilities at a time. We look at him as an adult, and then again as a child, and while each perspective is entirely convincing, each perspective also invokes the possibility of its opposite. Earles' onscreen appearances either in baby-drag or in the zoot suit of a hardened gangster each amount to the same thing — a moment-by-moment injunction to imagine the truth of the representation or its opposite, without ever settling on either. As in Chalfant's painting, or any instance of *trompe l'oeil*, it is not simply the deception, but *the deception seen again in the context of its seeing through*, which captivates. This dialectic of deception is both a remarkable exception to classical Hollywood's fetishization of a seamless realism and a crucial strategy within the cinema of Tod Browning more broadly.

What distinguishes Browning from his Hollywood contemporaries is not exclusively his strategic invocation of the *trompe l'oeil* effect, but the fact that the central object in this cyclical play of belief and disbelief is the human body — or, more precisely, the fact of bodily difference. To be clear, by "bodily difference" I do not necessarily mean sexual difference, dwarfism, physical deformity, or anything so categorical. Instead, I am referring to the obvious physical manifestations that would make it impossible for Lon Chaney to play a convincing Tweedledee, or vice versa. This sense of an absolute physical threshold — referenced in the popular 1920s schoolboy joke "Don't step on that spider...it might be Lon Chaney" — is precisely what makes Chaney a perfect leading man for Browning. Chaney's appeal hinges not simply upon all the things he *can* do (with his body, with makeup, etc.), but precisely upon what he *can and cannot do*. Browning cast Chaney in eleven separate films, and there can be little doubt that much of Browning's success depended on Chaney's ability to push the limits of disguise and bodily distortion, repeatedly calling those limits into question. With or without Chaney's nimble assistance, however, Browning's films repeatedly undermine the performative dimension of his characters' bodies by acknowledging various actors' real corporeality — forgoing nuanced personality distinctions in favor of an eschatological comparison of basic physical shapes and sizes, endowments and lacks.

The Return of the Really Armless Fake Armless Man

If a certain quotient of pleasure is produced through the repeated reminder that Tweedledee is an adult dressed up and acting like a child, he nonetheless remains a supporting character — part of the appeal of *The Unholy Three*, but not its narrative center. Two years later, however, in Browning's 1927 masterwork *The Unknown*, the bodily *trompe l'oeil* effect is even more aggressively exploited, accounting for much of the film's conflict and tension. Near the end of the first act, the audience learns that the film's protagonist is a fraud. Alonzo the Armless (Lon Chaney) — a gypsy circus performer who throws knives with great precision using only his feet — indeed has two healthy, functional arms. When in public, they are bound to his chest with a tight leather corset and covered with a shirt and jacket. The catch, of course, is that this diegetically crucial piece of information recapitulates something that most audience members would have already understood about Chaney — that the actor himself indeed had arms!

Consequently, when Browning reveals the deceptive mechanism beneath Alonzo's clothes, he confronts viewers with something they already know — a sort of knowledge-overlap or redundancy. We know that there are arms under Alonzo's cloak precisely because we know there are arms under Chaney's costume. As a result, there are only two options for Browning's narrative vis-à-vis Chaney, two possibilities that most viewers recognize at the precise moment the actual decision is made: 1) the film could remove Alonzo's cloak, revealing him to have arms, or 2) the film could refuse to remove Alonzo's cloak altogether. Though each of these options comes with its own set of risks, it is important to consider both of these narrative possibilities in opposition to a third, purely hypothetical non-option, a logical impossibility which no one in their right mind would believe, yet upon which the director's entire gambit depends, namely 3) the film removes the cloak to reveal the horror that both Alonzo, and Chaney, are in fact physically armless. Of course, we all know which option Browning chooses. However, in a precise homology with Chalfant's painting, the revelation of Alonzo's (and Chaney's) corseted arms is not an end in itself, but forces a dialectical step upward. Having seen the carnival chicanery that goes on behind the veil of Alonzo's clothing, the viewer is confronted with a strange problem when the phony "Armless Man" returns from his amputating surgery.

Unlike Tweedledee, whose diegetic body (in accordance with the dimensions of actor Earles' real body) remains an empirical constant throughout the film, Alonzo's body is supposed to change within the narrative of *The Unknown*, even while the viewer persists in knowing that Chaney has kept his arms. Long before Browning shows the audience the mechanism behind Alonzo's armless act, the viewer has presumably already equated Alonzo's silk shirt and embroidered jacket with Chaney's costuming, thinking "somehow, there must be arms under there." When the leather corset device is revealed, anyone who was originally deceived, or simply unquestioning, is brought into the fray. However, the scene of Alonzo's post-operative return to his beloved assistant Nanon (Joan Crawford) is something quite different. In terms of viewerly affect, the moment at which Alonzo arrives to finally confess his love for Nanon — the guarantee of which is his amputated arms — must be numbered amongst the most horrifying moments in all of Hollywood cinema, and not just because we know that Alonzo's supreme sacrifice has been in vain. When Alonzo returns to Nanon's apartment, opening the door with his foot, we cannot help but think to ourselves, "now he *really* has no arms!" The effect is only underscored when Nanon embraces Alonzo and says to him: "You are thinner, Alonzo! Have you been sick?" Alonzo replies with a perfectly gruesome suggestion: "No not sick," he says, "but I have lost some flesh." At this moment, however unconsciously, do we not briefly feel a surge of revulsion at the possibility that Chaney's own arms are now "really" gone — an abrupt but quickly fading sense that the impossible third possibility has indeed occurred?

Browning's tale of the really armless fake armless man is a perfect example of the Lacanian concept of double deception. Having admitted to his audience what they already know — that Alonzo's costume is a deception — Browning succeeds not by lying, but precisely by telling the truth. By fully disclosing (rather than artificially concealing) the mechanism of his protagonist's false disguise, Browning tips his hand, only to blindside the audience upon Alonzo's return by reiterating the very same deception — this time from a pre-established locus of honesty. The revolting, almost hyper-real sense that the post-operative Chaney's arms really are missing — or at the very least that something is dreadfully wrong behind the false veil — is mirrored in Lacan's most pointed discussion of *trompe l'oeil*, a passage from his 1964 Seminar entitled "What Is a Picture?" Here, Lacan identifies the doubly deceptive structure of *trompe l'oeil* in the classical tale of Zeuxis and Parrhasios. As the story goes, two friends are engaged in a painting contest. Initially, Zeuxis paints grapes so realistic that they attract even the birds. Parrhasios counters this effort, and "triumphs over him by painting on the wall a veil, a veil so lifelike that Zeuxis, turning towards him said, *Well, and now show us what you have painted behind it*" (*Concepts* 103). Lacan explicates the story by making a crucial distinction, a point that is easy to miss, especially given the temptation to misunderstand *trompe l'oeil* as an imaginary, rather than a symbolic (i.e. "double") deception. The point of the story is not that Zeuxis is fooled by the painting of the veil into believing that it is real, since, as in any instance of *trompe l'oeil*, the representation is self-evidently a fraud. Instead, as Lacan stresses, the point is that Parrhasios has presented Zeuxis with the representation of a veil (of all things!), and that, like any desiring human subject, Zeuxis presumes that *veils conceal*. Slavoj Žižek explains the paradox of double deception as follows:

> We can deceive animals by an appearance imitating a reality for which it can be a substitute, but the properly human way to deceive a man is to imitate the dissimulation of reality — that act of concealing deceives us precisely by pretending to conceal something. In other words, there is nothing behind the curtain except the subject who has already gone beyond it [196].

Having seen through the all-too-expected deception of Parhassios' fine technique, Zeuxis finds himself deceived nonetheless — specifically by the painting's blunt content. In the words of Henry Krips, "(D)espite seeing through the deception, indeed because he sees through it, he is trapped by the image since, in asking what is painted behind the veil, he mistakenly infers: veils conceal, therefore something must be painted behind the painted veil," presumably the final proof of Parhassios' great skill (28). A painting of a bowl of apples, Zeuxis anticipates, or perhaps of some vases of oil? For our part, we can just as easily imagine Zeuxis regretting his words as soon as he utters them, without Parrhasios having said a thing.

Alonzo's cloak in *The Unknown* is identical in structure to Parrhasios' painting of a veil — it is a deception which we are permitted to see through, only to be convinced that because we see a veil, there must be something behind the veil we see. Alonzo's clothing has already been positioned in the film as a locus of deception (we know all about Chaney's corseted arms), yet when the film signals (through intertitles, a fade-to-black, etc.) that Alonzo's surgery is complete, we are paradoxically inclined to believe that there is nonetheless something to it. In this case, the "something" is presumed to be a nothing — a horrifying lack of appendages — yet this momentary affirmative belief, and our positioning as dupes, arises directly as a result of, and not despite, our informed skepticism. Alonzo's covered torso, an image we have seen repeatedly prior to the surgery, on one level signifies "just more of the same old shtick." But having paraded Alonzo's veiled body throughout the film *as a lie*, Browning ultimately succeeds in convincing us of the impossible. Such is the paradox of human deception, according to Lacan: to deceive a human we must try obviously to fail in our deception, and only then will we succeed.

An admission: having screened *The Unknown* numerous times, never once did I myself consider the possibility that Alonzo's nimble feet belonged to an actor other than Chaney. This assumption, as it turns out, was simply incorrect; I was deceived. In terms of the history of the film's production, Alonzo's deft legs and feet were not always Chaney's own. In certain scenes they belonged to a hidden accomplice in the cinematic deception, a real sideshow "armless wonder" named Paul Dismute, whose head and torso were concealed off-camera while his exposed legs and toes performed the best of Chaney's stunts — lifting a cigarette to Chaney's mouth and lighting it, mopping his brow with a handkerchief, and strumming a guitar (Skal and Savada 113–14).

My misperception speaks precisely to the blanket effectiveness of Browning's doubly deceptive strategy — *of course they are Chaney's feet; Chaney is a master deceiver and he is deceiving me right now!* I am not alone in having been double-deceived, however. The success of Browning's trick is echoed in Mordaunt Hall's *New York Times* review of the film on June 13, 1927:

> Mr. Chaney really gives a marvelous idea of the Armless Wonder, for to act in this film he has learned to use his feet as hands when eating, drinking and smoking. He even scratches his head with his toe when meditating [17].

Reviewer Hall has clearly been fooled. Interestingly, however, four days later Hall recants his praise, greatly qualifying the actor's talents in a second column in the *Times*:

> [I]n the depiction of Alonzo using his toes to handle a knife and fork, to put a cigarette in his mouth, to scratch his head meditatively, or to fire a pistol and to throw knives, there is naturally a good deal of trickery. It is striking, but Mr. Chaney would have to be a contortionist to do some of the stunts he is supposed to do with his feet [X5].

It is as if some friend of Hall's — perhaps a movie industry insider — pulled the reviewer aside and chided him into questioning the reality of the illusion. Strangely, though, in his specific wording, the film critic still cannot seem to see beyond the film's double deception. Only half-convinced, Hall's retraction never quite pinpoints (and, I would argue, never quite *believes*) the lie behind the truth. One wonders if he ever finally figured it out.

Conclusion: Sizing-up Browning as Auteur

In his essay "The Myth of Total Cinema," André Bazin uses the idea of *trompe l'oeil* to distinguish the formative phase of cinema from its resolution in conventional realism:

[J]ust as the word indicates, the aesthetic of *trompe-l'oeil* in the eighteenth century resided more in illusion than in realism, that is to say, in a lie rather than in truth. ... To some extent, this is what the early cinema was aiming at, but this operation of cheating quickly gave way to an ontogenetic realism [19].

For Bazin, early directors such as Edison, Méliès, and the brothers Lumière were not engaged in successful deception — convincing audiences to believe their realistic illusions — but instead in an *"operation* of cheating" (emphasis mine). In such an arrangement, it is the operation itself, the mechanism behind the ostensible deception, which usurps the primary position in the text, and in viewers' minds. When sets appear excessively stagy, when costumes are overwrought, and when the sun appears as a painted wooden disc with a beaming smile, the experience of a cinematic audience is akin to theater. Pleasure derives from the ever-present knowledge that a trick is being played, and that something goes on, in Bazin's words, "behind the decor" (102). It is not straightforward deception, then, but the "trick" structure of double deception, which leads Bazin to connect early cinema with *trompe l'oeil*. Though such failed deception would seem to present an affront to viewers, the opposite effect is produced; to reveal the truth behind the deception lures an audience most profoundly.[6] Tod Browning clearly intuits this, although with the rise of classical Hollywood in the 1920s, many of his contemporaries were aggressively aiming at something different — overturning the pleasures of the *trompe* in favor of a seamless realism. In the context of classical Hollywood, Browning represents a marked reversion to early cinema's organic tendency to "tip its hand," but from within the context of realism proper.

As Tom Gunning suggests, viewerly pleasure in the early "cinema of attractions" derived not from being actually deceived (by the image of a train chugging directly toward the screen, etc.).[7] Instead, "(f)ar from confusing the film image with reality," audiences dismissed it "as mere trickery." Gunning continues:

Clearly the fascination and even the realism of early films related more strongly to the traditions of magic theater (with its presentation of popular science as spectacle) than to later conceptions of documentary realism. Méliès himself recognized this at his first viewing of Lumière, proclaiming the projection, "an extraordinary trick" ("un truc extraordinaire") [95–96].

Arriving at a moment when the conventions of Hollywood narrative cinema are becoming fully consolidated, Browning's early films do not simply manipulate his audience into accepting the verisimilitude of the world on screen. Instead, by refusing to "deceive the eye" in the way that Hollywood insists, the films position realism in a dialectical relation with behind-the-scenes insight, advancing a reflexive metacommentary on cinematic representation itself. In effect, the *trompe l'oeil* bodies that populate Browning's frame are the equivalent of the objective, blunt and inert, but nonetheless captivating hull of Lumière's steam engine — objects in which we do not actually believe, but in front of which we playfully imagine ourselves as believers.

A question remains, however, as to what extent this dialectic of double-deceptive trickery changes across Browning's body of work. Thus far, I have discussed two early Browning films — *The Unholy Three* and *The Unknown* — yet a great deal can be gained by comparing Browning's early work with his later (i.e. post–*Freaks*) films. To this end, I will conclude by offering two comparisons, each of which suggests that both the *trompe l'oeil* effect, and the related structure of double deception, can be understood as an evolving auteuristic signature over the course of Browning's career, with a striking phase shift occurring in Browning's last films. My first comparison involves two films — *West of Zanzibar* (1928) and *Mark of the Vampire* (1935) — which, in different ways, momentarily formalize the boundary-crossing behind-the-scenes view so prevalent in the films I have discussed above. At the very beginning of *West of Zanzibar* we see a magician named Phroso (Lon Chaney) set to perform a routine in which a skeleton in an upright coffin will be transformed into a curvaceous young woman. As in *The Unholy Three* and *The Unknown*, the point of the scene is not to dupe the audience. Instead, the director lets his audience in on the secret, cutting to an orthogonal shot from behind the coffin apparatus that reveals the woman to be standing on a revolving platform. This right-angle or cross-sectional view — a shot that encompasses both the audience-side and the backstage-side of the false coffin — perfectly encapsulates, in visual terms, Browning's position as the deceitful revealer of deceptions. What we see is neither the front nor the back of the veil, but its side — an ichnographic viewpoint in which all knowledge is relative. Like the decayed stamp that would seem to ruin the illusion of *trompe l'oeil*, such a revelation doubly deceives, setting the viewer up for all manner of subsequent deceptions, investments and pleasures.

The magic coffin scene exists in a tidy parallel with the infamous closing shot from Browning's *Mark of the Vampire*, in which we see Count Mora (Bela Lugosi) and his "daughter" Luna (Carroll Borland) behind the scenes of their phony haunted castle. For the first time in the film we receive positive confirmation that there are no real vampires here, just a couple of convincing actors, as we witness the two removing their makeup while discussing the brilliance of their Gothic performance-piece — the central deception in the film's mystery/horror plot. In this late Browning feature the dominant visual metaphor is that of a theater-house: behind the creepy, spider web–encrusted walls of the castle is a "green room" in which the vampire-actors receive their stage directions, don their makeup, and discuss technique. The fact that this revelation appears as a sort of offhand postscript — not even as the climax, but as part of the denouement — marks a striking shift away from Browning's tried-and-true narrative stratagem of revealing the mechanism of deception near the beginning of his films (as in *West of Zanzibar*). At the end of *Mark of the Vampire* the whole narrative is revealed to have been a fake, as is the process of filmmaking itself.

Though David Skal hypothesizes that *Mark of the Vampire* represents Browning "thumbing his nose at Universal for a particularly unhappy experience during the filming of *Dracula*," in my view we need not consider the director's biography in order to view the film as a subversive text (191–92). Indeed, it seems clear, given certain narrative repetitions within the Browning *oeuvre*, that to mysteriously withhold the truth of deception until a film-ending "a-ha" moment is far too hermeneutic, and, frankly, too *Hollywood*, for the Browning we know. Consequently, *Mark of the Vampire* can be viewed either as Browning's greatest failure, or as a passive-aggressive slap in the face to the audience's expectation of Browning as double-deceptive *auteur*—a deliberate autocritical inversion of films like *The Unknown*, *The Unholy Three* and *West of Zanzibar*. Instead of tipping its hand early on, the film maintains a strict adherence to the rules of the classical detective narrative — except with the addition of the most superlative Gothic vampires ever caught on film — and in doing so plays havoc with the generic contract that had, over time, been drawn between Browning's audience and his own unique brand of deception.

A second comparison can be drawn between two films, released a decade apart, that represent Browning's preoccupation with debunking phony spiritualism: *The Thirteenth Chair* (1929) and *Miracles for Sale* (1939).[8] Adapted from a stage play, the major appeal of *The Thirteenth Chair* centers on the talents of Madame Rosalie La Grange (Margaret Wycherly, who also appeared in the play), a fraudulent spiritualist who incorporates a healthy measure of real honesty as part of her deception. When LaGrange is invited to a wealthy private residence to conduct a séance, she begins by pretending to contact the spirit realm, speaking a whole series of questions into the air and receiving responses of "one rap for 'yes' and two for 'no.'" The point of this conventional exercise, in typical Browning fashion, is not ultimately to deceive or scare the assembled group (or the viewer), but to permit LaGrange to subsequently reveal the mechanism behind her deception, winning over her audience by way of an acknowledged trick so that the real deceptions can commence. Having disclosed the wooden sole in her shoe, which she motionlessly taps beneath her floor-length dress, LaGrange gets down to business:

"I'll tell you the truth now," she says, "Most of the time it's tricks, but tonight there'll be no faking. I can fool you, too, so you'll have to take my word for it that I won't." The word "skeptical" arises repeatedly in the discourse of the guests, but it becomes clear that the key, for Browning, is not to confound the audience's skepticism, but instead to underwrite it—showing the audience how the deception is performed so as to ground everything in an assumption of cynical manipulation. Later, LaGrange says, "I don't understand you at all. I show you my tricks. Would I have done that if I wanted to fool you? I would not. Well, then, why can't you give me credit for being honest?" This statement can be understood as a virtual epigram for Browning's *modus operandi*, a tendency that finds its place in many of the director's early story ideas, script selections and casting decisions, as well as in his directorial style.

A radical revision of the spiritualist hoax in *The Thirteenth Chair* comes in Browning's last film, *Miracles for Sale*. As in the ending of *Mark of the Vampire*, the climax of *Miracles for Sale* stages a deception at the viewer's expense, but this time it is a classic double deception—a genuine trick. The story's protagonist is Mike Morgan (Robert Young), a renowned designer of magic apparatuses. Early in the film, as the murder-mystery unfolds, Morgan espouses a philosophy that clearly echoes Browning's own:

> We're magicians. ... We entertain to people. We tell them that the hand is quicker than the eye and fool them legitimately. It's fun for them, and it's a living for us. But I hate these fakers that trade on human suffering and get money from heartbroken widows and mothers.

Unlike the "phony mediums" he detests, Morgan's deceptions are self-evidently harmless "tricks." But as the mystery plot nears its climax, and the time comes to flush the murderer out into the open, Morgan must put his skills as a trickster to the test.

In front of a large audience, Morgan gets set to perform "the late Sing Ling Fu's magic bullet trick," in which a woman catches a bullet in her teeth. He introduces his "new version of one of the most dangerous acts in magic" as follows: "Ladies and gentlemen, this is obviously a trick. Obviously the solution is in some deception, either with the weapons or the cartridges. My version dares you to find that deception." The disclosure is classic Browning, but the act that follows is far more complicated and mysterious than similar performances in earlier films such as *The Unknown* and *West of Zanzibar*. As is conventional in such magic acts, Morgan calls a random group of audience members up on stage to inspect two "regulation Army rifles" and some bullets. A rifle is selected and tested by firing it at an ordinary Ritz cracker, which explodes in front of the bull's-eye target. Morgan then asks one member of the committee to randomly select one more cartridge, and another man to mark it so that it can be identified as authentic after it is fired. What follows is a perfect double deception, put over not by Morgan, but by the structure of the film itself. In close up, only the audience is shown a set of hands surreptitiously exchanging the selected bullet for a second cartridge.

The switched cartridge is loaded into the rifle and handed to a U.S. Army marksman (whose official papers the committee has also reviewed). Judy Barclay (Florence Rice), Morgan's assistant and love interest, takes her place in front of the bull's-eye. The rifle is raised, then a tense pause, and BAM! Blood oozes out of Judy's mouth and she collapses. The audience gasps and the curtain is drawn, as a suspicious bearded man rushes toward the stage door. The man is summarily knocked unconscious by Police Detective Quinn (William Demarest); Morgan unmasks the man and the mystery is quickly solved. The real puzzle, however, concerns the fate of Judy. A quick cut reveals her to be alive and well and complaining about a bad taste in her mouth from the imitation blood capsule. But if the bullets were switched — a fact known only to the audience and the bearded man — then how did she survive? Interestingly, this is the wrong question.

The cause of the misdirection can be pinpointed in the supposedly truth-revealing close-up of the switched bullet, the cinematic equivalent of the newspaper clipping in Chalfant's painting. At the moment the bullet is switched, apparently revealing a veiled secret, the audience's viewing position changes to an insider's view: we know something that the protagonists do not. Because we have been "clued in," we draw an immediate conclusion about the scene's specific locus of deception — the lie is in the bullet. In a film full of magic and deception, the candid (and thus presumably true) substitution of a "real" second cartridge automatically presumes a prior (covert, deceptive) substitution, leaving no doubt about the solution to Morgan's "dare": the original bullet must have been a planted fake, i.e. a "blank" that was somehow included in the sealed box by the benevolent trickster Morgan. Otherwise, why would it have been switched? Yet by handing over this first deception, the film has craftily fooled the viewer with a second ruse, ensnaring us in the doubly-deceptive logic of Morgan's initial admission. The impossible-to-discern true situation is that *all* of the bullets were real — exactly as Morgan promised — a fact we discover only when Morgan's shill, the well-credentialed Army sniper, finally pipes up: "Well that's the first time I ever had orders to miss my target!"

Though this scene corresponds well with the trickery of earlier Browning films, the real issue in *Miracles for Sale*, as in *Mark of the Vampire*, concerns not the way in which the deception is revealed, but the point at which this truth-disclosure appears — namely at the very end of the film, invalidating the *trompe l'oeil* effect entirely. By withholding the moment at which the deceptive agents of the story tip their hand, it is as if Browning has given up on his role as trickster and drifted back into the simple first-order deceptions characteristic of Hollywood realism. However, it is tempting to give Browning the benefit of the doubt here. In the tacked-on ending of *Mark of the Vampire*, and the bullet-catching climax of *Miracles for Sale*, we witness two films not simply deceiving, but dialectically *failing to fail to deceive* their audience. In the context of Browning's long line of cinematic tricks, is this not the greatest deception of all?

Notes

1. Because *Freaks* has been analyzed by numerous scholars, I have deliberately limited my scope to Browning's other, relatively underwritten films. It should be clear, however, that my critical perspective on Browning might just as profitably be applied to *Freaks*.

2. As James W. Cook explains in his excellent chapter on "Queer Art Illusions," quite a few *trompe l'oeil* paintings included meta-textual clues such as newspaper clippings, usually praising the skills of the artists who painted them. One interesting variation on this structure, *Vanishing Glories* by George W. Platt, was initially shown at the 1888 St. Louis Exhibition, and included an exhibition card numbered "70" affixed to the canvas. Fairgoers marveled at the realism of Platt's large cowboy-themed canvas, but the real debate concerned whether the tiny exhibition card was genuine or painted (Cook 233, 240–45).

3. Most *trompe l'oeil* paintings do not contain such a literal "control" object as Chalfant's real stamp; however, it should be clear that other real objects surrounding a painting, including the frame in which it is mounted or the wall on which it is displayed, may perform an equivalent function.

4. As an indicator of the necessity of disclosure in producing the *trompe l'oeil* effect, consider the impossibly absurd error of a so-called "human mannequin" who stands perfectly still in a shop window for hours on end but never reveals himself to be human (by way of a sign, local newspaper advertisement, or simply by periodically "springing to life"). Such unflagging devotion to the success of the deception makes this imaginary performance artist not the world's best human mannequin, but the worst. His performance succeeds as a deception, but fails as a "trick."

5. The child's appearance is echoed three years later in *West of Zanzibar* (USA, 1928) when Lon Chaney's character appears for the first time on screen after his paralysis, using only his arms and dragging his legs behind him.

6. Though the goal of Hollywood's increasing use of computer generated imagery (CGI) would seem to be simple first-order deception of the audience, many of the most convincing special effects incorporate some form of reflexive double deception: digitally engineered "flaws," such as shaky hand-held effects or artificial loss of focus.

7. The film to which I refer is Lumière's *L'Arrivée d'un Train à la Ciotat* (France, 1895), though a number of films of the early silent period were rumored to have sent audiences fleeing from their seats for fear of being run over, shot at, etc.

8. In addition to the two films I discuss, *The Mystic* (1925, USA) also contains "several showy sequences demonstrating the elaborate methods of fraudulent mediums" (Skal 94).

Works Cited

Baudrillard, Jean. *Photographies 1985–1998*. Stuttgart: Cantz Editions, 2000.

Bazin, André. *What Is Cinema?* Trans. Hugh Gray. Berkeley: University of California Press, 1967.
Cook, James W. *The Arts of Deception: Playing with Fraud in the Age of Barnum.* Cambridge: Harvard University Press, 2001.
Gorman, Joan H. *Jefferson David Chalfant.* Brandywine, PA: Brandywine Conservancy, Inc., 1979.
Gunning, Tom. "'Primitive Cinema': A Frame-Up? or, the Trick's on Us." *Early Cinema: Space, Frame Narrative.* Ed. Thomas Elsaesser. London: BFI, 1990, pp. 95–103.
Hall, Mordaunt. "The Armless Wonder." *New York Times* (June, 13, 1927), 17.
_____. "Mr. Chaney's New Role." *New York Times* (June, 19, 1927), X5.
Krips, Henry. *Fetish: An Erotics of Culture.* Ithaca, N.Y.: Cornell University Press, 1999.
Lacan, Jacques. *The Four Fundamental Concepts of Psychoanalysis.* Trans. Alan Sheridan. New York: Norton, 1978.
_____. *Écrits.* Trans. Bruce Fink. New York: Norton, 2002.
Skal, David. *The Monster Show.* New York: Penguin Books, 1993.
_____, and Elias Savada. *Dark Carnival: The Secret World of Tod Browning.* New York: Anchor Books, 1995.
Žižek, Slavoj. *The Sublime Object of Ideology.* London: Verso, 1989.

The Big City
All of Browning's Universe in One Film

F. Gwynplaine MacIntyre

Tod Browning's 1928 crime drama *The Big City* has been called a "lost film," so let us begin by examining that term. A substantial number of silent films that were "lost forever" have returned from limbo. For fifty years after its original release, no clear print of Tod Browning's 1927 melodrama *The Unknown* was believed to exist, until a print surfaced in France lacking only the original English-language intertitles and one insert shot of a blackmail letter: these had been replaced with footage bearing French translations. Now *The Unknown* is available on video — a "lost movie" that found its way home. In April 2004, the Nederlands Filmmuseum located an excellent print of *Beyond the Rocks*, a 1922 romantic drama teaming two important silent-film stars — Gloria Swanson and Rudolph Valentino — and directed by the underrated Sam Wood. This film, with Dutch intertitles replacing the originals, was in the collection of an individual who neglected to catalogue his films properly. In April 2005, the same Filmmuseum screened *Out Yonder* (1919), starring Olive Thomas; this film was also "lost forever."

In 2005, a vast archive of "lost" silent films was discovered in the hangars of a neglected aerodrome in southern England. A few weeks later, I attended Cinecon 41 in Los Angeles, where — along with several hundred other people — I viewed *Sorrell and Son* (1927), another movie that was "lost forever" until somebody recently found it in perhaps the single most obvious place to look: a filing cabinet at the Academy of Motion Picture Arts and Sciences. *Sorrell and Son* was "lost" for 78 years only because nobody bothered to look in a very obvious place. (Admittedly, the last reel is still missing.) In October 2006, at the Giornate del Cinema Muto silent-film festival in Sacile, Italy, I attended the screening of several "lost" films recently rediscovered in France and England; appropriately, this screening was followed by a screening of two

Lon Chaney films that were also "lost forever" until somebody found them: *Mockery* (1927) and *Poor Jake's Demise* (1913).

Generally, a "lost" film resurfaces when a print is found in a private collection. These prints were usually placed on the exhibition circuit during the movie's original release, yet (due to negligence or theft) were never returned to the distributor. But time is the enemy. Almost all films released in the 1940s or earlier — including all the films of the silent-movie era — were printed on nitrate-based film stock which is highly unstable. The ideal policy is to locate such films and transfer their precious images to acetate-based film stock as quickly as possible. Some of the Hollywood studios have a higher percentage of "lost" films than others. It is encouraging to observe how many "lost" films have resurfaced. But very few of these rediscovered movies were produced by Paramount, or by the studio where Tod Browning spent the peak years of his career, Metro-Goldwyn-Mayer. This is because Paramount and MGM, far more so than the other Hollywood dream factories, were extremely vigilant about retrieving all their films at the end of their exhibition cycle. Yet this vigilance was imperfect. There is now in circulation an extensive clip from Lon Chaney's last silent film, MGM's 1929 drama *Thunder*. During its U.S. release, a projectionist removed several hundred feet of film from one reel of this movie as a souvenir, then returned the incomplete print to MGM, with nobody noticing that one reel contained less footage than its siblings.

Tod Browning's *The Big City* has been listed as a "lost" film — yet I have viewed, under very imperfect circumstances, an original nitrate print of this movie. More than ten years ago I met a private collector who owns a substantial amount of memorabilia. (At his attorney's request, I shall not disclose this gentleman's name. I am permitted to say that he lives in Europe.) Among the items in his memorabilia collection were many uncatalogued reels of film which his paternal grandfather had acquired in the 1920s and 30s, at the time of their original release.

It is my understanding — not verified — that these films were "bicycled" prints: unauthorized duplicates made illegally. During the period when a legitimately licensed print was in the temporary possession of a cinema manager, the movie reels were illicitly couriered to a film lab at night, after the evening's last performance. The reels were illegally duplicated, and the legal print was then rewound onto its spools and couriered back to the cinema in time for the next day's matinee. I stress that this is only a theory, which can be verified or disproven only if someone compares the film stock of these reels against legitimate prints from their original production companies. The current possessor of these reels of film had never archived them properly, and he was concerned about the films' safe keeping and storage. He was unaware that nitrate film stock can spontaneously disintegrate; when I told him about this, and I urged him to transfer his nitrate films to acetate stock, he asked me to inspect his collection and advise him as to which of his reels of film were most urgently in danger of disintegrating, and which ones would most greatly benefit from transfer to acetate. (At some point in its deterioration, a nitrate film is no longer worth transferring to acetate.) The collector refused to permit the removal of the films from his residence. He possessed an old Movieola flatbed, which his father had occasionally used for viewing these films without projecting them. I made arrangements to bring with me a hand-held Steenbeck viewer, as I am more familiar with this equipment.

In this gentleman's disorganized collection were eight film canisters labeled *Le loup de soie noire* (*The Wolf of Black Silk*). These turned out to be a partially deteriorated nitrate print of Tod Browning's film *The Big City*. Specifically, these reels were from that subgroup of silent movies known as "flash prints." In silent-film days, Hollywood studios prepared special prints of their movies for non–Anglophone audiences. These "flash prints" contained the same English-language credits and intertitles as the prints for U.S. distribution, but each intertitle was printed for only six or eight frames of footage; this was less than one second of screen time, so the titles seemed to "flash" upon the screen. These abbreviated film prints were much shorter than the Stateside prints, and cheaper to duplicate and transport. A typewritten list of each flash print's intertitles (in English) was included with the shortened film when shipped to a foreign distributor, who would then arrange for new title cards to be made, translated into the local language. The very brief English-language "flash" titles would then be sliced out of the film, and the translated intertitles — printed on longer film strips, running a greater number of frames — would be spliced in. If a silent film contained a close-up of a piece of text in English — such as the blackmail note in *The Unknown*, or Burke's calling card in the first reel of Tod Browning's *London After Midnight* — cinema exhibitors in other countries would have the option of slicing out this close-up, and replacing it with new footage translating the text into the local language.

Another consequence of foreign-language prints of American silent films is that the onscreen images often differ subtly from those in English-language prints of the same movie, due to parallax. In silent-era Hollywood, the studios often shot their movies through a double camera: two sidelong lenses, cranked simultaneously by one cameraman, exposing two negatives in separate film magazines. One negative was for domestic prints, the other for foreign distribution. Because of the parallax between these images, the two strips of parallel footage showed the same action from slightly different angles. Foreign prints tend to be slightly askew, as camera set-ups usually favored the camera taking the domestic negative. The flash print of *The Big City* which

I viewed (with its French name) retained its original MGM intertitles in English, but running only a few frames each. This was probably a print intended for distribution in France or Belgium, intercepted before French titles could be inserted. Or it may have been an unauthorized "bicycle" print duplicated from a legitimate release print before French intertitles were inserted. I have seen *The Big City* precisely once, in circumstances far short of optimal. This was partly due to the deterioration of the nitrate print. Some sequences had decomposed to the point where I dared not Steenbeck them at all, so I took brief glimpses at the frame images by tweezering the film and holding it towards a light source.

Another problem was the time factor. The collector had hired my services to inspect his film footage for damage, not to screen his movies for my own pleasure. Naturally, I took the opportunity to view as much of *The Big City* as I could. But I did not have the luxury of lingering over key scenes, replaying them for careful study. My favored projection speed for silent films is 21.5 frames per second. For this print of *The Big City*, I speed-cranked most of the undamaged footage through my patron's flatbed or my own Steenbeck, running the movie as rapidly as I dared without endangering the film stock. I took notes while I unspooled the film, but my notes were hurried and cursory. At some points I could only guess at the images on the partially melted footage. I hope that some later and better-informed cinephile will one day give the world a more detailed and more accurate analysis of *The Big City* than I can do here. I have done my very imperfect best.

The Big City is not Tod Browning's greatest film (I would nominate *Freaks*), but it is Tod Browning's most typical film, containing nearly all the themes of his universe. Only Browning's beloved freaks and cripples are absent. The plot devices and themes that recur most frequently throughout Browning's work — the criminal underworld, confidence tricks — are developed more fully in *The Big City* than in any other Browning movie. Stage illusions and magic tricks, so essential to some other Browning films (*The Mystic, White Tiger, The Show, Miracles for Sale*, the trick coffin in *West of Zanzibar*), are briefly included in *The Big City*, in the bizarre headless-dancers sequence.

The action begins in a Manhattan nightclub managed by a brassy hostess named Tennessee. Her name, as well as some catchphrases she speaks in the intertitles ("Now, suckers!" "Give the little girl a big hand!") indicate that this woman Tennessee is based on Mary "Texas" Guinan (1884–1933), a notorious personality of the 1920s who managed the El Fay nightclub in New York City. It was common knowledge that Guinan was the mistress of her club's true owner, gangster and bootlegger Larry Fay. In 1928, Browning would have expected audiences to recognize that some characters in *The Big City* were based on actual people.

The hostess Tennessee is played by actress Virginia Pearson, a casting choice which raises some questions. Pearson was a tall brunette with dark eyes and a medium build; Texas Guinan was short, blonde, blue-eyed and slightly plump. Because the woman named Tennessee is plainly meant to be recognized as Texas Guinan, why would Browning cast an actress who didn't resemble the person she is playing? One possibility occurs to me: Tod Browning had a very mercurial sense of humor. "Texas" and "Tennessee" are both names of states in the southern U.S.A., and so is "Virginia." Perhaps it amused Browning to cast an actress named Virginia as a woman named Tennessee who is really named Texas.

Between her criminal activities and nightclubbing, the real Texas Guinan occasionally performed as a movie actress, portraying thinly-disguised versions of herself. By a remarkable coincidence, in her first film — *The Fuel of Life* (1917) — Texas Guinan played a woman named Violet Hilton: the same name as one of the conjoined twins who later performed in Tod Browning's *Freaks*. Among the customers at Tennessee's club are a gangster named Red Watson (played by Matthew Betz, who was red-haired in real life but not discernibly so in this monochrome film) and his chief henchman. The latter is played by an actor who appeared in several Browning films under the screen name John George. The name of his role here — "The Arab" — suggests that Browning may have conceived this role specifically for John George, a Syrian by birth. A short man of stunted appearance, John George was often cast as dwarfs or hunchbacks. In *The Big City*, he conveys the pathos and pathology of a physical defect without displaying any obvious deformity.

Into the nightclub strides a gaudy character named Chuck Collins (Lon Chaney). Here, and for much of the film, Collins is dressed in a motif of stripes: he wears tailored suits with pinstripes, striped shirts, and striped bow ties. In a later sequence with Marceline Day, Chaney wears a tattersall suit with matching bow tie. Chuck Collins is a flashy dresser, the sort of criminal known in Britain as a "spiv." (None of the characters in this film wear black silk, despite the movie's French title.)

Now comes the most distinctively Browning scene in *The Big City*. As the chorus girls finish their floor show, Tennessee introduces the next act: "The Headless Dancers." These turn out to be a man and woman performing a foxtrot, but with no heads! The illusion is very convincing for a moment, but after the initial surprise its secret is obvious ... and it has already been given away by the title cards, as well as by a brief shot of the dancers waiting to make their entrance. The "headless" dancers wear hoods of black velvet, and they dance in front of a black background: when lighted from the sides, to eliminate shadows, the dancers' hooded heads are nearly invisible. This "black art" technique had been used for separating characters' heads from their bodies in previous films, such as 1925's *His Majesty, the Scarecrow of Oz* (in which the Tin Woodman chops off a witch's head without killing her). Browning would use this same "black art" effect in 1927 in *The Show*, featuring Edna Tichenor as a carnival gaff (a counterfeit freak) — a woman's head on a giant spider's body, her own body concealed behind black velvet. Fake grotesques, especially as part of a confidence trick, are a recurring motif in Browning's films. Other examples are the phony clairvoyant in *The Mystic*, the counterfeit vampires in *London After Midnight* and *Mark of the Vampire*, Lon Chaney's fake cripple in *The Black Bird* and the chess-playing robot (with a man concealed inside) in *White Tiger*. The latter is especially interesting: Browning based his fake robot on an actual (but equally fake) chess-playing "Automaton" that toured Europe and America in the 19th century, and which was witnessed by Edgar Allan Poe in Richmond, Virginia, when it was exhibited in that city's museum during the period December 15, 1835, through January 2, 1836.

The dialogue titles in *The Big City* establish that the Arab has abducted Tennessee's headless dancers and replaced them with two of Red Watson's minions; the black hoods conceal their identities. Now the dancers, still hooded, whip out handguns and proceed to rob the customers. At gunpoint, Chuck surrenders his diamond cufflinks to the dancers, but he informs his rival that they both know who's really behind this robbery: "Take good care of this sparkler, Red," says Chuck in an intertitle, "I might want it back some day." The room is full of witnesses; to make it seem as if he too is a victim of the robbers, Red meekly hands over his own wallet and watch to the male dancer ... but Red tips a wink to him, and — in close-up — we see the male dancer winking at Red through his hood's eyehole. Later that night Red and the Arab are at Red Watson's place, waiting for the fake dancers to arrive with the swag. They should have been here hours ago; has Red been betrayed? "Well, I'd like to see anybody double-cross me!" he snarls.... Then he suddenly glances towards a nearby closet. An instant later, the closet's door moves as if pushed from within.

Here we have something unusual. In silent films, when the actors onscreen react to a sudden noise (which the audience cannot hear), there is typically an insert shot of a telephone bell ringing or a hand rapping a door to show the noise's source. But here — and later, in this same film — Browning makes the unusual decision to show characters responding to a sound without first establishing its origin. The Arab breaks open the closet to discover a young man and woman in dancing clothes, bound and gagged. These are the two minions who were supposed to substitute for Tennessee's dancers. When the Arab ungags the she-dancer, she ungrammatically protests: "How could we be there ... when we was here?" We cut back to Tennessee's nightclub. She and Chuck are seated at a table near the orchestra. A comical-looking tough-guy waiter

(Eddie Sturgis) brings Chuck a covered dish. The waiter lifts the lid, and we see in close-up a mound of spaghetti, without sauce. The waiter forks aside some of the spaghetti to reveal the stolen valuables, including Chuck's diamond cufflinks.

Here we encounter another motif which Browning used frequently: the confidence trick with multiple double-crosses. The headless dancers employed at Tennessee's nightclub were fakes (not really headless), but they were genuine fakes who were honestly employed. The genuine fakes have been replaced by phony fakes: Red Watson's assistants, who were supposed to rob the customers on Red's behalf; they committed a genuine theft against Chuck Collins (stealing his jewels) while committing a phony theft against Red (who gives up his valuables willingly, confident he'll get them back). Yet now, with typical Tod Browning ingenuity, it appears that the genuine phony fake dancers (working for Red) have been replaced by fake phony fake dancers, working for Chuck: the people actually wearing the hoods were Chuck's brassy girlfriend Helen (Betty Compson) and his handsome henchman Curly (James Murray). The business of stashing the jewelry beneath a pile of spaghetti is a clever visual device. Browning was fond of planting valuable objects in unlikely places (in *The Unholy Three*, we have stolen jewels concealed in a toy elephant).

A dissolve brings us later that night to Chuck's hideout, a cabaret in Harlem. After the First World War, this neighborhood in northern Manhattan had become a haven for Negroes who were often unwelcome elsewhere. In the 1920s and later, it was not unusual for white tourists to visit Harlem in the condescending belief that black performers offered entertainment that was more sensual and primitive than the performances in white establishments. In Chuck's nightclub we see a black chanteuse singing while black chorus girls dance in grass skirts, evoking the African jungle. Browning would also use such imagery in *West of Zanzibar*.

The name of Chuck's nightclub is significant: the Black Bottom Cabaret. In the 1920s, the Black Bottom was a popular dance (invented by Negro performers) that was slightly scandalous for its hint of sadomasochism: the dancers thrust their rumps towards the audience while spanking themselves. Tod Browning was probably aware of a popular stage act performing in vaudeville at this time, who climaxed their performances with a rendition of the Black Bottom: Daisy and Violet Hilton, the conjoined twins who would later appear in Browning's *Freaks*. Sexually attractive and joined at the pelvis, the Hilton sisters danced the Black Bottom to show off both their female charms and their biological oddity. While performing on the Gus Sun vaudeville circuit, Daisy and Violet Hilton were taught the Black Bottom by an American vaudevillian who (like the Hilton twins) was born in England: the comedian Bob Hope. In *The Big City*, by naming Chuck's hideout the Black Bottom,

Browning and his scenarist Waldemar Young have cleverly invoked a contemporary dance craze — as well as sadomasochism, buttock fetishism and popular perceptions of African-American sensuality. However, the Negro performers we briefly see in this scene are merely local color, unrelated to the plot.

The handsome Curly is Chuck's right-hand man, but now the dialogue establishes their relationship: lately Curly has been defying Chuck's orders, and growing more and more independent. Curly is younger than Chuck, and taller, and could probably beat him in a brawl. But now Chuck shows who's the boss by giving Curly a punch in the jaw that knocks him down. Curly rubs his jaw as he explains to Chuck's moll: "It's nothin,' Helen. I was bad ... and Papa spanked!" Here again is a whiff of fetish, so beloved of Browning. Chuck has punched Curly — a man's way of dominating another man — yet Curly describes it as a spanking, casting himself as an infant in his relationship with Chuck. To make sure we get it, he refers to Chuck as "Papa." Actor James Murray was almost 18 years younger than Lon Chaney, and could plausibly be cast as Chaney's biological son. A year after *The Big City*, Murray did play Chaney's son in *Thunder*, although in that film Chaney (in heavy make-up) played a character substantially older than himself.

Now we encounter another Browning motif: the false identity, seen in *The Black Bird*, *The Unholy Three*, *The Devil Doll*, *White Tiger* and elsewhere. Helen has been established as Chuck's assistant in crime, but now we see that she also runs an ostensibly honest business, with Chuck pretending to be her customer. Helen manages a costume shop across the alley from the Black Bottom. In Helen's shop, in the presence of her seamstresses, Helen and Chuck address each other as "Mister Collins" and "Miss Helen." Yet another of Browning's recurring themes appears now: a shop stocked with unusual merchandise that is actually a "front" for criminal activity. The pet shop in *The Unholy Three*, the toy shop in *The Devil Doll*— and here a shop that makes theatrical costumes.

In Tod Browning's films, as in Poe's "The Purloined Letter," people disguise unusual items by hiding them in plain sight. The miniaturized humans in *The Devil Doll* are on display as inanimate dolls. A criminal midget, evading the law in *The Unholy Three*, appears in public as a baby. Chuck and Helen hide their valuable stolen jewels in Helen's costume shop by stashing them in a box of worthless costume jewelry. And just in time, for now we see an insert shot of Helen's doorbell ringing. This technique of insert shots (to establish a sudden noise) was a standard part of the grammar of silent film. Browning intentionally follows the rules here, to set us up for a later event when he will break the rules.

The new arrivals are "Grogan and O'Hara from Headquarters," who think that Chuck knows more than he's telling about the robbery. Helen protests that she was robbed by the same "dirty crooks." One more major character in *The Big City* is now introduced. Helen employs in her shop a slavey maid, played by Marceline Day. Barely 20 years old at this time, actress Day specialized in playing virginal "good-girl" roles, her portrayals enhanced by the fact that she was completely flat-chested. (Moviegoers of the 1920s apparently expected flat-bosomed women to be more virtuous than busty ones; to judge from some recent movies, modern audiences think so too!) Marceline Day's complete lack of a bustline had been useful a year earlier when she was cast in Browning's *London After Midnight*. The convoluted plot of that film required Day to portray a woman her own age — Marceline Day was 19 at the time — who, for bizarre reasons, must impersonate herself when she was five years younger. At the climax of *London After Midnight* the heroine's impersonation of an underage girl is — because of Day's utter lack of endowments — considerably less ludicrous than it might have been with a more bosomy actress. Marceline Day's movie career suffered drastically with the arrival of talking pictures. Although she was born in Colorado Springs (also the birthplace of Lon Chaney), Day spoke with a bizarre diction that sounds vaguely European. In *The Wild Party* (1929), cast as a student who is presumably American, she pronounces the words "selfish" and "college" as if they were "selfeesh" and "colleetch." Marceline Day's ingenue role in *The Big City* is named Sunshine, a blatant attempt at character definition. She is the sole support of her invalid father, who implausibly lives in a bedsit above Helen's costume shop. When we first see Sunshine with her father, he sits weakly in a chair, barely moving.

Here we have two recurring themes of Browning's films that are less welcome than his other motifs, because they weaken his plotlines and make them less plausible. One is the theme of the innocent naif who is employed in the criminals' shopfront, rendering the entire crooked enterprise vulnerable because of the naif's ignorance (Sunshine in *The Big City* fulfills a similar role to Hector MacDonald, the honest clerk in the crooked shop of *The Unholy Three*). Why do Browning's cynical crooks endanger themselves by employing these innocents? Equally implausible is Browning's running theme of criminals who compromise their crooked enterprises for no sensible reason. Helen's shopfront is part of Chuck's criminal empire, but she compromises herself and Chuck by giving shelter to Sunshine's father, an honest man who is extremely ill. If he recovers, he might notice the criminal activity and inform the police. If he dies in the room above Helen's shop, the police might be summoned — something Helen can't afford. Is it possible that Helen, and other criminals in Browning's universe, actually *want* to get caught? A likelier explanation is that some aspects of Browning's plotlines are simply flaws, which weaken the plausibility of his films. In the presence of Grogan and

O'Hara, the child-like Sunshine babbles a comment implying that Chuck is guilty of the jewel heist, although she actually has no knowledge of this. Sunshine even shows the box of fake jewelry to the detectives, not suspecting that it contains the genuine gems they're seeking.

Curly, meanwhile, is at the Black Bottom, directing the chorus girls in their dance routine. Browning presents Curly as the dominant male, wielding authority over the sexy chorus girls while they exhibit their bodies. But at the same time, Browning shows Curly in a feminized context. Dancing is "girly" stuff, and males who show expertise in this activity (as dancers or choreographers) are often suspected of homosexuality. The chorus girls are more obviously sexual than the subdued Sunshine. As Curly rehearses the chorines, Sunshine arrives and watches him with a look of deep longing on her face. (Marceline Day was a talented actress; her problem was her voice.) Sunshine takes a balloon from the nightclub's décor; while gazing wistfully at Curly, she cradles the balloon in her arm. This simple visual device cleverly deepens Sunshine's character: the child's plaything establishes her childishness, but at the same time — because she cradles the balloon in her arm as if it were an infant — the balloon implies that Sunshine's desire for Curly might involve dreams of marriage and motherhood. Browning brilliantly uses physical action here to establish his heroine's inner thoughts.

And now, literally, the balloon bursts. This is a clever foreshadowing of later events; Sunshine has good intentions, but she will be the troublemaker in this drama, the one who bursts the balloon figuratively as well as literally. If the balloon in this sequence symbolizes Sunshine's maternal ambitions, the sudden burst of that balloon is an omen. And the bursting balloon triggers a funny sight gag, one which might have worked better if this film were not silent: when the balloon breaks, the chorus girls and Curly react to the sudden bang — heard by them, but not by the movie's audience — by leaping into a "hands up" position, with Curly drawing his pistol.

When Curly sees it's a false alarm, Sunshine reveals her sexual envy: "Why don't you never want to be nice to me?" The cynical Curly responds: "I suppose you'd like me to boil over, like one of those movie actors?" This gives James Murray a chance for a deft parody of silent-film romance, as Curly sarcastically pitches woo to Sunshine. But what began as a joke becomes serious, as Curly kisses Sunshine with genuine ardor. Just now a chorus girl walks past, well-rouged and blatantly sexual. The newcomer sees what's happening and laughs. Curly literally drops Sunshine on the floor, while telling the chorus girl: "I was just showin' Sunshine how they act in the gallopin' tintypes." While Sunshine watches, Curly flirts openly with the chorus girl. (The actress in this role is uncredited, but she strongly resembles — and I believe that she is — Edna Tichenor.) The chorus girl wears heavy make-up and a short skirt;

Sunshine watches enviously as the girl applies even more lip rouge to her mouth while Curly admires the view. "Do you like it, Big Boy?" asks the slutty chorus girl, anticipating a line spoken by villainess Cleopatra to strongman Hercules in *Freaks*.

Cut to the police station, where detectives are getting their orders to watch both Chuck and Red. Now Sunshine is in her bedsit. Before, her invalid father was in a chair; now he is bedridden. She stands before the mirror, posing in a tight-fitting dress with a short skirt, and applying lipstick. Sunshine's father is helpless. His eyes watch his daughter, but he is too weak to protest as she sluttifies herself. The dress worn by Marceline Day in this sequence has a very subtly padded bosom. We see Negro performers in a frenzied dance at the Black Bottom, symbolizing wild lust. At the stage door, Curly is confronted by Sunshine in her tarted-up outfit. "Do you like it, Big Boy?" she asks, echoing the chorus girl. Chuck arrives, now wearing his tattersall suit. He barks an order to Sunshine: "Gwan home and wash that paint off your face!" Suddenly the cops raid the joint. Chuck dashes to his office to retrieve the stolen jewels. Into the room walks Red Watson, who sees Chuck wearing the cufflinks that were "stolen" from him by the headless dancers. Now Red knows who double-crossed him in the robbery at Tennessee's nightclub. Curly's arrival distracts Red. Curly and Chuck easily escape the police raid, but Sunshine is not so lucky. In her sluttish get-up, the cops mistake Sunshine for one of the bad girls of this place, and she is arrested. We next see Sunshine in a prison cell, still dressed in her sluttish outfit but now more bedraggled. "They won't tell my father, will they?" she timidly asks a matron.

Cut to Chuck and Curly with Helen in her rooms. Policemen stand outside. The dialogue establishes that Sunshine has been in prison for ten days, and something unfortunate has happened to her father. Now Sunshine is released from prison. At the door of her bedsit she is confronted by a woman who is apparently the landlady. At this point I found the movie very confusing, and I cannot tell whether this is a fault of Browning's film as MGM released it or a result of my imperfect viewing of a deteriorated nitrate print. The shot-matching implies that Sunshine and her father live above Helen's costume shop, but another (unnamed) woman, who appears briefly — only in this sequence and soon after — is apparently Sunshine's landlady. The landlady speaks her one line to Sunshine and departs: "Your father was buried yesterday." Sunshine falls weeping beside her father's empty bed.

Cut to Helen's apartment, across the street from her costume shop. Here, again, the physical relationship between the story's various settings harms the plausibility: if a bedsit above Helen's shop had been available to let, surely *she* (not Sunshine) would be living there. But the unlikely spatial arrangement in Browning's film enables a visual device, allowing him to show Chuck hiding in Helen's flat while staring out the window to watch the police staked out in front of her shop. (If Helen lived above her own shop, Chuck's viewpoint would require the camera to point straight downwards.) Chuck and Curly smoke profusely, reminding modern viewers that Lon Chaney died of throat cancer. Chuck has concealed the stolen jewels in Helen's flower pot. This is another example of Browning's penchant for hiding valuable objects in mundane places, and it's also a visual pun: Chuck has "planted" the jewels. (Some of them are "seed" pearls.) Sunshine timidly visits Helen's flat. The geography of the film is truly confusing here; again, I cannot tell if this is due to Browning's direction, MGM's editing (credited to Harry Reynolds), or my own imperfect viewing of a flawed print. Sunshine's bedsit appears to be located abovestairs in Helen's shop, but she also seems to be living in the same block of flats as Helen, in the building *across the street* from the shop. Either this is a continuity error, or I missed something. The naive Sunshine opens the door to Helen's apartment without knocking. Why does Helen keep her door unlocked while harboring criminals? As Chuck sees the door opening, he draws his handgun. The gun, a Colt .45 1911A automatic, is deeply blued, but cameraman Henry Sharp's photography makes this weapon gleam incandescently. Chuck holds his fire when he sees who's at the door. Here a close shot of Lon Chaney displays his acting talents, as he simultaneously registers contempt for the damp Sunshine and relief that she isn't the police.

In the next room, Curly overhears Chuck berating Sunshine while she pleads for his forgiveness. "Every day they tried to make me say you were a thief! That's why they kept me in jail!" she whimpers. Helen has somehow got herself downstairs, where she meets Sunshine's landlady. Is this woman Helen's landlady too? Again, the geography is unclear. Helen takes pity on Sunshine, and permits her to move into Helen's flat. She must have quite a lot of room, since Chuck and Curly are staying there too. It seems deeply implausible that these three criminals would allow Sunshine to stay with them, risking the chance that she might innocently betray them while the police are right outside. Browning's direction, and the dialogue, make it clear that Chuck and Helen feel genuine pity for Sunshine. This sympathetic emotion in unsympathetic characters serves to set up later developments. Still, it beggars belief that Helen has enough room and enough furniture for two men and two women to sleep in four separate beds and couches, but this decision may have been imposed on Browning by MGM's chief of production, Irving Thalberg, so as to avoid the censorship problems of depicting any two or more of these characters sharing a bed.

Curly walks into Sunshine's room, puts his hand on her shoulder, and kisses her. She perceives this as an expression of sympathetic affection, and she returns his kiss until Curly becomes more ardent. Sunshine struggles as

Curly attempts to rape her. (Hey, mister, the cops are right outside!) Chuck bursts into the room and attacks Curly. The "Papa spank" scene established that Chuck is a better brawler than the younger, taller Curly. But now there is an exciting, well-edited fight sequence in which James Murray outfights Lon Chaney and nearly strangles him ... until Chaney whips out his handgun and coshes the other man. This powerful and thrilling scene is immediately rendered ludicrous when Chuck thrusts his Colt .45 into Sunshine's hands and tells her "If anybody bothers you ... use this." Chuck should realize that Sunshine can't be trusted with a firearm, especially with the police right outside! And I found it hugely implausible that the police would devote so much manpower to a stakeout for a robbery in which no murders were committed. But the previous year's *London After Midnight* has already proved that Tod Browning's universe is filled with police officers who apply their resources unrealistically.

Helen wants Chuck to tell her where he's "got the stuff hid," but he refuses. This is typical Browning territory; as in *White Tiger* and *The Unholy Three*, here are partners in crime who cannot trust one another.

The camera showed Chuck bashing Curly in the top of his head, but now Curly is seen rubbing his jaw. Either this is a continuity error or Browning is intentionally echoing the "Papa spank" scene. Despite the fact that he's just tried to rape her, Curly has no difficulty getting with Sunshine alone and asking her, "Ain't you sore at me for what I done?" Marceline Day's eyes brim over with glycerine tears as Sunshine happily shakes her head "no," prompting Curly conclude, "I can't figure you dames no-how." Sunshine has already been shown to be in love with Curly, yet here she seems to love him even more because he tried to rape her!

The cops are still doorstepping Helen's shop. Sunshine naively tells Chuck, "If you'd go tell the police you didn't rob those people, they'd believe you." Sunshine's naivete is so extreme she genuinely believes that Chuck is innocent. Helen cynically tells Curly, "Chuck's startin' to sprout wings!" ... then she tells Sunshine to fetch the bible for Chuck. Although Chuck has taken a protective attitude towards Sunshine (becoming the orphan girl's surrogate father), the dialogue makes it clear that Helen is sexually jealous, mistaking Chuck's motives. Helen goads Chuck until he raises his hand to strike her, just as Sunshine enters the room. Chuck lowers his hand. Browning's staging of this scene, and Chaney's subtle acting, make Chuck's action brilliantly ambiguous. Did Chuck refrain from hitting Helen because he retains some respect for her? Or does he merely want to avoid upsetting Sunshine? Perhaps it's only the nearness of the police that restrains him. Any or all of these motives could be the truth.

Helen's comment about the bible seemed to be a wisecrack to goad Chuck and get Sunshine out of the room. But now Sunshine indeed returns with a bible which Helen has conveniently kept in her apartment, even though we've seen no evidence of religious piety from her. Now she bluntly tells Sunshine that "he and we" (herself, Chuck and Curly) stole the jewelry. And now Helen demands her share of the swag. When Chuck defies her, she walks out of the building, aware that Chuck can't follow her while the police are outside.

At this point there's a "trick" camera set-up that serves no purpose to the plot or character development. We see the shadow of a boxer silhouetted against a wall. He moves back and forth, but his movements are stiff and unnatural. A cut reveals that Curly is sitting in a chair, fiddling a statuette of a boxer; it looks like part of an athletic trophy. Helen has returned. When Curly tells her that Chuck is alone with Sunshine, the jealous Helen interprets this sexually. She suggests to Curly that she and he should run off with the jewelry. (Won't the police grab Curly?) Anyway, neither of them knows where the swag is hidden. Sunshine has been applying her good influence to Chuck. She assures him that if a man sincerely repented his crimes "it would make me love him more than ever." Sunshine tells Helen and Curly that Chuck has decided to go straight, and he decrees that Curly will go straight, too. Curly interprets this as a double-cross, but Chuck threatens Curly with the best line in this movie: "I'm gonna make an honest crook out of you!" For a moment, it looks like Chuck and Curly are going to brawl again. But the older man stares Curly down, and it's clear that Chuck has won. (Splendid acting by both Chaney and Murray here.) Curly goes to the flower pot and retrieves the jewels. Have I missed something? I would have sworn that only Chuck knew where the jewels were planted.

Now Helen opens her closet door to reveal Red Watson and two of his henchmen: the Arab and the male dancer who was previously tied up in Red's closet. How did they get in here, past the police, without Chuck or Curly hearing them? This sort of legerdemain was barely plausible in silent movies, in which nobody ever makes a sound unless it serves the plot. Helen's dialogue reveals that her trip outside was to summon Red; she has double-crossed Chuck and Curly, and now Helen and Red will scoot with the loot. (With police in pursuit?) As Red snatches the bag with the swag, Chuck suavely tells him, "Just leave 'em in the bag. I'll call for 'em some evening." He cautions Red not to do any shooting, as the cops will hear it. "The cops can't hear a knife," says the Arab, and John George caresses his switchblade lovingly (the blade gleams in the light) as he draws it forth. Having built to this climax, Browning proceeds to squander it on some thick-ear dialogue containing one useful plot point: Red knows that the police won't trace the jewels to him because Chuck's gang have been blamed for the robbery.

Just when Chuck laughs off Red's latest threat, suddenly they all look towards the door. Once again, Browning's silent-film actors are reacting to a sudden noise which Browning hasn't established. His use of that device earlier in the film was a set-up for this moment.

The Arab goes to the apartment's outer door, which has an old-fashioned warded lock with a large keyhole. Through the keyhole we see what he sees: two brass buttons and the badge of a policeman's tunic. Two uniformed cops enter the apartment. One of them thanks Red for telling them where Chuck and Curly are. The cops seize the stolen jewels, and handcuff Chuck and Curly, giving Red the credit for the arrest. As they leave with their prisoners, one cop filches the key to the apartment ... and locks the door on the way out, locking Red and his men inside. Through the keyhole Red observes the police officers releasing Chuck and Curly, then doffing their tunics and hats to put on civilian jackets and trilby hats: the "cops" were really two of Chuck's men! Browning stages this scene very effectively. He introduces the fake police with a tight close-up of a tunic and badge, concealing their faces; this convinces us that the intruders are genuine police, but hints that something is being withheld. And the payoff for this scene is one of Browning's best double-crosses.

Fade to a brief scene of Sunshine and Curly becoming affectionate. Next is a dissolve to Chuck in a barber's chair, getting a shoeshine and a facial massage while speaking to an apparently genuine policeman, who tells Chuck: "I'm glad you turned in that stuff ... and I'm glad they're going light with you."

Ouch! Here, alas, is the single most implausible theme that recurs through Browning's films: the lifelong criminal who undergoes a sudden total reformation, and who completely escapes punishment for his crimes. We saw it in *The Unholy Three* (1925 version) and *White Tiger*, and here it is again. Browning's world is cynical; why does he repeatedly spoil that cynicism with this implausible reversal? The cop asks Chuck why he has reformed, and Chuck replies, "I'm goin' to marry the greatest little girl that ever lived." Lon Chaney's performance, throughout the film, has carefully prepared for this moment. He has convinced us that his interest in Sunshine was paternal. Now we see that he is interested in her for other reasons ... but we accept that he is sincerely in love with her, not motivated by mere lust.

Cut to Sunshine's bedsit, the same room where her father died. Apparently the landlady has kept it available for Sunshine all through Sunshine's absence during the police stakeout. Curly is here, and he nervously proposes marriage. Sunshine joyfully accepts, just as Chuck arrives, intending to propose to Sunshine. When she gives him the news, Curly adds: "I'm on the level, Chuck. I love her." Lon Chaney's face registers several emotions as Chuck makes his decision: "To make sure there'll be no mistake, you two are gonna be married tonight!" Then he leaves, concealing his face from the camera so as to hide his thoughts. Chuck goes to Helen's apartment, where she tells him she had him "all wrong." Having got himself all primped to marry Sunshine, Chuck tells Helen to get dressed: "Me and you are goin' to be married!" As Helen smiles broadly and rushes off, Chuck has one more line — to remind the audience that he's a cynic after all. "I ain't gonna buy you nothin'," he tells the departing Helen, "I'm just gonna marry you!" Fade out with a backlit shot of Sunshine kissing Curly.

The Big City is probably Tod Browning's most typical film, containing the best examples of his major themes, and some of the most extreme examples of his flaws. At its heart, *The Big City* is very similar to the 1973 caper film *The Sting*, which it seems to anticipate. Both films employ the device of "good crook/bad crook," in which a criminal protagonist (the ostensible "good crook") gains the audience's sympathy because he is charming and well-dressed, and because most of his criminal activity is directed not against innocent victims but rather towards a "bad crook" who is less charming, less attractive and less sympathetic than the "good crook." Chaney's portrayal of Chuck Collins is only intermittently charming; in many scenes of this film he is a very nasty character indeed. Several shots in *The Big City* show Chaney glancing sidelong, indicating to the audience that Chuck Collins cannot be trusted. But his rival Red Watson — played by Matthew Betz, an actor even less handsome than Lon Chaney — is always less charming, always more thuggish than Chuck Collins. Chuck is a snappy dresser, in tailored suits, and much of his dialogue is witty as well as cynical. As portrayed by the toad-faced Betz, Red Watson is very believable but utterly repellent. All of Red Watson's (Betz's) speeches in this film's intertitles conform to the type of dialogue known in Britain as "thick-ear": all snarls and threats, lacking any wit or grace.

Chaney and Browning employ their skill to make the audience admire Chuck Collins before the plot gives us any reason to like him. I am hopeful that a complete print of *The Big City*— ideally a print in better condition than the one I Steenbecked — will become available for conversion to video or DVD.

Lost in Proto-Performance
West of Zanzibar *and the Last Stand of the Primal Father*

BJÖRN QUIRING

In postcolonial studies, a lot of ink has been spilt concerning the difference between Africa and "Africa," i. e. the exotistic dream of Africa invented by white Europeans and North Americans, particularly in the nineteenth century. An expert in the field considers Tod Browning's silent movie *West of Zanzibar* from 1928 the best American movie about the phantasm "Africa":

> The best movie ever made in America about "Africa" was silent and black-and-white. It used all the African clichés and stereotypes that undergirded the imperial and fantastic films, and nonetheless rose above them to greatness [Cameron 75].

It's a somewhat opaque statement, since Kenneth Cameron leaves it basically unexplained. This article provides an attempt at an explanation: the enduring interest of the film is due to the fact that it mirrors its own phantasmatic status into itself and plays with it in the typically Browningian fashion. *West of Zanzibar* thus provides no information whatsoever about Africa, but a lot about "Africa," i.e. a certain structure of Western obsessions and projections; and the movie becomes a lot more interesting if that is kept in mind. The palpable influence of expressionism on its imagery might be taken as an indication of that fact.

Browning unfolds his melodrama in an artificial Africa where everything is fake exotic (by necessity, since the whole movie was shot on a low budget in and around Culver City, California). The first part of the movie connotes a European location by dress and architecture, but the movie mainly is set in the Congo, which in the early twentieth century was the favorite location for exotic "African" dreams. This fact is to be explained historically: for many European freebooters, the Congo was a dream come true when the Belgian king Leopold XI grabbed the whole Congo basin for himself personally by an ingenious diplomatic coup in 1884. Under Belgian occupation, unscrupulous adventurers had the opportunity for systematic freebooting in the service of the king, and got rich quick in case they didn't die of the rampant epidemics (see Hochschild). The systematic, violent plundering of the Congo's riches, of which the first was ivory (to be succeeded by rubber in the course of the 1890s), involved a brutal industry running on the forced labor of native blacks (of whom literally millions died under Leopold's reign), and which harvested the king and his helpers several billions of dollars in the bargain. All this happened under the pretence of a humanitarian mission: the colonialists justified their presence in the country by a reference to mythical despots who were reported to cruelly enslave their subjects and whose removal by enlightened Western civilization was a sacred obligation. The Belgian king and his cronies accordingly took great care to demonize some Arab and black slave traders from North Africa who actually were a comparatively minor problem in the Congo. Belgian propaganda depicted them as sexual predators and absolute despots to whom the life and death of their subjects didn't matter one whit (Hochschild 27–28, *et passim*). Joseph Conrad, who was in the country at that time, described his experiences in his novel *Heart of Darkness*, even today both the most famous exposition of the phantasm "Africa," as well as deconstruction of that phantasm: what Conrad's narrator finds in the heart of the Congo is a cruel, self-deifying, slave-owning despot, but he's the white ivory trader Mr. Kurtz. In the *Heart of Darkness*, the colonizers have been lost in a phantasm they fabricated themselves, and subsequently don't fail to become everything they ascribe to their phantasmatic enemies and the "brutes," just as Dead-Legs does in Browning's movie. Conrad's book was obviously an inspirational source for *West of Zanzibar*, although in the movie we hear no more pious smoke screen talk of missionary idealism: it's clear from the start that every white in the Congo is looking for his or her own material or spiritual gain there.

Conrad emphasized the threatening irreality of an acquisitive despotism gone out of control, and so established a topos which already was familiar terrain to Browning. Accordingly, *West of Zanzibar* plays with the tenuous difference between phantasmatic performance and reality, as most Browning movies do. As always, Browning unfolds this problem within the parameters of a tragic family romance, an Oedipal triangle's fatal opening into a traumatic world beyond. *West of Zanzibar* begins in Browning's favorite setting, a vaudeville theater. The main protagonist is the stage magician Phroso, played by Lon Chaney. The status of this protagonist already poses the problem of representation: every stage magician is an actor and director at the same time, organizing his own ritual mastery over the limitations that hem humans in. In this function, he is a parody of the absolute, mythical despot. In the dramatic hyperbole of side show magic, the absolute power over life and death is conjured up again and again only to be spoofed. This is just what Phroso does at the start of Browning's film when his words "Ashes to ashes! Dust to dust!" seem to transform a skeleton into his young and beautiful wife. At the same time, the words hint at the old motive of the equivalence of love and death. However, since no one is really deceived by this sort of magical performance, since the mastery is based on a blatant but elusive trick, the magician is a master only at the level of masquerade. His über-masculinity is a sham which even makes his very masculinity fall into doubt, along with Phroso's false moustache.

At the same time, Phroso seems to merge with his role: we never learn his "real" name, he changes from "Phroso" directly to "Dead-Legs," both of them being "stage names." He is exposed to the danger which most of Browning's heroes face — to get lost in performance, to take their roles for realities. His wife Anna seems to feel that danger; at least her distance and her affair with Crane, a "real" man with a "real" job as ivory trader, seems to point in that direction. What's more, Crane seems not only to be a trader, but also to have some governmental function, since he is addressed as "gov'nor" (as would have been necessary for effective business in the Congo, since it was not exactly a free trade zone; see Hochschild, 117–18). He is a genuine "master," endowed with real *vitae necisque potestas* instead of its playful equivalent. However, his constantly hard and cruel ways suggest that women might actually be better off with "unreal" men. "Crâne" in French signifies the "skull," and Crane indeed seems to be an executive of the grim reaper — the Dead-Head who gives Phroso his Dead-Legs. The clash between the real and unreal man and subsequent accident changes the body of Phroso, reduces him to a new position of abandoned paralytic that he comprehends as a new role from which he remains dissociated. He doesn't completely identify with it, even though he is permanently attached to it. He explores the potential of his new role in different contexts outside of the vaudeville theater (especially in the cut scenes in which he manages to make money out of his disability). The main result of these experiments is that Phroso gets servants — two supporting actors (Tiny and Babe, fake children in whom childish stupidity and cunning cruelty meet) and one technical advisor (the alcoholic fixer "Doc"— to help him "keep crawling." The fact that as a paralytic he is more dependent on others does not contradict his fake despotism: the sitting and lying position iconographically is the position of the powerful — the king doesn't rise from his throne, only the inferior stands up when his superior enters the room. And the movie strongly emphasizes this convergence of power and the sitting position: the two black chiefs depicted in the movie are constantly carried around sitting, as is Crane when he arrives at Dead-Legs' post.

Phroso finds a new plot fitting for his new role in a church, in which he discovers his dead wife with a baby beside her, a mysterious "primal scene" for him to make sense of. He interprets it as the deed of the "real man" and at the same time inserts himself into the picture through an oath to the Virgin Mary, establishing a metonymical relation to the ethereal present absence of his wife. He vows revenge toward Crane and his offspring. This oath is a conditional self-curse: by swearing, the subject enters into a new order of obligations. That way, the oath establishes "sense," it gives meaning to the world and allows the speaker to orient himself in the ambiguous complexity of the symbolic system by fixating himself within it. By his vow, he not only posits Crane as an absolute cause of his misery; his designation of his wife's child Maizie as Crane's "brat," to whom the same oath applies, is also to be considered prescriptive, not descriptive. It's less an expression of a mistaken belief and more a performative act, reconstituting Phroso himself by rejecting filiation, which Maizie seems to incarnate. With filiation, he also renounces the normal, regulated bounds of representation and phantasmatic performance. This oath-giver sets himself up as the serpent in the genealogical tree of knowledge: "He made me this thing that crawls. Now I'm ready to bite." Nevertheless, the maxim *pater semper incertus* is probably also known to Phroso/Dead-Legs. Even the movie itself doesn't establish a conclusive resolution of the matter of Maizie's parentage, since Crane may be lying cleverly when he affirms that she is not his daughter but Phroso's. Alternatively, she may be the daughter of a third party; indeed, it doesn't matter much. In any case, Phroso finds his new role in a self-directed, self-enacted plot of revenge, which repeats what he has decided to be his own experience with a different cast and in the same turn posits his strange new mock sovereignty. He takes on the role of a "hyperreal man" by reconstructing himself as the pure representation of the subject position beyond the law, the phantasmatic primal father who is not only master over life and death, but also stands above the laws of filiation. The primal father in Freud's *Totem and Taboo* is defined not so much by his actual sexual possession of all women in his territory, but by his ability to command or prohibit sexual alliances without being bound by the laws of parentage and filiation, without being inscribed in the order of descendance and exchange (cp. 185–86, 203–05). The primal father leaves no trace in the genealogical chart, has no real place in the chain of the generations, since in any structure of kinship a primal filiation is impossible (see Lévi-Strauss 563, and *passim*). In this peculiar manner, Phroso complements the statue of the immaculate Holy Virgin in front of which he vows his protracted revenge.

Phroso/Dead-Legs thereupon follows Crane into the African jungle, and beats him at the trade game by his own theatrical means overflowing their bounds. He subverts Crane's power through show effects, the trappings of illusion and deception: Dead-Legs exhibits himself as a magical freak and directs ghostly apparitions which are enacted by his white servants appearing as evil "voodoos" to Crane's slaves in order to appropriate the ivory they're carrying. The ivory is accumulated in Dead-Legs' shack, which figures as a receptacle of symbolic riches: the tusks are never sold, just stored up. Since the phallic status of the ivory imagery is constantly emphasized, the theft is perceived by all parties involved as a symbolic castration.

The reactionary surrealism of *West of Zanzibar* is saturated by the fact that the movie depicts Africa itself as a side show, that the jungle seems to be a vulgar and blatant arrangement of exotism created for the white gaze. It becomes increasingly clear that Dead-Legs really has come into his own in "Africa" only because it is a freak-show decoration, a wall of exotic leaves in front of which the magician sits on a porch, which also serves as the stage for his conjurations and sleights of hand. Even the tribal world appears as a cardboard hallucination. A sign of this is the fact that there seems to be no language difficulties, since the natives speak a decelerated Pidgin English even among themselves. Another sign is that everything but the fake jungle looks distinctly American: the "African" masks resemble Halloween masks, the "African" statues look like something one might find at a fairground creepshow, the silly "ritualistic" gestures of the blacks recall inebriated American fraternity rituals of the Roaring Twenties more than actual Central African ceremonies (as is apt, since the "Congolese" were mainly played by black Hollywood studio workers). Throughout the movie, Blacks are never addressed by whites but ritualistically, and vice versa, so that it's hard to say who started all this pompous silliness.

Despite constant references to it, there would be no signs of cannibalism and bestiality to be found anywhere in Browning's "Congo" either, were it not for the Europeans who keep symbolically feeding on each other. In particular, the monstrous aspirations of Dead-Legs, his desire to be seen straddling the frontier between human and nonhuman, are expressed not only by his occasionally caressing a chimpanzee like a baby but also by his reference to himself as the "thing that crawls, ready to bite," his serpent-like movements and crocodile-like lurking. Dead-Legs is himself extraterritorial, "a strange man," as Maizie puts it. (His assumed role as a cruel despot who has left civilization behind to become a savage quasi-divinity, as well as his threatening immobility in the shadows with an "impressively bald" [Conrad 59] head, are bound to remind present-day viewers of Brando's Colonel Kurtz in Coppola's *Apocalypse Now*, another free adaptation of Conrad's *Heart of Darkness*.) Dead-Legs has created ideal conditions for his performance as primal father in this "African" environment. He designates his own foreclosure of filiation as the one and only "law of the Congo": the prescribed union of man and woman in death, in which daughter and wife are not distinguished, appears as a law promoting incest instead of prohibiting it. Its application would be an absurdity in any actual, functioning kinship system, yet it makes perfect sense in the staged realm of an aspiring primal father impersonator. For all we know, Dead-Legs himself may have instituted this particular "law of the Congo" ("Dead Lex").

However, all his endeavors seem to lead him into a dead end. Ironically, in some scenes, just as in Conrad's novel and, to a lesser degree, in *Apocalypse Now*, it becomes apparent that the mixture of deceit and despotism instituted by people like Dead-Legs is not an unprecedented aberration, but the very figure of colonialism itself. Crane, too, tries to strengthen superstition in order to keep his native servants in line instead of enlightening them ("White master ... no ... 'fraid ... voodoo!"). He only seems somewhat less successful than Dead-Legs in his obscurantist endeavor. That he, just as his declared opponent, looks down on blacks and women as expendable property becomes palpable in his grinning approval of Dead-Legs' cruelties toward Maizie: "Well, Phroso, you're putting on a great show!" The only remaining difference between Crane and Dead-Legs would consist in the fact that Dead-Legs seems uninterested in the trade and profit that Africa has to offer. Dead-Legs is interested in ivory not as an object of value but as a medium of communication: through his thefts he contacts Crane and transmits his own superior status to him. Yet the movie dissolves even this difference; not only the natives but also the colonizers treat the ivory as a fetish object whose phallic connotations are frequently emphasized, most strongly in a shot in which a tusk seems to grow out of Crane's groin. Ivory itself appears as an embodiment of power (whereas money plays no palpable role in the movie; it just greases palms). Ivory is to all parties involved an object communicating prestige, a quasi-cause with no practical value whatsoever. Magic and capitalism are not mutually exclusive, but can support each other in all the myriad figures of commodity fetishism (see Benjamin 15–18)—"The word 'ivory' rang in the air, was whispered, was sighed. You would think they were praying to it" (Conrad 27).

The prayer to ivory is obviously also a prayer to Death. Not only because "ivory" is also a slang word for "skull," establishing again the equivalence of (phallic) love and death, but also through the metonymical relations between the tusks, the skull masks worn by the "natives" (as well as by the fake "voodoos"), Dead-Legs' bald skull "like an ivory ball" (Conrad 60), his stage skeleton, and Crane the "crâne." Dead-Legs is much closer to Crane than he thinks, since their aims, methods and position converge, and this convergence has fatal consequences. Dead-Legs re-discovers his own projected image inscribed in the dark heart of colonialism, hence his self-appointed dramatic task turns out to be redundant. He cannot top Crane by artifice, because colonialism itself is a show out of bounds, all its "masters" being make-believe primal fathers. Crane, even in the face of death, cannot help returning the message Dead-Legs has conveyed to him back to sender. After Crane has dissociated himself from Maizie, there is no longer any difference left between the two men. Dead-Legs has no longer a symbolic system to distance himself from and to demolish. It dawns on him that not only himself, but the whole world might be "lost in performance," a perspective of absolute horror concomitant with the onset of paranoia.

> Everything belonged to him — but that was a trifle. The thing was to know what he belonged to, how many powers of darkness claimed him for their own. That was the reflection that made you creepy all over. It was impossible — it was not good for one either — trying to imagine. He had taken a high seat amongst the devils of the land — I mean literally. You can't understand. How could you? [Conrad 60].

After the tables have been turned on him, Dead-Legs is obliged to reconstruct the structures he worked so hard to destroy in order to ward off psychosis. He can only escape from his deadlock and re-establish filiation by an *acte de passage* involving the reverse image of the established phallic love-death equivalence, by a self-sacrifice. He symbolically "sacrifices" Maizie in order to save her from the "law of the Congo" with the help of his old stage contraption with embedded skeleton. And, at the same time, he reaffirms his bond to the kinship system as well as to Maizie by actually substituting himself as the burnt offering to the primal father. He hands his "daughter" over into the responsibility of the "fixer" in his double qualification as doctor and qualified "stage technician." By this theatrical act a new dream couple is produced and sanctified, so that the cycle can begin anew, with all problems of the white man and his phantasmatic burden still remaining unresolved.

Works Cited

Benjamin, Walter. "Kapitalismus als Religion." *Kapitalismus als Religion*. Ed. Dirk Baecker. Berlin: Kadmos, 2003, pp. 15–18.
Cameron, Kenneth M. *Africa on Film, Beyond Black and White*. New York: Continuum, 1994.
Conrad, Joseph. *Heart of Darkness*. New York: The Modern Library, 1999.
Freud, Sigmund. "Totem and Taboo." *The Origins of Religion*. The Penguin Freud Library, vol. 13. Harmondsworth: Penguin, 1990, pp. 43–224.
Hochschild, Adam. *King Leopold's Ghost*. Boston/New York: Mifflin, 1999.
Lévi-Strauss, Claude. *Les Structures Elémentaires de la Parenté*. Paris/La Haye: Mouton, 1962.

Films

Browning, Tod, dir. *West of Zanzibar* (MGM, 1928).
Coppola, Francis Ford, dir. *Apocalypse Now* (Zoetrope Studios, 1979).

You're Better Off Without Your Parents:
Where East Is East *Seen Through a Daughter's Eyes*

SARAH DELLMANN

Between 1919 and 1929, director Tod Browning shot ten silent movies with actor Lon Chaney in leading roles. Most films enjoyed great financial success and were very popular. *Where East Is East* was the final product of this cinematic partnership, as well as the last silent movie for both Browning and Chaney.

Rich in themes, Browning's films allow various approaches and are open to interpretation from a wide range of perspectives. Recently, Stephan Brandt pointed out the ambiguity of the category "race" and identity in this film, and Lars Nowak examined transgressions of difference and modes of repetition of identity. In this essay, I will offer a feminist approach to *Where East Is East*, taking sides for the (position of the) daughter in that movie and defending her pleasure. To do so, I need to leave psychoanalytic interpretations behind and turn to the carnival as interpretative background of Browning's films instead — which, as I see it, can be justified by simply looking at the tradition of Tod Browning's movies.

Before the start of Browning's career in cinema, the carnival and other forms of popular culture had grabbed his attention. As his biographers write, various forms of popular culture were part of the entertainment of Browning's hometown of Louisville. Once a year, a big carnival took place: "An annual city event of the early 1890s that could not have escaped the boy's attention was a spectacular carnival called the Satellites of Mercury, evoking all the splendor and pageantry of Mardi Gras with its parades, floats, and exotica" (Skal and Savada 18). Tod Browning left Louisville around 1902 and worked as a contortionist and vaudeville artist in traveling shows before he became an actor in 1913, and, later, scenarist and director. Browning was very firm with the tradition of popular and carnival culture and knew the side show business very well—in front of and behind the curtain. The carnival tradition in Browning's work is evident and present in many of his films: show numbers and tricks are performed throughout the film (sometimes linked to the narrative, sometimes not); the fairground and circus are the setting of the story; or the main characters try to escape by using abilities they learned in show business. Nevertheless, this carnival tradition still remains an underrated aspect in the discussion of his work. Nowadays, the tradition of carnival and its — although not explicit — power-critical content of the grotesque are not familiar to today's spectators anymore. In order to understand this background, I wish first to turn to the Russian comparative literature specialist Mikhail Bakhtin.

The Critique of the Grotesque

Bakhtin reconstructs the medieval carnival tradition in analyzing the works of François Rabelais. He looks at festive descriptions, links them to various kinds of carnival references and promotes the carnival season as an opposition to the power and influence of the Roman Catholic Church in medieval Europe. During the carnival season, one sets aside fear of reprisal and is thus free to mock the entire social order, including oneself. During this period, the everyday hierarchies were abolished, the laws were repealed and thereby the possibility of looking at the world from a different viewpoint and with a different perception was given.

> Thought and word were searching for a new reality beyond the visible horizon of official philosophy. Often enough, words and thoughts were turned around in order to discover what they were actually hiding, what was that other side. The aim was to find a position permitting a look at the other side of established values, so that new bearings could be taken [Bakhtin 272].

This "look at the other side" is achieved through the strategy of degradation, which, according to Bakhtin, is the main aesthetic principle of grotesque realism. Degradation means "the lowering of all that is high, spiritual, ideal, abstract; it is a transfer to the material level, to the sphere of earth and body in their indissoluble unity" (Bakhtin 19–20). Degradation is the inversion of all principles: the high becomes low, the spiritual corporeal, the holy profane, the old dies and is reborn a new and better way.[1] In inversing the official order, degradation uncrowns the powerful and empowers the powerless. Bakhtin concludes that the carnival was a lived utopia. Degradation confronts everything stable that refuses change. Therefore, the grotesque "discloses the potentiality of an entirely different world, of another order, another way of life. It leads men out of the confines of the apparent (false) unity, of the indisputable and stable" (Bakhtin 48). It points out the relativity of each form of power and supremacy, even its own, and leaves room for imagining another world.

So whenever Browning strips words and abstract metaphors down to their physical meanings, or illustrates them in their literal meaning in images on screen — a technique he uses quite often in his films — we might find ourselves involved in degradation: at the non-official, and carnivalesque side of society.[2] Keeping this tradition in mind, I will now look for grotesque elements in *Where East Is East*.

Where East Is East: *The Story*

As in the previous Browning-Chaney film *West of Zanzibar,* the action is set in a jungle, this time not in Africa but in the jungle of Indochina. And as in the previous film, the father has sole custody of his daughter and sacrifices himself for her happiness.

Tiger Haynes (Lon Chaney) lives alone with his beloved daughter Toyo (Lupe Velez) and employees in a villa in a town at the edge of the jungle. Tiger Haynes catches tigers that are then exported to zoos. He loves his daughter more than anything else — and when Toyo falls in love with the son of the tiger export manager, Bobby Bailey (Lloyd Hughes), he first is opposed to their relationship because he sees the happiness of his daughter endangered. But realizing her to be truly happy and in love, he gives in and agrees to her marriage. Bobby Bailey and Tiger Haynes are to transport a tiger to a faraway port and board a ship. Among the passengers is Madame de Sylva (Estelle Taylor), who seduces Bobby; she is, as we find out later, Toyo's mother and in earlier days had broken the heart of Tiger Haynes. Tiger Haynes catches Madame de Sylva and Bobby in the act of kissing and is especially angry with Sylva, who, he feels, is endangering the happiness of his (in fact, their) daughter. Bobby and Tiger Haynes then discuss the matter and Tiger Haynes pardons Bobby's escapade. Still, Bobby's desire for Madame de Sylva has not been doused, and, even worse, she tries to seduce him again and again. Back home, Tiger Haynes tries to exclude Madame de Sylva from the engagement party, but she insists on coming. Toyo, naive and innocent, is ignorant of these previous events and is simply glad to have found her mother. Toyo insists that she stay — and Madame de Sylva continues to make eyes at Bobby, wanting to take him away from her daughter. Madame de Sylva proposes Bobby take a ship and elope, but fails herself to appear at the harbor. Toyo is devastated because of the inexplicable absence of her beloved. As Bobby finally returns from his (unpremeditated) trip and still hesitates between mother and daughter, Tiger Haynes attempts to force Madame de Sylva to leave the villa once more. Madame de Sylva grabs her pistol, but Tiger Haynes snatches it away from her. Toyo hears the noise and discovers who her mother really is. Madame de Sylva refuses to refrain from seducing Bobby, so, in his anger, Tiger Haynes unleashes a gorilla. Although he is able to calm the ape, Tiger Haynes is seriously wounded and Madame de Sylva is mauled to death. Toyo and Bobby marry in the presence of the wounded father and leave the town immediately after the ceremony. Tiger Haynes then dies of his wounds.

Where East Is East *within Oedipus*

Tod Browning's films, especially those with Lon Chaney, have often been interpreted with psychoanalytic and, more precisely, Freudian theory, especially with regard to his theory of the oedipal stage and the castration complex. Maybe it is because of all the kissing that's going on in this film that critics favor a psychoanalytic approach to the analysis of this movie: Not only do Bobby and Toyo kiss each other, but so do Madame de Sylva and Bobby, and Toyo and Tiger Haynes, every time they meet and leave. Their intimacy is more intense than what one would tend to accept within a "normal" father-daughter relationship. For example, in one scene, Tiger Haynes carefully tries to calm his daughter, caresses her naked back, wipes away her tears and holds her on his lap. And when they "play tigers," they tickle each other. Intra-familiar borders are transgressed: the mother kisses her son-in-law, the father kisses the daughter. These incestuous structures are what attracts Freudian oedipal theorists: The animals are then regarded as a regressive solution of the oedipal stage via infantile states and/or stages.

As feminist (film) critics have pointed out, the daughter's position within oedipal constructions blocks her way to autonomy and satisfaction. According to Freud, the female child becomes aware of not having the penis that males possess, and thus defines herself as the incomplete other, thereby desiring the father, who is in possession of what she does not have. The male, complete in himself, can walk ahead self-assuredly, despite his fears that his penis could eventually be removed. This deeply rooted fear is constantly reinforced by the existence of the woman. The female, however, is never complete in and of herself: her desire is directed towards, and absolutely dependent on, the male and his penis.

This concept of desire can be criticized for being contradictory: desire is never anything purely passive; and so the daughter's desire within oedipal structures remains an impossible logical operation, a deception. As Teresa de

Lauretis argues: "no one can really see oneself as an inert object or a sightless body; neither can one see oneself altogether as other. One has an ego, after all, even when one is a woman" (140). A simple inversion of roles would not destroy these structures: although the determining fact of a social position justified by a biological characteristic would be wiped out, the myth that does not grant liberty and fulfillment in desire for everyone would be reinstalled.

Oedipal interpretations offer the convenience of a consistent description of desire and identity, searching (and finding) an authentic truth of the subject and its place in the world, re-orientating the subject when it becomes confused. The carnival logic, however, understands identity as performative and vacillating, rather describing a subject "in process" than attributing authenticity to it and (meta-historical) truth. It thus is open to rearrangements; this may result in *various forms* of identity and desire — at the price of not being able to describe the world in already known terms and patterns. In order to avoid repetition, to nourish curiosity and to look for something better for the daughter, I will follow the tradition of the grotesque in carnival and offer an interpretation of family structures as depicted by the animals shown in *Where East Is East*.

East of Oedipus: Familiar Animalism, Unfamiliar Animals

If we stick to Freud, the animal is another image of regression. But we can also look at the animals as a reference to the fairground tradition. We can interpret the tiger as a symbol of sexual emancipation, as Stefan Brandt proposes (Brandt 141), or look at animals in Browning's films as metaphorical representations of the characters or one of their qualities, as Boris Henry does. He observes an alarming function of animals for the narrative: they refer to repressed moments, which offer a possible relationship between two bodies (Henry III.2., 2–4). "The animal is thus a kind of mark and it is one of the traitors of the human body.... It is thus a demand of the body, a necessary transition to affirm one's state of being after it had been questioned" (III.2., 12). The narration of *Where East Is East* is punctuated by the appearance of animals. During the whole film, animals are present on various levels. First, they are physically present: there are tigers, elephants, cows, oxen, and in the house and the courtyard, a goat, a parrot, white doves and a gorilla in a cage. A small monkey accompanies Madame de Sylva on her journey. Animals appear in language and in images, too: Tiger Haynes calls the lovers whispering sweet nothings to each other "parakeets"; Toyo wears elephant figures as earrings; and the sash around Tiger Haynes' pants is decorated with an embroidered dromedary. Not all the animals in *Where East Is East* take an apparent role in the narration. The animals also bring the circus tradition and the viewer's desire for the spectacular back to the cinema — quite some time after movies had left the fairgrounds behind.[3]

The original family (Tiger Haynes, Toyo, Madame de Sylva) is bounded by their relations to animals. First, all of them "are" tigers and/or are named as such: Tiger Haynes has the tiger in his name; has stripe-formed, tiger-like scars on his face; and is a tiger catcher. Toyo and Tiger Haynes "play tiger" together by forming hands into paws and claws, and hissing. The recognition between Madame de Sylva and Tiger Haynes underlines the family's bond to the tigers through a tiger characteristic: "You are unchanged, Tiger, except some more scars" are among Madame de Sylva's first words addressed to Tiger Haynes. Madame de Sylva's servant, when seeing Bobby in danger, warns Tiger Haynes "She is bad! White boy like sheep with tiger! Keep him away from her!" and introduces Madame de Sylva as part of the tiger family.[4] Bobby's status is defined by a link to an animal as well: the sheep is a symbol of victim and sacrifice. Bobby is not part of the family, as he is not a tiger. In contrast to Bobby, other animals surround the tiger family members: Tiger Haynes is accompanied by a gorilla (at the beginning, together with his daughter by an elephant), Madame de Sylva by a little monkey and Toyo by white doves. Bobby and Toyo meet by venue of a tiger: he is the son of Tiger Haynes' business partner. Bobby and Madame de Sylva meet through the small monkey — on the ship, the monkey plays with a ball. Madame de Sylva then rolls it towards Bobby, who picks it up — he then has the monkey's toy and instantly becomes the toy or pet of Madame de Sylva.

Neither Bobby nor Toyo see through Madame de Sylva's strategies. Toyo even argues with her father that her (biological) mother should be present at her engagement party — being completely naive about her (as the spectator knows, the mother is the real menace to Toyo's happiness). "Please, it will make me so happy," she begs him; and "happy" is the word that finally prevents her father from throwing Madame de Sylva out of the house. Even as Madame de Sylva comes to the party, wearing a marvelous dress that Toyo wore in an earlier scene, Toyo is proud of her mother and her beauty, announcing this to all the guests. When Madame de Sylva tells her daughter at the end of the evening, "I compliment your choice," kissing Toyo quickly on her forehead, and then Bobby's lips, longer, Toyo only seems to be irritated for a short moment.

Animalistic Revenge: The End of the Game

Toyo performs roles, acts childishly and uses adult gestures that are never sincere. She is only upright and authentic in her love for Bobby; in one scene at the beginning, Toyo attacks a woman who was making eyes at Bobby. Bobby was about to follow the seductive woman, but Toyo caused that woman to fall out of her sedan so that she herself would regain Bobby's attention. It is only at the end of the film, when Toyo is deeply saddened by Bobby's unexplainable absence, that she refuses to act: engaged in playing with her father, she suddenly lets her hands fall down and announces, "No, no more play. I can't hide anymore. I am so unhappy."

The decision to stop playing is the beginning of the revenge. The showdown between Tiger Haynes and Madame de Sylva is paralleled by scenes of the gorilla. At the beginning of Madame de Sylva's stay, she asks Tiger Haynes, "You still have old Rango? She remembers me?" Tiger Haynes replies, "Yes! Gorillas never forget those who hurt them!"[5] The fight begins with Madame de Sylva's provocation "Who will make me leave?" when Tiger Haynes, about to explode in anger but not really knowing what to do wants to remove her from his house. The following image shows the gorilla shaking the bars of her cage. As Madame de Sylva shows up at the engagement dinner, throwing seductive glances Bobby's way, the gorilla becomes agitated. And when Madame de Sylva, after failing to kill Tiger Haynes, still tries to seduce Bobby, the gorilla's force increases; she rages more violently in her cage. As Madame de Sylva refuses to apologize for her behavior and instead smiles without remorse, Tiger Haynes unleashes the gorilla from her confinement. The gorilla takes part in the revenge for all the frustrations, rejections and injuries. It is the "embodiment of a past that haunts the present enriched with rejected desires, hatred-poisoned love and unfulfilled drives" (Uzal, 73). In *Where East Is East*, the violence of animals and humans are powering moments of estrangement and monstrosity, causing the blurring of their boundaries. Tiger Haynes, who had until this point only played the tiger (hands and mouth become paws and jaw), transcends the game by really transforming into a tiger and now literally tears Madame de Sylva to pieces. His name is degraded, becomes material reality; the animalistic truthfulness of his name is grotesquely revealed. Tiger, who was dedicating his life to the happiness of his daughter, dies after his daughter is happily married. Just as in *West of Zanzibar*, the father, thwarted by his wife, sacrifices himself for his daughter.

Gaylyn Studlar observes this in films with Lon Chaney in general. "Chaney may destroy his enemies, but only in his own sacrifice can (feminine) purity and innocence be sustained. The moral order of the patriarchy is restored after it is revealed as being deeply perverse" (214). But does patriarchal power really get restored? *Where East Is East* shows that one — if one is a daughter — cannot live happily together with one's family because the parents, especially the mother, always stand in the way of lustful and satisfying relationships. Only after both parents have left earthly life does Toyo have the opportunity to make something out of her love and her desire. *Where East Is East* even contains a double negation of the parents: first, they are to die, and later they are to be left behind when the happy couple leaves the town immediately after the wedding ceremony.

What's in It for the Daughter? Animal-Grotesque Conclusions

The animals open up ways for rearranging family settings and for explaining interpersonal relations. In this perspective, *Where East Is East* cannot be reconstructed through an oedipal focus: Oedipal relationships are subverted, the roles are inversed and the father as well as his position fails and is degraded in the end. An oedipal perspective would mean seeing every image of three people together as a proof of the oedipal triangle, ignoring the end, and squeezing all the role inversions into the original oedipal scheme. Animalistically speaking, the family does not seem to be a place of patriarchal power or masculine supremacy. Bobby cannot be described in terms of traditional male characteristics — he is the sheep(ish), the victim, he remains passive and is the film's central object of desire, almost being passed from one woman to another; he is seduced but does not seduce. Bobby is an object rather than a subject of desire. Both male characters, Bobby and the father, find themselves in a position of (relative) powerlessness; it is Tiger Haynes, the father, who desires the daughter — and not vice versa. With the loss of his daughter, Tiger Haynes loses for a second time the person of his desire, just as years before he had lost Madame de Sylva. It seems that he does not have what the female characters desire and must let them go. He cannot defend his house against Madame de Sylva; he must rely on the help of the female-attributed gorilla for his revenge. The scars in his face show the vulnerability of the masculine body rather than its physical perfection. In the scene of Tiger Haynes and Toyo playing tigers, Toyo wins the fight, sitting on her father's stomach as he lies on the ground. The servants laugh at their master. In Bakhtin's words, the high is degraded, lowered to the ground, while the employees (and the daughter) rise over their employer (and father), and thus experience themselves the position of power and supremacy — at least for the duration of their laughter.[6]

At the engagement dinner, Toyo promotes her mother to the invited, taking a role traditionally not held by a daughter. Toyo has the power to decide when to play and when to stop playing. She defends her desire and (illusions of) love against her father and against her mother, while everybody else is forced to step down. Although evidently only a few oedipal structures remain and little patriarchal power is left over, Browning's films are nevertheless often seen as candidates for psychoanalysis. But why, after having had the chance to see the world from a carnivalesque point of view, do film-historical and theoretical reconstructions often reinforce the structures that already have been subverted? Why not take the opportunity to look at the world and the films from a carnivalesque standpoint? Is it the fear to look right into something that violates our deepest ideas about the family (and patriarchal structures within)? If not useful for emancipation, why not leave these myths behind instead of perpetuating them?

If we try to change the narrative image[7] of women, or at least to describe it in other terms than those of Oedipus, and then turn to Freud again, we might not get that far, as Freud calls a woman's moving away from the Oedipus a "regression." Although he does not use this term in an offensive way, the linear way to progression is clearly pointed out:

> Progression is towards Oedipus, toward the Oedipal stage (which in his view marks the inset of womanhood, the initiation of feminity); regression is away from Oedipus, retarding or even impending the female's sexual development, as Freud would have it, or, as I see it, impending the fulfillment of the male's desire, as well as its narrative closure [de Lauretis 142].

If we look for fulfillment of the daughter's desire and cannot find it at the end of the development Freud sketches, we should allow ourselves to take one step back and have a look at possibilities that other points of departure provide, without fearing "regression." We then are able to ask other questions: Why shouldn't we destroy myths and mechanisms that underline the story of a one-and-only submissive feminity and, finally, start off with something else? For, if we understand filmmakers and spectators to be subjects constituted by history and social relationships, we can change these images and the imaginary of women and other genders; we can even understand these myths as *historical* narratives—and therefore do not need to repeat them the same way across the centuries.

Obituary to the Father

Where East Is East does not only offer a new perspective to outline the narrative image of the daughter, but also that of the father, as the characters performed by Lon Chaney do not match the traditional role of men. Gaylyn Studlar analyzes characters performed by Lon Chaney as incarnations of a masochistic perversion of loss. These "narratives of male loss" (231) do not lead to the affirmation of an active sexual identity in which patriarchal power manifests and reproduces itself. Instead, those male characters find themselves in a position of powerlessness. "Instead of patriarchal sexual identity, his characters only can achieve a redemptive, masochistically romantic transformation through their thwarted desire" (Studlar 213). Completely devoted to love and ready for sacrifice, revenge and maybe redemption can occur, but never romantic fulfillment of desire:

> The mystery that Chaney's stardom exploited was the revelation of what may have been the equivalent of "the final forbidden mystery" in an age that glorified men's physical perfection and unflappable "bully" optimism. Chaney's roles offered a revelation of the "exposed obscenity of the self"—as Other—as masculinity allowed to be failed and freakish [Studlar 209–10].

Interestingly enough, the masculine's Other is not projected onto the woman, but can be found in the deviating male body—and thus explains the man's fear of becoming "Other"—differently from terms of the castration complex. *Where East Is East* thus offers more possibilities for everyone: The father is no longer identical with himself but can be the "Other" at the same time—without needing a feminine character to bear his projections. The daughter fights for her love and desire and (a rare ending until today) gets away with it—without compromise, happy and alive.

It really is time for something new. Let us overcome the old and open our eyes to other perceptions of family structures and interpersonal relationships between people. Let us go to the movies and leave Mom and Dad and Freud at home in order to free our view for something we might not have known before. Let us dare the adventure of a non-oedipal look at films: through a daughter's eyes.

The author thanks Bernadett Settele, Karen Teuber-Genn and Katharina Voss for helpful comments on the essay and its translation.

Notes

1. This is not to be seen as subsequent actions (first holy, then profane; first birth, then death). In the sense of carnival, these—from a nowadays perspective contradictory and only as separated understandable—spheres merge; they are one and the same. The body was not yet the private, individual, ready-made and atomized one it came to be with bourgeois conception. The private and the universal are still interwoven in ambivalent and contradictory manner (Cf. 23–25). Bakhtin refers to statues of pregnant elderly women: birth and death *are one*.

2. Pascale Risterucci analyzes this usage of language in her essay *Ce Qui Est Dit Est Dit* ("What Is Said, Is Said"): The body is shaped according to the word; there is no reality besides the one that is written or spoken—even if the spoken words turn out to be lies. Nanon promises Alonzo that she hates the arms of men (*The Unknown*), Dead Legs believes Crane that Anna

will follow him to Africa (*West of Zanzibar*), Cleopatra swears to Hans she will marry him for love (*Freaks*). The protagonists cling so strongly to these words — and it is only afterwards that they understand the divergent usage of language. Subsequently, the protagonist tries to reestablish the truth of the words said in modifying his/her body according to the words so it can fulfill its nomination. Thus, besides tearing off his own arms, those of the rival need to be torn off (*The Unknown*); one does need to burn oneself instead of one's daughter (*West of Zanzibar*); or modify the brute bride to be the real queen of the freaks (*Freaks*) (Cf. Risterucci 51–56). In Browning's scenario to Emerson's *The Mystery of the Leaping Fish*, the gangsters "wash the money" in a launderette; and the protagonist, Coke Ennyday, is always sniffing cocaine; etc.)

3. The cooperation of circus or fairground and movies in *Where East Is East* is not just part of the setting of the story but has certainly also taken place outside of the narration, during the production process: Tigers and elephants obviously need a tamer, and thus they must have worked together.

4. This happens before the film explicitly brings to evidence that Madame de Sylva is Toyos' mother.

5. This intertitle is not part of every version of the film: the recently restored version does not contain this scene.

6. As in all of Toyo's acting and playing, the effects are more than mere simulation. Simulation and playing games both reveal possibilities, but playing momentarily does "really take place," thus offering a (material) experience, not only imagined results of simulation. When the game gets serious, the material aspects of the transformed body win over the merely imagined simulation.

7. De Lauretis invents the term "narrative image of woman" as not only the image of woman but as "the join of image and story, interlocking of visual and narrative registers effected by the cinematic apparatus of the look" (140).

Works Cited

Bakhtin, Mikhail. *Rabelais and His World*. Trans. Helene Iswolsky. Cambridge, MA, and London: M.I.T. Press, 1968.
Brandt, Stefan. "White Bo(d)y in Wonderland: Cultural Alterity and Sexual Desire in *Where East Is East*." (Herzogenrath 129–149).
Buchmann, Sabeth, et al. (eds.) *Wenn Sonst Nichts Klappt: Wiederholung Wiederholen*. Hamburg/Berlin: b_books, 2005.
De Lauretis, Teresa. *Alice Doesn't: Feminism, Semiotics, Cinema*. Bloomington: Indiana University Press, 1984.
Henry, Boris. *Tod Browning, le spectacle du Corps*. Marseille, unpublished PhD thesis, 2003.
Herzogenrath, Bernd (ed.). *The Films of Tod Browning*. London: Black Dog Publishing, 2006.
Nowak, Lars. "Different Wiederholte Differenzen: Zur Filmischen Praxis von Tod Browning." (Buchmann 258–72).
Risterucci, Pascale. "Ce Qui Est Dit Est Dit." (Risterucci and Uzal 51–56).
_____, and Marco Uzal (eds.). *Tod Browning, fameux inconnu*. CinémAction n°125. Paris: Éditions Corlet, 2007.
Savada, Elias, and David Skal. *Dark Carnival: The Secret World of Tod Browning, Hollywood's Master of the Macabre*. New York: Anchor Books, 1995.
Studlar, Gaylyn. *This Mad Masquerade: Stardom and Masculinity in the Jazz Age*. New York: Columbia University Press, 1996.
Uzal, Marco. "Le Corps est un Animal Encombrant: L'Animalité Dans les Films de Tod Browning." (Risterucci and Uzal 70–73).

Films

Browning, Tod, dir. *West of Zanzibar*. (Metro-Goldwyn-Mayer Corporation, 1928).

Browning, Tod, dir. *Where East Is East*. (Metro-Goldwyn-Mayer Corporation, 1929).
Browning, Tod, dir. *Freaks*. (Metro-Goldwyn-Mayer Corporation, 1932).
Emerson, John, dir. *The Mystery of the Leaping Fish*. (Keystone Komedy/Triangle Film Corporation, 1916).

Tod Browning vs. George Melford
Dracula's *Doppelgänger*

FRANK LAFOND

Dracula, directed by Tod Browning, premiered at the Roxy Theater, New York City, on February 12, 1931. Along with James Whale's *Frankenstein*, which was released later the same year, it undoubtedly stands as a landmark in the history of talking horror film. Yet another adaptation of Bram Stoker's famous story was simultaneously filmed by Universal studios, using the same sets as well as the same shooting script, and had been released about a month before. Entirely shot at night, when the regular crew was then long gone, this film deliberately targeted the Latin American market by using Mexican actors and Spanish dialogue, since for various reasons subtitles were not really considered as an option in the early days of the talkies.[1] Paul Kohner supervised the production, as he did with *The Cat Creeps* in 1930, and George Melford, who had already made Latin actor Rudolph Valentino a star in *The Sheik* (1921), directed it. The resulting picture has since been overshadowed by Tod Browning's phenomenal hit, although its technical merits have quite often been underlined by critics and genre fans alike. However, a DVD edition containing the two versions seems to invite us to closely compare them, and upon successively watching them, one can't help experiencing an uncanny feeling. That is not to say, however, that our essay will focus on this alternative version, but rather that we are going to use Melford's work as an instrument for a better understanding of Browning's.

The first thing that strikes the spectator is the difference of length between the two films. While Browning's feature film lasts approximately 75 minutes, Melford's version is about 24 minutes longer. Since both pictures are supposed to be based on the very same — although translated — shooting script, one can justifiably imagine that some scenes were edited out (or perhaps even not shot at all) while others were simply shortened. But then why did the director, who is given credit as a writer on the final draft of the screenplay but not on the opening credits, choose not to include these scenes in his own cut (see Dracula Shooting Script)? And, more importantly, what are the effects of such narrative options on the American film? Thanks to its Mexican *doppelgänger*, we will also examine Browning's *Dracula* from other angles, including direction and acting (notably how the portrayal of the living dead by the two actors differs). Having done all that, we will finally be in the position to define with precision Tod Browning's conception of the horror genre at work in this film.

A First Overview

Much has already been said about the staginess and verbosity of the all–American production, mostly due to the fact that the script was based on the play written by Hamilton Deane and John L. Balderston, thus avoiding a beneficial return to the original novel, and that the main actors came from the stage version. Exception is widely made for the first act located in Transylvania, where the fluid camerawork, signed by Karl Freund, who became famous in Germany in the 1920s for his work with directors such as Friedrich W. Murnau (*The Last Laugh*, 1924) and Fritz Lang (*Metropolis*, 1926–1927), has a few wonderful moments.[2] For instance, Freund uses an impressive tracking shot toward Dracula (Bela Lugosi) for the first onscreen appearance of the vampire, which brilliantly illustrates the monster's irresistible attraction for the audience and the other characters alike. It's a known fact that the crew headed by Melford used to have a close look at the dailies of Browning's picture in order to try and improve their own work. There's no doubt that they succeeded in some places, but elsewhere, like here with the introduction of the monstrous character, standard was obviously set much too high.

Since the two *Dracula*s released in 1931 are based on the very same screenplay, few differences of importance can be noticed by the spectators at first sight: the characters and the story are, of course, identical. The Latin picture adds some bits of dialogue or description here and there, mostly to little avail (during the inn scene at the very beginning; Renfield's (Dwight Frye) protracted supper at Dracula's table; Renfield's first meeting with doctor Van Helsing (Edward van Sloan); etc.). Overall, already talkative scenes seem even longer, and narrative is only made more coherent at one point, when Van Helsing and John Harker (David Manners) take care of Lucy, known in her "after-death" as the Lady in White — an episode surprisingly cut from the other film. However, even if Melford's *Dracula* lasts much longer than Browning's, this does not mean that it incorporates every single detail. The killing of a young flower vendor by the vampire once he arrives in London is, for example, replaced by a long shot where he is seen slowly raising from his coffin in Carfax Abbey. Although the modernity of the Western world depicted in the two narratives is most questionable, this particular scene of Browning's film, whose soundtrack appears to be filled with car honks and urban life sounds, assumes an important meaning: central to the movie — at least at this point — is the infiltration into, the contamination of, *our* civilization by an ancient evil force from the East. This is the reason why we see Count Dracula walking through the crowded streets of London, clad in formal dress and followed by a flowing tracking shot that makes his great ease frightening. Needless to say, his awakening in a gothic set such as the abbey seriously minimizes this idea; and, from that standpoint, Melford's work follows more closely the classical horror narratives of the 1930s in which monstrosity was always clearly distinct from normality.

Furthermore, even in the case where the action of the two pictures is similar, the editing can differ to a significant extent. Near the end, Mina/Eva, who has just drunk blood from Dracula's arm (and not from his chest as in the novel), is talking with John/Juan, and then tries to bite him, as the vampire himself attempts to hypnotize Van Helsing in another part of doctor's Seward asylum. Unlike Melford and the shooting script, Browning refuses to dramatize the events by crosscutting between the two actions, which echoes the restraint found at work in the numerous melodramas he has made (*The Unknown*, 1927; *West of Zanzibar*, 1928; etc.). The same thing could be said about his use of music. Except for Tchaikovsky's *Swan Lake* played over the opening credits — as well as like in other Universal horror films — Wagner's *Die Meistersinger* and Schubert's *Unfinished Symphony* heard during the concert hall sequence, the picture does not feature any musical soundtrack; but that shouldn't be considered only as a characteristic of early talking films, as the Latin production briefly resorts to it on some rare occasions (to punctuate Dracula's rising from his box in London, etc.). Rather, in both versions dead silence works as a way to efficiently emphasize the eeriness expressed by the images; most contemporary horror films should learn from them.

Portrait of the Monster as ...

Although Tod Browning's adaptation of *Dracula* was apparently not shown nationwide until March 31, a still widespread rumor claims it was released on Valentine's Day in the United States. Anyhow, as Rhona J. Berenstein has demonstrated at great length, Universal studios conceived at the time "an explicitly romantic campaign targeted at women" (Berenstein 66).

In fact, the film's most important input probably lies in the representation of the vampire as an attractive aristocrat, an irresistible seducer whereas, in contrast, its most famous cinematic predecessor, Murnau's *Nosferatu, a Symphony of Horror* (1922), insisted upon the vampire's physical abjection. However, the final American version appears to be more complex and interesting from this particular standpoint. Near the beginning of the movie, Renfield is not overcome and fatally bitten by Dracula's sensual brides, like his counterpart in the Latin version is. Rather, Dracula repels the three young women, and then is shown dangerously leaning over Renfield's unconscious body. Thus, the omni-sexuality of the undead character — a crossing of boundaries established by patriarchal society which strongly contributes to his monstrosity — is put to the fore by Tod Browning; whereas the homoerotic innuendo was perhaps judged too explicit by the Spanish production and the original shooting script. In all versions, however, Dracula almost manages to hypnotize/seduce Van Helsing, the narrative main figure of authority; but, due to his failure and the absence of female rivals, of course, the scene has other implications.

After her first meeting with Dracula, a playful Mina Seward (Helen Chandler) imitates his particular phrasing in the presence of an already fascinated Lucy (Frances Dade). Needless to say, this unusual accent will soon become one of Bela Lugosi's most famous trademarks, but is here parodied in the most biting way. Interestingly enough, this joke does not appear in the screenplay or in the Latin feature film, which could easily suggest that it was an addition made on the set by Tod Browning after seeing the Hungarian actor's eccentric performance.[3] According to David J. Skal, Carlos Villar, Lugosi's Spanish-speaking doppelgänger, was the only actor that Universal allowed to see the dailies of Browning's production "because the studio wanted him to be as close to Lugosi as possible" (Skal). Alternate takes of shots featuring Lugosi were even used for the Spanish version. Villar lacks the allure of the Hungary-born Lugosi, although his face, which can remind us of a rat, is somewhat closer to Bram Stoker's own description of the character. However, note the significant difference in acting between the two actors when Dracula is confronted by the little mirror that has revealed his true nature to Van Helsing: while Villar gives a demonstration of force and violence, smashing the box into pieces with his stick, Lugosi simply makes it fall with his hand, and grimaces with pain or in disgust as he moves away. The performance of the latter manifests a relative simplicity that finds an echo in Browning's extremely simple choices of mise-en-scene here (a single shot, with no close-ups showing the absence of mirror image). Bela Lugosi looks fixedly at doctor Van Helsing; Carlos Villar continuously rolls his eyes in such an exaggerated way as to stop being frightening. As Cynthia Freeland has noted, the vampire's power resides first in his possession of a "Medusa-like gaze" (129), a mesmerizing look that is repeatedly enhanced by isolating light effects. However, Tod Browning uses different strategies in order to represent the other, coded as aberrant.

A Creature of the Night

As critics Alain Silver and James Ursini have rightly argued

> [t]hroughout the narrative, the most extraordinary events are reported rather than visualised — "He came to me; he opened a vein in his arm and made me drink" — as Browning is content to cutway at the critical moment of every attack and indulge in ironic touches (as when Harker seeing the wounds on Mina's throat asks, "What could have caused them, Professor?" or the maid announces "Count Dracula" in voiceover before Van Helsing can reply) [Silver and Ursini 67].

For instance, when Renfield slowly crawls towards a maid who has passed out and fallen to the floor, Tod Browning chooses to cut away before something really happens. Is the madman going to bite her neck or does he intend to do something else? The spectators will never be able to tell. The answer lies in Melford's version, however, which follows more closely the description of the shot E-93 appearing in the original English shooting script and is described as follows: "Maid in fore, as Renfield reaches out slowly, with infinite caution, and then with a swift swoop, makes a grab for the fly, which gets away" (*Dracula* Shooting Script). Shot E-92 of the screenplay also features a large close-up of the maid's neck. Yet Browning voluntarily leaves it out, and, contrary to Melford, he even rejects large close-ups, such as the one showing "two little red marks with white centers" on Mina's neck (shot E-36). Even when both versions resort to this kind of shot, the Latin *Dracula* goes as far as multiplying them. For instance, when Renfield slits one of his fingers in front of a bloodthirsty Dracula, three close-ups are used: twice we see the real estate agent's very bloody thumb (in this film, he hurts himself with a knife, not with a simple sheet of paper) from the point of view of the approaching vampire, and once Carlos Villar's glowing eyes in a shockingly close shot. In order to shoot the same sequence, Browning only needs a single image of Renfield's hands, filmed closer and from a much higher angle than Melford's, with a Christian cross falling from his off-screen neck suddenly entering into the frame by the top of the image and stopping dead the menacing Count.

Overall, the rather small number of inserts found in the all–American picture may be another argument for its staginess; but, perhaps more importantly, the fact that many of the "missing" close-ups display (potential) supernatural elements — the marks on Mina's neck, the absence of Dracula's mirror image, etc. — could be said to slightly undermine its horror nature. The use of sound also contributes to it: for instance, compare Browning's film with the repeated creaking and self-opening of the heavy doors in Dracula's castle that we find in the Latin version. They are either much shorter and less resounding (as Renfield is about to enter the vampire's lair), or have been voluntarily neglected — note the "absence" of the last one (when the Count finally walks out of the bedroom) that leaves Renfield desperately gasping for air. This does not mean, however, that the aesthetics of Browning's movie follows the definition of the fantastic given by Tzvetan Todorov — that is to say narratives constantly oscillating between a rational and an irrational explanation until their very end (see Todorov). The first indisputable uncanny event occurs, in fact, quite early on, when the vampiric host goes through a huge cobweb at the top of the stairs without tearing it. At the crucial moment, Browning interrupts a long shot of Bela Lugosi heading for the web with a cutaway showing Renfield, who stares at him — the supernatural happens off-screen and is left to the spectator's imagination; whereas Melford brutally puts part of the cobweb right in front of the terrified witness. Here, Dracula looks like a magician doing conjuring tricks that the spectator — diegetic, as the young real estate agent, or not — is not capable of imitating (see Lenne 90). Therefore, this scene brings to the fore the director's tastes and thematic preoccupations (*The Mystic*, 1925, or *Miracles for Sale*, 1939, for example) and foreshadows *Mark of the Vampire* (1935), where the vampire, again played by Lugosi, is finally revealed to be an actor.

The "anti-climatic finale" (80) of the film, as Silver and Ursini put it, is another example of Browning's handling of the horrific aspects inherent in the mythical figure he is dealing with. Against all expectations, at least for a modern audience, the death of the Count occurs completely off-screen: Van Helsing is first seen leaning over the box in a long shot, his back to camera, and when he plunges a wooden stick into Dracula's heart, we only hear the faraway screams of the latter while the colorless John Harker appears onscreen looking for Mina. In other words, the director is not trying to shock the spectator, to horrify him with gruesome or violent images; whereas Melford lets him see the monster's prone body in a closer shot and hear his agony in a more demonstrative and protracted way as the half-clad Eva (Lupita Tovar) is painfully seizing her chest — thus implying some kind of link (physical? moral?) between the two characters. Were the horror elements toned down, as well as the eroticism, because of censorship? Maybe so, but there is much more to it. Despite all its unquestionable flaws, Tod Browning's *Dracula* shouldn't be too quickly rejected in favor of the Spanish-language version. In many ways, George Melford's effort was praised — and still is — because of the way it spectacularly handles all the supernatural aspects of Bram Stoker's story. Central to Browning's picture, however, is a conception of horror more restrained and demanding from the audience, just like the shadow in the form of a bat that is cast by a lampshade on the background wall of Lucy's bedroom, suggesting a menace before Dracula himself appears onscreen. It's no surprise that this subtlety is not present in its Latin *doppelgänger*.

Notes

1. For instance, Gary D. Rhodes writes that "subtitles were technically possible, but illiteracy rates in Mexico were very high and thus eliminated that option" (Rhodes 93). The very same year, a third *Dracula*, in other words a silent version of Browning's movie, was even made by Universal for the theaters that were not yet equipped for the talkies.
2. For instance, Patrick Brion argues that *Dracula* is "superb from the point of view of form but very stagy" (8).
3. Actually, Browning had chosen his long-time partner Lon Chaney to play the role of the Count. Unfortunately, the actor died of throat cancer in 1930.

Works Cited

Brion, Patrick. "Une vie dans le Fantastique." *Cahiers du cinéma* 550 (October 2000).
Dracula (The Original 1931 Shooting Script). Universal Filmscripts Series, Classic Horror Films — Volume 13. Absecon: MagicImage Filmbooks, 1990.
Freeland, Cynthia. *The Naked and the Undead: Evil and the Appeal of Horror*. Boulder and Oxford: Westview Press, 2000.
Lenne, Gérard. "Mélodrame et illusion chez Tod Browning." *Positif* 476 (October 2000), 86–94.
Rhodes, Gary. "Fantasmas del Cine Mexicano: The 1930s Horror Film Cycle of Mexico." *Fear Without Frontiers*. Ed. Steven Jay Schneider. Godalming: FAB Press, 2003.
Silver, Alain, and James Ursini. *The Vampire Film: From Nosferatu to Interview with the Vampire*. Third edition. New York: Limelight Editions, 1997, 67.
Skal, David. Audio commentary for Tod Browning's *Dracula* (Universal DVD, 1999).
Todorov, Tzevetan. *The Fantastic: A Structural Approach to a Literary Genre*. Trans. Richard Howard. Cleveland & London: Case Western Reserve University Press, 1973.

Browning. Freak. Woman. Stain.

EUGENIE BRINKEMA

Twins, doubles, partial objects, the grotesquely mutilated, little people, too-big people, good mothers, bad mothers, law-giving fathers, ghosts and freaks, betrayal and murder — Freud would have loved Tod Browning's films. And yet, there is almost no psychoanalytic criticism on the works of this auteur. There is, in fact, little criticism on Browning in general — and what is written tends to focus on biographical curiosities (his early years in the circus), or deploys strictly formal analyses of his themes, lighting, or collaboration with Lon Chaney.

When Browning criticism makes its occasional detour into the murky waters of psychoanalysis, it circles around familiar Freudian theory-objects: castration anxiety, the Oedipal crisis, and the uncanny. These statements are typical: David Skal and Elias Savada posit, "*The Show* again echoes Freud's essay 'The Uncanny'" (108), and "In Browning's next project, Freudian theory would be bizarrely literalized into a weird and spectacular circus attraction" (110). Stuart Rosenthal writes, "Alonzo, in *The Unknown*, commits what amounts to an act of self-castration" (43); and Nancy Margaret Bombaci argues that "Browning's films ... inscribe Freudian dramas that materialize as family melodramas" (188). Though the language of psychoanalysis seems to materialize, the writers appear more interested in the Freudian than in Freud. The terms tossed about — castration, the uncanny — are not only well-known to the non-psychoanalytic theorist, they are popular idioms that, even in Browning's time, would have been familiar to spectators, given that in the 1920s "new words and phrases began to be bandied about the cocktail-tray and the Mah Jong table — inferiority complex, sadism, masochism, Oedipus complex" (Allen 28). Psychoanalytic theorists would, of course, argue that the power of Browning's films does not reside in his appropriation of Freudian concepts, but that notions like the uncanny as described (not created) by Freud are ahistorically unsettling. As Freud explains in his famous essay on the phenomenon, "This uncanny is in reality nothing new or alien, but something which is familiar and old-established in the mind and which has become alienated from it only through the process of repression" (217).

The use of Freudian concepts in an analysis of Browning is not without merit. It is undeniable how significantly mutilation, partial bodies, wounds, and trauma figure in his films. Narratives focus on mommy-daddy-me triads (the title *The Unholy Three* is a wonderful characterization of the Oedipal players in Freud's drama), and there is a strong visual presence of automatons or doll-like humans, cited by Freud as examples of the uncanny. Furthermore, Browning's 1932 film *Freaks* is, in many ways, a story about the development of the fetish. Such a reading goes thusly: the midget Hans' body visually brings into existence the discourse of childhood, and his aggressive/sexual urges are freakish and disruptive for the very same reason that are infantile ones. Freud writes of the traumatic infantile moment in his analysis of fetishism, "the inquisitive boy peered at the woman's genitals *from below*" (155). The sight of the absent maternal penis throws the child into such libidinal disorganization (mine is losable as well!) that a fetish object is erected in place of the missing penis and the process of fetishistic disavowal instated (the famous "I know very well, and yet...."). The "big woman" whom Hans adores, Cleopatra, is constantly shot from below—"normal sized," she looks enormous in Browning's world. While some of these low shots are from Hans' point of view, such as the opening one of Cleopatra on her trapeze, others (in scenes where Hans is not present) are the apparatus taking up the position of a child in relationship to her statuesque body. When Cleopatra drops her cloak in front of Hans, this moment unearths the maternal body, while her costume resembles fetishistic substitutes (cloaks, undergarments, garters). Hans' own disavowal takes the form of: "I know very well that she cannot love me, and yet I hope/believe she loves me." His insistence that he is a man, not a child (despite appearances), and his heated sexual interest in Cleo, make him a *Doppelgänger* for Freud's aggressive desiring infant. Hercules, then, figures as the punishing father, in competition with the child for the mother's love and threatening castration should he lose this competition. In the wish-fulfillment scenario of *Freaks*, the spiteful "child" kills the "father," and literally cuts the "mother" down to size. Because of this, the mother is no longer available as a sexual object, and Hans finds a substitute in the form of gentle, patient Frieda.

A Freudian reading of *Freaks* can be taken quite far. Masud R. Khan offers an etiology of fetishism in which one of its elements is "the terror panic of incest" (qtd. in Dadoun 40). Hans' obsession with Cleo, made possible through the development of the fetish and its correlate structure of disavowal, thwarts his romantic relationship with his fiancée Frieda. The actors who played Hans and Cleo were real-life siblings, Harry and Daisy Earles. The romantic entanglement with Cleo, then, prevents the love scenes between Hans and Frieda that would effect real-life incestuous scenarios. The film can end in no other way than Hans crying on Frieda's lap, not only because she comes to take up the mother position abandoned by Cleo, but because a passionate romantic kiss would itself create an extradiegetic perverse and taboo situation! In short, the Freudian reading works.

Browning and his collaborators may have had access to some psychoanalytic texts: he and his screenwriter Guy Endore "likely took some inspiration (for the 1935 film *Mark of the Vampire*) from Ernest Jones' pioneering psychoanalytic study *On the Nightmare* (1931), which explicitly linked vampire fantasies to incest guilt" (Skal 191). The least persuasive explanation for why Browning's films drip so strikingly with Freudianism resides in rumors that Browning lost his genitals in a car accident and thereafter became obsessed with castration imagery. Skal has demonstrated that this was never the historical case, but no matter; I am not interested in these *whys* but prefer to instigate a series of *hows*. How does a psychoanalytic reading provide richer insights into Browning's films, both as separate entities and a motley assortment of works that have intertextual relationships and connections? How might psychoanalysis help us theorize the distorted and distended bodies of Browning's works? How does psychoanalysis explain both the corpus and the corpse?

To answer these questions, we must move away from castration, the uncanny, and Oedipus; for existing Browning criticism, when it takes up psychoanalysis, focuses on mainstream (and often flimsy) Freudian ideas at the expense of the more fascinating possibilities offered by a (re)turn to Jacques Lacan. Lacan's work on anamorphosis, the gaze, and courtly love allows us to theorize a complex interaction in Browning's films that previous criticism has not adequately addressed: the relationship between women and "freaks." The unholy triad of *this* essay will be Freak-Woman-Stain. Freaks in Browning's films are, of course, not limited to *Freaks*; I will look primarily at that film but also at *The Unholy Three* (1925) and *The Unknown* (1927).

The Anamorphic Freak

In *Seminar VII: The Ethics of Psychoanalysis*, Lacan defines anamorphosis as "any kind of construction that is made in such a way that by means of an optical transposition a certain form that wasn't visible at first sight transforms itself into a readable image" (135). He insists on the affective and temporal dimension of the device, whose "pleasure is found in seeing its emergence from an indecipherable form" (135). Although limiting himself in *Seminar*

VII to fairly proper examples of its manifestation (such as in Holbein's famous 1533 painting *The Ambassadors*), four years later, in *Seminar XI: The Four Fundamental Concepts of Psychoanalysis*, Lacan playfully connects the image of anamorphosis with "the effect of an erection" (88). He imagines a tattoo traced on a limp penis that comes into existence contemporaneously with tumescence. Sex, pleasure, picture — these are not accidental signifiers but rather a network along which we can slide from the visual disruption of a stained image to the material disruption of the freakish body.

Anamorphosis is visual freakery — unruly, disorienting, distinctly not part of the normative world of representation. The freak is associated with the same language — Pascal Bonitzer conflates the two when he writes that "the-object-which-makes-a-stain is thus, literally speaking, an object which goes against nature" (21). The "radical ambiguity" of anamorphosis is a phrase fit for freaks whose liminal position is largely due to their ambiguous position between fixed normative categories of identity. Slavoj Žižek writes that "anamorphic distortions of reality may function as repellent horror, like the forehead protuberance of the 'elephant man,' yet phallophany may also occasion an effect of sublime beauty" (*Enjoy Your Symptom* 140). Not coincidentally, because Woman is never too far from anamorphosis or freakery, Žižek locates this beauty in the face of Virginia Woolf. When he writes of the stain (his word for anamorphosis) that its intrusion "disrupts this safe distance: the field of vision is invaded by an element which does not belong to the diegetic reality, and we are forced to accept that the pulsative stain which disturbs the clarity of our vision is part of our eye" ("Bold Gaze" 237), this is an exact account of the perception of the freak — intrusive, invasive, disturbing — epitomized in the reaction of Jon from *Freaks* when he says, "Monsieur Dubois ... I could not believe my eyes. A lot of horrible, twisted things crawling, whining, globbering."

Inherent in the perception of both the freak and anamorphosis is a visual and constitutive trickery: how does it all work? The pleasure of anamorphosis is not simply in seeing the image emerge, but also in deciphering the exact details of its construction. The attention to the physical details of the anamorphosis brings an awareness of the pleasure in seeing the trick succeed, in figuring how the image deceives our senses. In *Seminar VII*, Lacan speaks with fetishistic interest of a Jesuit chapel in which "there existed a whole wall some eighteen meters long ... that was completely unreadable from any point in the room, but if one entered by a certain corridor, you can see for a brief moment the extraordinary dispersed lines come together" (*Ethics* 135). Is this all that different from the "perverse kind of sexual curiosity" Elisabeth Grosz argues people have about freaks: "'How do they do *it*?' What kind of sex lives are available to Siamese twins, hermaphrodites, bearded ladies, and midgets?"

(64). Though one asks how the freak *does* it and how the stain *is done*, a web of curiosity descends over both aberrations and makes them into subjects of obsessive inquiry.

Freaks are a visual block — put on show, they are to be gazed upon and are simultaneously that which we are told not to look at (the parental imperative, "Don't stare!"). *Freaks* is, in many respects, a flimsy frame around the spectacular attractions of freakish bodies — how else to explain the camera's obsessive interest in bodies in disorder doing the most ordinary things: rolling a cigarette, drinking wine, eating bread? The anamorphosis in *The Ambassadors* is a death's head, a skull, that which haunts the entire picture and yet what we almost do not see. For both the freak and the stain we look, we look away, we look awry, we look again. Each time our gaze is captured by something disturbing, something new. The familiar environment of the painting is made different, made uncanny, made other. Žižek's characterization of the anamorphic stain as that which "does not fit" and "sticks out" is exactly the position of those with marginal bodies. Both the stain and the freak exist as relational — they do not take shape independently of the normative context against which they are defined. When Gilles Deleuze writes that "the monsters in *Freaks* are monsters only because they have been forced to move into their explicit role, and it is through a dark vengeance that they find themselves again" (72), he highlights the constructedness of the position of the freak and the violence of the manner in which the transformations of othering/othered bodies occurs.

It is not an accident that the image askew in Holbein's painting is death's head, the ultimate stain — what emerges as surplus in the picture is the image of our own negation. So, too, what the freak points to is our own thinly-masked distortion, our own freakery. Browning asks us to look again, look at freaks aslant; his freaks are an anamorphosis necessitating a visual and ideological double-take. What is freakish, different, askew, about these freaks, Browning's film demands, when seemingly "normal" Cleopatra is so monstrous, so consuming, so evil? Holbein's stain gives great, perhaps the only, meaning to his painting, and here lies the radical possibilities of the blot — because it is almost not there, it fills the space fully; almost unseen, it escapes flat surveillance and speaks, unmediated, to the spectator. *The Unholy Three* illustrates the freak's ability to pass for another (an adult midget for a child), while *Freaks* exemplifies the significance of the ambiguous position in the figure of Joseph/Josephine, whose desire is not limited to one sexed body.

The impurity of the freakish painting is also a characterization of the disrupting/disrupted body. The freak is social, visual, bodily disruption — not to wholeness, but to the fantasy of wholeness. The freak ruptures just as the grotesque ruptures — by calling attention to inside space. The sleek, smooth, static, closed space of non-anamorphic painting becomes supremely open by the inclusion of the stain. Anamorphosis forces a painting fluid, organic, new. The bodies of Browning's freaks are regularly in a state of change, not least because as performers in diegetic sideshows they are often changing in and out of costume and performative disguise. They comprise doubled sensory-motor surfaces (one of the Siamese twins in *Freaks* feels a kiss given to her sister), double masks (embedded costumes, such as in *The Unholy Three*), and double passings (one for another, such as the Roman "Lady" crossdresser in *Freaks* distracting from the actor's stutter, or Alonzo in *The Unknown* passing as one type of freak, a man with no arms, covering for his other freakishness, as a fugitive criminal with an extra thumb). Anamorphosis functions identically: collapsing the binary of interior/exterior, it pulls the punctum of the painting out from its inner recesses while simultaneously hiding it in a public space. Like the letter in Poe's *The Purloined Letter*, anamorphosis is the great secret of the painting precisely because it is visible and over-exposed. The covered, flat, smooth surface of the painting is an alibi for the pleasures and horrors of the tiny smudge at the bottom of its frame. Just as *Freaks* stages the marginal bodies of its characters, *The Unknown* gives us a double pleasure in the simultaneous shot of Alonzo the Armless throwing knives with his feet and the undressed figure of Estrellita (a young Joan Crawford)—the love story exists solely to produce scenarios for the display of these embodied figures.

We are all too aware, once having seen the stain, of its presence. There is a temporal divide, before and after—like the logic of trauma, it possesses a self-conscious temporality, foreclosing the space before the vision. Disability studies locates a similar temporal disruption in the figure of the marginalized body, defining disability as "that in the body which exceeds deterministic efforts to predict a life trajectory" (Mitchell and Snyder 377). "Diseases 'follow a *course*' and therefore prove familiar and domesticated by virtue of a belief in their determinate status.... Disability might be characterized as that which exceeds a culture's predictive capabilities and effective intervention" (Mitchell and Snyder 3). In other words, the grotesque body is temporally grotesque because it cannot be integrated into a teleology of the life cycle or contained within a linear progression. Anamorphosis is a similar temporal problem: the stain necessitates a second look, a turning back. Writing of *The Ambassadors* in *Seminar XI*, Lacan describes this process:

> What, then, before this display of the domain of appearance in all its most fascinating forms, is this object, which from some angles appears to be flying through the air, at others to be tilted? You cannot know—for you turn away, thus escaping the fascination of the picture. Begin by walking out of the room in which no doubt it has long held your attention. It is then that, turning round as you leave ... you apprehend in this form.... What? A skull [88].

The trappings of time saturate even Lacan's lecture — his ellipses, pauses and repetitions extend this speech act, spell out in time the temporal effort and gap introduced, even required, by the anamorphosis. The painting is made theatrical — Lacan's instructions are reminiscent of those by a director to an actor in a play or film. Anamorphosis — like the freak, like the Woman — makes the world into a surreal stage.

Photographer Diane Arbus, who cited Browning as an influence, is worth quoting for her perception of freaks:

> Freaks was one thing I photographed a lot. It was one of the first things I photographed and it had a terrific kind of excitement for me. I just used to adore them ... they made me feel a mixture of shame and awe. There's a quality of legend about freaks.... Most people go through life dreading they'll have a traumatic experience. Freaks were born with their trauma. They've already passed their test in life. They're aristocrats [3].

The freak who has already experienced his or her trauma is reminiscent of the woman in psychoanalysis: born "already castrated," she has already experienced the great loss that haunts phallus-obsessed male subjects. She "lacks lack" as Montrelay posits, and therefore has, literally, nothing to lose. While a feminist response rightly notes the problems inherent in this formula (Cixous: "supposedly, she misses the great lack, so that without man she would be indefinite, indefinable, nonsexed, unable to recognize herself" [235]), — it emphasizes the negativity of psychoanalysis' account of lacking lack at the expense of the radical possibilities and freedoms afforded to the freak and woman.

Trauma is the great return, as what is foreclosed in the Symbolic returns in the Real. To what, though, can the freak who is born under the sign of trauma return? To have no trauma to return to is to return, precisely, to nothing. Traumatized bodies circle around the rend, the negative space of the stain. If the freak and woman lack, if they lack their trauma because it is already overpresent, they are also aligned with Lacan's formula for anxiety, articulated in his unpublished seminar on the affect — "if all of a sudden all norms are lacking, namely what constitutes the lack — because the norm is correlative to the idea of lack — if all of a sudden it is not lacking ... it is at that moment that anxiety begins" (11/28/62, 12). The freak and woman return to this encounter, return to the foreclosed kernel, return to death as full subjects. Put another way, the freak and the woman are already too-sutured in the Real. The ethical possibilities afforded by having already experienced one's trauma, by having already endured the great subject-defining loss, align the freak and the female, neither by making the female freakish nor by feminizing freaks, but by disregarding those categories in favor of a more fundamental one: the freak and the woman are those for whom trauma is already made flesh and who therefore have nothing left to (forec)lose.

Hans is born with his trauma, and his earthly/secondary tragedy is the realization that his beloved, Cleopatra, never loved him and regarded their wedding as a joke. *Freaks* suggests that Hans' near-hysterical collapse when he discovers this, and his horror at Cleo's mutilation at the hands of his fellow freaks, leads to his total isolation in the epilogue to the film. We might follow Hans' statement to Phroso and Venus at the end of the film, "I can't see no one," to its doubly negated conclusion: I can see something. Perhaps Hans is glimpsing clearly for the first time the position he was already in, the trauma he had already experienced. Hans' overproximation to his Cleopatra-trauma is the realization of what he had previously undergone. Cleo did not betray Hans so much as compel him to recognize his already-betrayed social and physical status.

When Hans tells Cleopatra, "Most big people (laugh at me). They don't realize I'm a man, with the same feelings they have," and protests to Frieda, "Please, Frieda, don't tell me what to do! When I want a cigar, I smoke a cigar! I want no orders from a woman!"—psychoanalysis would tell us not to take his words at face value. Hans protests too much that *he is a man, not a child*, and these protests ring with the anxious desperation of defensive truth. If Hans' desire is precisely the opposite of what he says—to be treated like a child, not a man—then the ending of *Freaks* is a textbook wish-fulfillment scenario. Hans receives in Frieda the good mother, having eliminated Cleo, the bad mother. Cleo's horrific wrong is not in treating Hans like a baby, giving him a piggyback ride at their wedding and humiliating him, but rather in actually giving Hans what he always wanted and answering his regression fantasy. Nothing is more terrifying to the subject than to be given its desire, for it is by repressing foundational fantasies that subjects function. Žižek, writing on the scene in David Lynch's *Wild at Heart* in which Willem Defoe abuses Laura Dern by forcing her to say "Fuck me," then, when she finally says it, responds, "No, thanks, I've got to go...," says: "The subjects are humiliated when their fantasies are brutally externalized and thrown back at them" (*Ridiculous Sublime* 11). Hans' near-hysterical grief after Cleopatra's mutilation (witness his traumatic repetition of her cruel words "dirty ... slimy ... freaks!") suggests a total loss, the result of a confrontation with the real of one's desire.

The anamorphic moment that separates out from the continuous scene is also the traumatic realization of Hans' desire for precisely that which he disavows. Cleo's threat lies not in pretending to love Hans, but in the possibility of her real desire for him. Her sweet looks and intrigued side glances threaten to offer Hans "absolute satisfactions," the very presence of which would extinguish his desire. When Cleo exposes Hans' fundamental fantasy to be loved by the desiring mother, she closes the fantasy screen that kept the

Real at bay. Hans' great psychic disruption in *Freaks* is to see his fantasy for what it is and to simultaneously feel seen by it. This great betrayal can only end in Cleo's mutilation and display as a freak — having seen too much, she becomes the object of the freaks' surveillance (under the carts, through windows and doors), and finally nothing more than a spectacle for a paying audience.

This returned gaze of Hans' desire is also the stain in the picture that sees us: "It is by means of the 'phallic' spot that the observed picture is subjectivized: this paradoxical point undermines our position as 'neutral,' 'objective' observer, pinning us to the observed object itself" (Žižek, *Looking Awry* 91). The freak sees us because the freak is there in order to be seen. One of the most disturbing moments in *Freaks* occurs right before Cleopatra's exposure as guilty and her subsequent punishment: one of the freaks, standing near a bedridden Hans, plays an eerie tune on a harmonica, providing a soundtrack for the scene that is occurring and that is about to occur. The film is made filmic, the attack on Cleopatra made real precisely by being made diegetically theatrical, by being constructed as a performed spectacle. The off-stage world becomes stagelike, and it is worth asking what an off-stage world would consist of for the freak or the woman. Neither the woman nor the freak appears to have access to a space apart from spectacle, instead existing in various modalities of theatrical fictions that are either more or less acknowledged in the diegesis itself.

The horror freaks inspire is not merely the horror of the composite or the ambiguous body, but the defiantly unambiguous relationship between the freak and the gaze. Freaks and anamorphosis pull us into the picture and locate us in the insecure position of being visually interrogated. *Freaks* is a horror film not because Cleo is mutilated and Hercules killed, all lightning and dark shadows — no, *Freaks* is a horror film because the gaze itself is horrific, because locating the gaze is work in terror. The freaks see too much, and have this ability precisely because they are otherwise — their marginal bodies produce their surveilling powers. Little bodies fit under carts and behind doors; partial bodies slide over the ground unencumbered by arms or legs. The Lacanian subject is caught in the field of vision by the stain — "the singular object ... is there to be looked at, in order to catch, I would almost say, *to catch in its trap*, the observer" (*Four Fundamental Concepts* 92). We cannot deny our unstable subject position in Browning's unstable world — the non-objective reality of the psychoanalytic subject is far too precarious. As surely as the freaks spy on Cleopatra and Hercules, we feel for certain that they see us too, that our punishment is next.

Unlike Browning progeny Hitchcock, whose use of the stain is local, specific, and related to crime, the anamorphic freak saturates Browning's films with no motivation or narrative purpose whatsoever. The anamorphosis offers not an escape but a pull into representation; the excessive presence of this figure, in Browning's entire oeuvre, makes an encounter with the abject unavoidable. And unlike Hitchcock, where the stain is used to effect the pleasure of anamorphic discovery about which Lacan wrote, Browning's films do not *use* the stain, but are themselves mere and perfect vehicles for its display. Browning's anamorphosis is non-productive; it is a sublime disruption, purposeless, aw(e)ful. Hitchcock's desire of discovery and furtive network of decoded representations are replaced with Browning's simple frame around the disruption itself. Pleasure is everywhere replaced with a strange, odd anxiety. The cinematic subject slowly peeled from itself is the I that can no longer approach the film from a position of mastery, but finds him or herself subtly ripped to shreds, no longer recognizable as unified, but instead constituting a shattered web of non-transcendental all-too-human matter-stuff. Is there any other spectator to a Browning film than the masochistic one?

The Anamorphic Woman

In an interview with Bela Lugosi that, according to Skal, "reads suspiciously as if the actual person interviewed was Browning" (126), Lugosi/Browning posits that women in America

> are unsatisfied, famished, craving sensation, even though it be the sanction of death.... They go to circuses and cast restless, unseeing eyes on clowns and trapeze artists ... [for] a profound biological reason. Before a woman bears a child she goes through successive phases of horror, lest the fruit of her body be a monstrous thing [qtd. in Skal 127].

The desiring female spectator has a unique connection with the abject subject of abject films because she herself is monstrous. Woman is a stain; woman is *the* stain — the site of a new way of seeing and disruption to the field of vision itself. Woman's specular essence, well documented by feminist film theory, aligns her with the freak and the stain — passive, erotic, displayed, she "freeze(s) the flow of action" and "performs within the narrative" (Mulvey 19). Both she and the freak are punished — specularly, spectacularly — and fetishized for their difference. Woman, like the freak and stain, fractures space. Browning's crime narratives exist as distractions, excuses for watching bodies in revolt. What is more memorable from *The Unholy Three* — the sketchy, clichéd plot, or Lon Chaney in drag and Harry Earles as a sadistic midget posing as a creepily aggressive baby? The similar narratives of Browning's films, their nearly interchangeable plots, and their recycled casts all deprioritize the language and the form of the film in favor of pure visual shock, located in the freak and in the eroticized female on display. Woman exists in a strangely liminal space; assigned a position of pure fantasy, like the freak, she exists as the seminal perpetual other. Like the stain, she is a partial object that does not fit, is not quite right—despite the phallic suggestion of the descriptions of anamorphosis, it is woman who sticks out of every picture.

The "looking back at us" quality of anamorphosis that is linked to mask/woman and freak functions as another trace of the multiple differences at play in Browning's films, at once shielding and providing, blocking image, offering image. Womanliness masks woman but is simultaneously the production of a positive mask. "What causes such uneasiness is the impossibility of discerning behind the masks a consistent subject manipulating them" (Žižek and Dolar 192). If there is a central threat in *Freaks*, *The Unholy Three*, and *The Unknown*, it is not a local threat of a crime or an unrequited love that will be alleviated by the end of the narrative, (indeed by the process of narrative), but is rather the unassignable, undecipherable movement of systems of differences that no narrative can possibly account for or neutralize. Once again we return to the freak and the female's to-be-looked-at-ness, often deemed a misogynistic feature of Hollywood cinema; but this time we locate in it the possibilities of being that which can never be taken in fully by narrative. Cleopatra and Estrellita escape their films precisely by falling deeper into the sutures of representation.

In his discussion of anamorphosis in *Seminar VII*, Lacan instructs, "The important thing is that at a given moment one arrives at illusion. Around it one finds a sensitive spot, a lesion, a locus of pain, a point of reversal" (140). The sensitive spot in both *Freaks* and *The Unknown* is located in the problematic elevation of a female love object. When Lacan writes how one finds in a Rubens painting "the fact that what we seek in the illusion is something in which the illusion as such in some way transcends itself, destroys itself" (*Ethics* 136), we should think back to the reading of Hans' desire for Cleopatra to take up the bad mother position and humiliate him on their wedding night. Hans seeks in the illusory love relationship for Cleopatra to transcend her own lie, her own false profession of love, in order to destroy it and adopt the position he really desires. If the "interest of anamorphosis is ... a turning point when the artist ... reverses the use of that illusion of space, when he forces it to enter into the original goal" (*Ethics* 141), then the anamorphic love relationship forces the love object to enter into their original goal, one that stands behind the fantasy screen. This relationship is nothing other than the model of courtly love, the model for love relationships in Browning's films and provider of the final link in our Freak-Woman-Stain series.

In courtly love, "the object involved, the feminine object, is introduced oddly enough through the door of privation or of inaccessibility" (*Ethics* 149).

The primary love relationships in *The Unknown, The Unholy Three*, and *Freaks* consist of two men, at least one of whom is somehow freakish, and an inaccessible woman — Cleopatra to Hans (*Freaks*) because she is both beautiful and big; Estrellita to Alonzo (*The Unknown*) because she is disgusted by men's arms, and later to Malabar for the very opposite reason (or perhaps because disgust has become pleasurable); and Rosie to Echo (*The Unholy Three*). The barrier surrounding the Lady of courtly love, and in these films, is not a quality of the Lady's but of the freakish male suitors. *Their* difference, their marginal position is what raises the female protagonist into the position of the Lady. In this act she "is emptied of all real substance," for "what man demands ... is to be deprived of something real" (*Ethics* 149–50); that deprivation takes the form of converting a real-life woman into an empty signifier. Hans' desire is not for Cleopatra as a flesh-and-blood woman, but for the Symbolic network in which he would be deprived of that which she signifies.

Cleo-as-Lady is a silent signifier: her punishment is the permanent foreclosure of speech (she issues squawks instead of words, and the corners of her mouth turn down as though to foreclose even the possibility of speaking). Her defeat is not bodily but structural; she loses her position as anything other than the forever inaccessible object. The famous quick zoom in on Cleopatra's face as she utters the words "Midgets are not strong ... he could get sick" — and it is the zoom more than the words that horrifies — is not only an exclusion of the world, a collapse of a larger universe into the close ahistorical lines of her face, but a sign of detachment, of the indifference of the signifier to which this plot ultimately leads. This zoom does not correspond to a diegetic viewpoint — it is the apparatus closing in, an impossible, non-human sight, itself experienced as freakish.

What makes the Lady desirable and necessarily inaccessible are her other suitors, rivals for the signifier. We glimpse this structure in Browning's films repeatedly, for we have not only the freakish desiring male and the elevated Lady on the pedestal, but always also a third party, a rival, not only to bear witness to the desiring male subject, but to help maintain the Lady's position as prohibited object of desire. Lacan coins the word "jalouissance" — what Geneviève Morel describes as "the jealous hatred provoked by the confrontation of the subject with an ideal image that possesses the desired object which the subject lacks" (158). This *jouissance* in, of, and towards jealousy is the essential animating presence of Browning's love triangles. For example, at the end of *The Unknown*, not only does Malabar possess Estrellita's love, he is a fully formed man; Alonzo's jealousy is for both Estrellita and for Malabar's whole body. Confronted with the man who possesses his desired objects, he is confronted with his double lack.

Lacan locates in courtly love a process of "holding back, of suspension, of *amor interruptus*" (*Ethics* 152); this is the historical requisite of courtly love, for the Lady was often married — truly inaccessible — and the prolongation of desire required its non-fulfillment. It is only through the disembodied Symbolic position of the Lady that she becomes and remains desirable. This endless prolongation is the source of the erotic pleasure of Browning's films. Unlike most Hollywood narratives (especially in the 1920s — think screwball comedies), Browning's films work very hard *not* to form a couple. Every time the grotesque desiring male gets too close to fulfilling his desire, gets too proximate to the Lady, gets too near to closing the gap between his fantasy and reality, he refuses her by exposing her crime, mutilating himself, or simply telling her to leave. None of these acts are done by a single subject acting alone; the ambivalent trace of the rival's success is always there: Hans' guilt at the end of *Freaks*; Alonzo's self-doubting grimaces, played out on the ravaged face of Lon Chaney in *The Unknown*; Echo in *The Unholy Three* and his ventriloquist dummy uttering words of love even as Echo covers his wooden mouth with his hand.

It might seem as though a couple *is* produced in these films — for Hans ends up with Frieda, Estrellita with her armed lover Malabar, and Rosie with Hector after she is "released" from her duties to Echo. However, the operative structure of all three films is the very *amor interruptus* that Lacan associates with psychoanalytic ethics. *Freaks'* narrative continues, through the very end, in order to taunt us with the question: Can Hans *have* Cleopatra? Cleopatra's punishment, her symbolic castration from the waist down, is a final desperate attempt to close that query; for even if Hans were able, as a little man, to have intercourse with her, as nothing more than a torso by the end of the film, Cleopatra's genitals are no longer even in the equation. Hans is the epitome of the *unvermögender Mann*, the man without means — he has means (money) but not means that *mean* something sexually. Cleopatra is foreclosed entirely as a sexual being so that the question of Hans having her can be adequately redirected into his quick and unmotivated reconciliation with Frieda. In *The Unknown*, we never get a sense of Malabar as a character and never find out why Estrellita falls in love with him; Alonzo and Estrellita's impossible joining and its prolongation provides the narrative desire that moves the film along. The same is true for Rosie and Echo in *The Unholy Three*. These films are structured around a love relationship, and its impossibility, that does not lead to a climactic joining at the end, but to its dissolution and somewhat haphazard redirection towards another (less interesting) love object. None of the final love pairings in Browning's films are of much interest to the spectator; what fascinates us is the affair that never happened and could never possibly happen. What makes these suspended films fascinating is not in the production of a beautiful partnership, but rather in how the freakish couple is *de-formed*.

In the logic of Browning's films, the freak as fantasy object participates in creating freakishness in the subject who looks. The introduction of sexual signifiers onto the figure of the freak does not function to exploit the desired objects; what is at stake in *Freaks* is how our desiring cripples, distorts, and stains us. Fantasy elides loss, absence, and difference; when Browning gets us uncomfortably close to our own fantasy screen, the ability to imagine things otherwise disappears, hence the overwhelming sense of fate and determinism in his works. The real trauma of *Freaks* is not the marginalized freakish body, nor is it the self-imposed mutilation that occurs in *The Unknown*; the great trauma of these films is the exposure of the freakish excess that drenches every subject. The disconcerting stare into the camera by the "living worm" as he rolls a cigarette with just his lips and mouth, and the visible obvious disfigurations of surplus or lack (too many bodies as in Siamese Twins, or too few limbs), confront us not with an image of the body deformed, but our own freakery. When Alonzo says, after his operation, "I lost some flesh," this is not the locus of the horror in *The Unknown*; the lost flesh has no substance in itself, it functions to propel the narrative — and Alonzo's death — forward. What shocks about Browning's films is not an occurring trauma, but the realization that trauma actually changes nothing at all: Alonzo's amputation goes unnoticed by Estrellita; Cleopatra becomes a mutilated spectacle just as she was once a beautiful trapeze artist.

If, in part, Browning's films seem to be moralistic tales on the surface, they also evince a classical Lacanian interest in, and admiration for, villainous figures whose single-minded hatred, malevolence, or desire for revenge drives their character. Cleopatra and Alonzo stand firm in their hatred right until their mutilation/death; they are fiercely committed to their narcissism and vengeance. In a very real sense, Cleo escapes ever being guilty. The moment that Cleopatra is emptied of herself into the signifier Lady at the beginning of the film, her exclusion from the Symbolic order (through a fall too deep into it) is fixed, and she is already mutilated, already dead. Hans' desire, then, is the source of Cleopatra's mutilation, not the knives and guns displayed in the final scene. His tremendous visible guilt at having caused her disfiguration — despite Frieda's reassurance that "Hans, you tried to stop them.... It wasn't your fault"— speaks to the truth of the film. The great crime of *Freaks* is *not* Cleopatra's plot to kill Hans, nor the revenge on Cleopatra and Hercules; rather, it is Hans' initial desire for the big beautiful woman, for mother. *That* is the transgression that structures the entire film. Estrellita in *The Unknown* is similarly dead to the Symbolic order when she is elevated to the position of Lady and specularized early in the film in her diegetic performance. The crime for which Alonzo must be punished is not the attempt on Estrellita's lover's life, but for his desire for the Lady alone.

If Browning's films punish not the obvious criminal but the *one who desires*, what does this mean for our role as desiring spectatorial subjects? When we see ourselves seeing, find ourselves trapped in the gaze, we anticipate the punishment levied against the seeing subject of the film and therefore feel, too painfully, too fully, our own complicity and guilt. For what is most distressing about Browning's films — and while formally beautiful, they are at heart distressing works — is not that women are the freaks, nor that the "normal but evil" are freaks, but that the term itself disappears into the space of representation. There is no opposition to the term "freak," no picture or frame around the stain — "It is as if ... the anamorphic stain acquires clear and recognizable outlines, while all the rest, the remaining reality, becomes blurred" (Žižek, "Bold Gaze" 253). Like Arbus' photographs, in which Hamptons socialites are as freakish, indeed more so, as the giant in his New York apartment, everyone is disfigured, everyone is missing a pound of flesh, everyone is a desiring punishable subject. In Browning's world there is one large stain, one universe that constitutively sticks out; there is no place from which we can safely place others as Other. Every subject is caught in the gaze, and this refusal to allow for an outside is ethically claustrophobic. Instead of comforting binaries — male/female, freak/normal, stain/picture — there is simply the endless slippage of differences, the endless deferral of traumatic resolution.

Works Cited

Allen, Frederick Lewis. *Only Yesterday: An Informal History of the Nineteen-Twenties*. New York: Harper and Row, 1931.

Arbus, Diane. *Diane Arbus: An Aperture Monograph*. Ed. Doon Arbus and Marvin Israel. New York: Aperture, 1972.

Bombaci, Nancy Margaret. *Freaks and Desire: Fetishizing Bodily Difference in Late Modernist American Culture (Nathanael West, Djuna Barnes, Tod Browning, Carson McCullers)*. Dissertation, Fordham University, 2000.

Bonitzer, Pascal. "Hitchcockian Suspense." *Everything You Always Wanted to Know About Lacan ... but Were Afraid to Ask Hitchcock*. Ed. Slavoj Žižek. London: Verso, 2000, 15–30.

Cixous, Hélène. "Castration or Decapitation?" *Psychoanalysis and Woman, a Reader*. Ed. Shelley Saguaro. New York: New York University Press, 2000, 231–44.

Dadoun, Roger. "Fetishism in the Horror Film." *Fantasy Cinema*. Ed. James Donald. London: British Film Institute, 1989, 39–61.

Deleuze, Gilles. *Cinema 2: The Time-Image*. Trans. Hugh Tomlinson and Robert Galetta. Minneapolis: University of Minnesota Press, 1989.

Freud, Sigmund. *The Standard Edition of the Complete Psychological Works of Sigmund Freud*, vol. XXI. Ed. James Strachey. London: Hogarth Press, 1953–66.

_____. "The Uncanny." *Writings on Art and Literature*. Ed. Werner Hamacher and David E. Wellbery. Foreword by Neil Hertz. Stanford: Stanford University Press, 1997, 193–233.

Grosz, Elizabeth. "Intolerable Ambiguity: Freaks as/at the Limit." *Freakery: Cultural Spectacles of the Extraordinary Body*. Ed. Rosemarie Garland Thomson. New York: New York University Press, 1996, 55–66.

Lacan, Jacques. *Anxiety, Seminar X, 1962–63*. Unpublished translation by Cormac Gallagher from unedited French typescripts.
———. *The Four Fundamental Concepts of Psycho-analysis, Seminar XI*. Trans. Alan Sheridan. London: Vintage, 1977.
———. *The Ethics of Psychoanalysis, Seminar VII*. Ed. Jacques-Alain Miller. Trans. Dennis Porter. New York: Norton, 1992.
Mitchell, David T., and Sharon L. Snyder. *The Body and Physical Difference: Discourses of Disability*. Eds. David T. Mitchell and Sharon L. Snyder. Ann Arbor: University of Michigan Press, 1997.
Morel, Geneviève. "Feminine Jealousies." *Sexuation*, SIC 3. Ed. Renata Salecl. Durham: Duke University Press, 2000, 157–69.
Mulvey, Laura. "Visual Pleasure and Narrative Cinema." *Visual and Other Pleasures*. Bloomington: Indiana University Press, 1989, 14–26.
Rosenthal, Stuart. *Tod Browning: Vol. 4, The Hollywood Professionals*. London: Tantivy Press, 1975.
Skal, David J. *The Monster Show: A Cultural History of Horror*. New York: Faber and Faber, 1993.
———, and Elias Savada. *Dark Carnival: The Secret World of Tod Browning, Hollywood's Master of the Macabre*. New York: Anchor Books, 1995.
Žižek, Slavoj. *Looking Awry: An Introduction to Jacques Lacan Through Popular Culture*. Cambridge, MA: MIT Press, 1991.
———. *The Art of the Ridiculous Sublime: On David Lynch's* Lost Highway. Seattle: University of Washington Press, 2000.
———. "'In His Bold Gaze My Ruin Is Writ Large.'" *Everything You Always Wanted to Know About Lacan ... but Were Afraid to Ask Hitchcock*. Ed. Slavoj Žižek. London: Verso, 2000, 211–72.
———. *Enjoy Your Symptom! Jacques Lacan In Hollywood and Out*. New York: Routledge, 2001.
———, and Mladen Dolar. *Opera's Second Death*. New York: Routledge, 2002.

Mark of the Vampire
Seeing Is Believing

Reynold Humphries

My first memory (a very distant one) of Browning's controversial film of 1935 is of a reaction where surprise gave way first to a feeling of frustration, then to one of considerable irritation, and finally to an impression of a waste of time. Why bother to make a vampire movie that turns out not to be about vampires, only an elaborate plot to confound a murderer and, at the same time, an elaborate hoax to deceive the audience? Bryan Senn has evoked "the cheat ending which few horror fans can forgive and no one can forget" (269). When discussing how the film was received when it opened in May 1935, however, he points out that it "was well received by both critics and audiences alike. So perhaps Browning's assessment of what moviegoers (of the time) truly wanted was not far off after all" (Senn 272). There was, however, another reaction at the time of the film's release, one whose tone and content have nothing in common with either enthusiasm or an annoyed rejection. In July 1935 the *New York Times* published a letter under the title "Concerning Horror Films" by one William J. Robinson, M.D., of New York City. He evoked *Mark of the Vampire* and claimed: "Several people have come to my notice who, after seeing that horrible picture, suffered nervous shock, were attacked with insomnia, and those who did fall asleep, were tortured by most horrible nightmares" (PCA file). This letter smacks of the hysterical reactions with which sections of the British press greeted Michael Powell's *Peeping Tom* in 1960 and David Cronenberg's *Crash* in 1996, albeit in a less excessive form.

However, it is surely clear that something is going on within the film which is not immediately apparent. My own engagement with assorted vampire films since my early rejection of *Mark of the Vampire* has led me to modify my judgement considerably—or rather to adopt a totally different standpoint in an attempt to approach the film's narrative and representational strategies, the way Browning directs his actors and actresses, places his camera, and uses special effects and trick photography, not to mention certain ambiguous features of the dialogue. A close appraisal of these elements will enable us to grasp the significance of the film, what it means for the spectators and how this meaning is created. For it is clear that the film addresses the spectators in a wide variety of ways, through individual shots and scenes on the one hand to point-of-view shots on the other. If my approach is first and foremost formal, I have had recourse to psychoanalysis to show that a particular logic is at work — not the logic of some "cause/effect" of a conscious kind, but the logic of desire, of the unconscious. Like Bryan Senn, I find that "logic seems to fly, batlike, out of the window" and have asked myself the questions he asks: "If the pseudo-vampires have no supernatural power after all ... how does Luna fly on giant bat-wings down from the castle rafters...? Plus, if there truly were no vampires, then what accounts for the victim killed prior to Sir Karell's murder?" (Senn 270). I believe that there are answers to these, and many other, questions, but that the answers are not the same, just as the questions do not necessarily address the same (lack of) logic.

For some 45 of the film's 60 minutes, we the spectators believe that we are dealing with a sort of follow-up to *Dracula*, except that this time the vampire is called Count Mora (Bela Lugosi), and he has a daughter, Luna (Carroll Borland), whom he encourages to vampirize the heroine, Irene (Elizabeth Allen). This is in marked contrast to the earlier film, where the powerful patriarch Count Dracula would not tolerate his three wives feasting on Renfield; he alone had that right. Now, if the logic of the plot is to persuade Baron Otto (Jean Hersholt) that vampires exist (the better to confound him and prove he killed Sir Karell (Holmes Herbert), then every single detail in the plot must address Baron Otto as a very special sort of spectator. In other words, he must be a witness to events the only explanation of which is supernatural. From the moment the Baron is absent from an occurrence which is vampiric in nature, the film can only be addressing other witnesses — namely, the film's spectators. We can therefore put forward a hypothesis that would go something like this. All events in the film must be witnessed by Baron Otto or by the spectators (or both) if the film is to be coherent in deceiving us and making of us dupes in the elaborate *mise en scène* conceived by Professor Zelen (Lionel Barrymore) and Inspector Neumann (Lionel Atwill), and involving the murder victim's daughter Irene and other characters.[1] That, however, is not sufficient: Everything in the film must be part of that *mise en scène* in order for there to be a coherent address to the spectators. To express it another way: For there to be coherency, Browning's *mise en scène* of the film entitled *Mark of the Vampire* must correspond, on the level of scenes and use of the camera, to both the form and the content of the plot hatched by the Inspector and Zelen (with the collaboration of the other characters, who thus themselves become *actors* within that particular *mise en scène*).[2]

Now this is all too obviously *not* the case, as the film's opening scenes bear witness. The opening shot is of a cross; as the camera cranes down, we see that it is atop a church spire. We then discover a group of villagers or peasants gathered round a fire, singing.[3] It is night. Cut to a woman placing a sprig in front of a window. Cut to another woman praying, her little daughter watching her. Cut to a baby in its cradle, playing with an identical sprig. The scene then moves to a graveyard where an old woman with a load of sticks on her back is moving among the graves. A cart rattles by at great speed in the far background.[4] Suddenly a bat appears out of nowhere and frightens the old woman away. Again the scene shifts, this time to the local inn where a couple of travellers are talking with the innkeeper. They want to know why the doors and windows are festooned with the same sprigs we have just seen. The inn-keeper informs them that it is bat-thorne, there to ward off the vampires, but that they are quite safe. Needless to say, the couple are scornful, much as Renfield was at the opening of *Dracula*. Suddenly a little old man rushes into the inn, visibly flustered and out of breath. It is the doctor (Donald Meek) who has an important role to play later. He makes light of his state, claiming that it is not he but his horses that are in a rush. He too pretends to scoff at the idea of vampires, but once his back is turned, the innkeeper's wife tells the travellers that he won't leave the inn again that night for any call whatsoever.

What conclusions, if any, can we draw from the three minutes of film we have just witnessed? Firstly, none of the film's main characters are present, including Baron Otto; he does not appear until the next sequence, where he announces to the servants in Sir Karell's mansion that their master has been murdered. What we have seen is addressed to us alone and cannot be part of the Inspector's *mise en scène*. That, however, fails to take into account one simple and naturalistic factor — the two travellers, a man and his wife. What are they doing there? I would argue that they, too, are spectators, and that we are being invited not to react as they do but to believe what we have seen. Or, to put it differently, since the villagers believe in vampires, we would be well advised to do so too. This entire opening is therefore something akin to an "opening gambit" in chess: the way you play and which pieces you choose to move *and how* is crucial for your beating or being beaten by your opponent. An apparently "banal" move can, in fact, hide a strategy destined to deceive your opponent, the better to defeat him. However, that is only one aspect of the opening and perhaps not the most interesting. Clearly it is designed to encourage the audience to believe, especially if they have seen *Dracula* and remember the fate of the unfortunate Renfield; but the function of the doctor is quite a different matter, and it is this narrative strategy that I wish to address now. For the doctor is clearly frightened when he enters the inn, although both he and the innkeeper's wife refer only to the fact of being in a rush. That he should deny this by blaming it on his horses is surely a detail we would be wise not to neglect. For the cart that rattled by at a great rate, and to which I referred above, was also in a rush, a rush presumably caused by the fact that its driver was lashing the horses to go ever faster. To claim that horses are in a rush is to bestow upon the creatures a human capacity for thought. More to the point, it is a question of what Freud called "disavowal": acknowledging that something is true, while at the same time believing in the existence of that which is invalidated by this acknowledgement. The doctor knows full well he's in a rush because he's frightened, but nevertheless one can do nothing with horses when they take it into their silly heads to rush home. I shall now argue that this psychic structure of disavowal takes us to the heart of the matter and will help us understand the incoherent elements in the film, as well as a certain number that appear perfectly limpid. To help us in our quest, I suggest we turn to *Dracula,* the film's peasants and the characters of Renfield and Van Helsing.

When we first meet Renfield in Browning's earlier film, he is in a coach which drops him off at the village from where he is to take another coach to Borgo Pass and the castle of Count Dracula, with whom he has an appointment. Readers will note, therefore, that Renfield fulfils, from the standpoint of the literal level of the script, the function of the couple in the inn in *Mark of the Vampire*: they are all *travellers,* and skeptical ones at that. As we shall see presently, Renfield is a witness to a certain number of phenomena under circumstances that cannot but lead us to ask certain questions, both about him and ourselves. First, however, let us turn to the peasants. Like those in *Mark of the Vampire,* they are God-fearing and superstitious, and the film shows that they have every right to be — it is Renfield's refusal to believe which dooms him to become one of the living dead, an eternal servant of Count Dracula. Van Helsing says in *Dracula* that "the superstition of today" becomes "the reality of tomorrow," and the entire film is based on the suspension of spectatorial disbelief: we don't believe in vampires, but nevertheless one has to take precautions against them. Thus we are willing to take Van Helsing seriously. As he points out to Dr. Seward after Renfield has been incarcerated in the latter's asylum, "The strength of the vampire lies in people's *not* believing in him." However, if Renfield remains true to this refusal to believe until it is too late, we shall see that Van Helsing is far from carrying out in reality what he urges upon others in his various declarations.

On four occasions in *Dracula,* in the space of his journey to Dracula's castle and his encounter with the Count, Renfield's senses inform and warn him that something is amiss, yet he refuses to act on this information. The first occurs when he leans out of the coach the Count has sent to meet him to tell the driver (whom both he and the spectators have seen earlier) not to drive so fast. There is nobody in the driver's seat, only a bat hovering above. With a look of amazement and horror, Renfield draws back into the coach, as if he were anxious to disavow what he has seen. He knows, yet nevertheless.... The second occasion is a continuation of this. When the coach finally stops, Renfield alights and addresses the driver again but stops in mid-sentence when he sees there is nobody driving. The third instance occurs when the castle door opens. Renfield mounts the steps, his hesitation indicating a psychic conflict, a conscious awareness that something is very wrong. Finally, when the Count descends the huge interior staircase to greet him, he passes through a huge spider's web as if it were not there (or as if he were not a material being), whereas Renfield has to brush it aside with his cane when he follows the Count upstairs. It is worth pointing out here that a door opens, seemingly of its own accord, in *Mark of the Vampire* when the three "vampires," Count Mora, Sir Karell and a third man, make their way through the castle crypt back to their coffins.[5] There is no doubt in *Dracula*, however, that we are dealing with the supernatural, so Renfield's hesitation is akin to that of someone witnessing a magician's trick. The formula "as if by magic" would fit perfectly the door's opening and underpins Renfield's reaction. Just as we cannot see how the magician does his trick and hence admire his skill, as if there were no trick involved, so Renfield understands full well that something is happening but prefers not to face up to the implications.

Ushered into a large but cosy room with a fire, Renfield makes a strange remark: "It's different from outside, more cheerful." Clearly it is the homely aspect of the room that elicits this comment, but a moment's reflection shows that the remark is not as banal as it might seem. What is Renfield referring to when he says "outside"— the exterior of the castle or the staircase he has just mounted? If both are inhospitable, it is the encounter on the staircase and the role of the spider's web that must remain uppermost in Renfield's mind and provoke a feeling of unease. I would argue that we are in the presence of what Freud called "the Uncanny," *das Unheimliche,* and that the very words of the character introduce the theme. For "cheerful" is another way of saying "homely"— in other words, "heimlich." As Freud has pointed out, "heimlich" can mean "homely" but also "familiar," the word taking on the meaning of its opposite "unheimlich" when this familiarity starts to produce unease — in other words, a sense of the uncanny. This occurs for the subject when the uncanny turns out to be "something which is familiar and old-established in the mind and which has become alienated from it only through the process of repression" ("The Uncanny" 241). Renfield has felt that unease, which he then disavows linguistically by calling the room "cheerful," while at the same time unwittingly acknowledging that he has recognised the unconscious significance of his encounter with Dracula. We must now turn to the case of Van Helsing to solve the enigma.

As I pointed out above, Van Helsing remarks in *Dracula* that the vampire's strength derives from the fact that people do not believe in him, which we can rewrite thus: Should a person notice a phenomenon indicating unequivocally that a vampire is at work, the person will deny the testimony of his or her senses in favour of a belief that there's no such thing as a vampire, thus enabling the living dead to continue, unchecked, their infamous activities. However, later in the same film Van Helsing evokes "the little-known facts which the world is perhaps better off not knowing." This would seem to contradict the earlier remark by encouraging ignorance, the vampire's greatest ally according to Van Helsing. What would at first sight seem to be a contradiction, an incoherence on the level of the script, is in fact something quite different. If the remark remains in the script, it is because its significance addresses the filmic text, and thus the spectators, in a very special fashion, providing a way to understand what is being signified. For Van Helsing is even more careless than Renfield when it comes to neglecting the information his senses provide, which is surely worthy of our notice.

Renfield has been locked up in Dr. Seward's asylum where the doctor and Van Helsing can keep an eye on him. However, Renfield keeps on escaping from his cell, and is given to wandering through the hospital and participating in the conversations between the two men. This is obviously completely illogical on a conscious, literal level, but its meaning has nothing to do with such logic. A nurse by the name of Martin is in charge of Renfield, and we are surely entitled to ask how such a professional can allow his patient to escape all the time. Feebly, the film tries to explain this by representing Martin as hardly superior to the village idiot, but to no avail. The fact that Van Helsing pays no attention to what Martin tells him is a striking instance of refusing information that contradicts what he knows: Van Helsing should be the first person to surmount any prejudices he may have about Martin's intellectual capacities when he learns about Renfield's constant escapes. For there are no traces of Renfield having actually broken out of his cell — except on one occasion the bars have been broken. Surely the alert vampire hunter should be able to draw the obvious conclusion: that Renfield has been able to pass through the walls of his cell because he is no longer a material being, or that he has superhuman strength, another trait of the vampire. Whichever way Van Helsing's intellect turns, he should come up with the same answer: Renfield is not simply insane but a vampire. Yet he does not.

We can draw a parallel between Van Helsing's refusal to act on the information provided by Martin and Renfield's refusal to take into account the testimony of his vision when Dracula passes through the spider's web. From the very outset Van Helsing has refused to pay heed to what Martin has to relate, such as when he claims to have heard wolves. Now Van Helsing knows full well that vampires can turn into wolves as well as bats. When Jonathan Harker says he saw a dog running across the lawn after Dracula has left Seward's Sanitarium, Van Helsing suggests, "Or a wolf?" So Van Helsing is taking the situation seriously, *except* when Martin gives him a piece of information that proves everything he claims to believe. Something far more radical is taking place than mere class prejudice or scientific hubris. We are in the realm of the reactivation of the mirror stage where the young child at once jubilates at its own image in the mirror and becomes aware that it exists thanks to the other. Readers will remember that Van Helsing proves to his own satisfaction that Count Dracula is a vampire by noting the absence of the Count's reflection in a mirror. This lack of a reflection heralds within the subject's unconscious an uncanny return to the mirror stage from the vantage point of the Symbolic Order where the subject has resolved its Oedipus complex and come to terms with sexual difference — the mother is not endowed with the all-powerful signifier, the phallus — and its own mortality. If there is no other person alongside the subject when the latter is reflected in the mirror, then this absence represents the lack that constitutes each and every subject. The shock of this absence triggers the feeling of the Uncanny due to the absence reactivating an unpleasant fact which each subject must accept but which they repress, while carrying the unconscious traces of this knowledge with them for all time. *The vampire is thus the locus of castration.*

This, however, begs the question of the role of women and their relation to vampires — Mina in *Dracula* and Irene in *Mark of the Vampire*. At one point in the former, Mina is "visited" by Lucy. Although Mina has already received the "visit" of Dracula, she is not yet under his control, whereas Lucy, the first victim, has died and is now therefore a vampire. Mina's way of describing the encounter with Lucy to Harker and Van Helsing is remarkable. After telling them of it, she adds, "Then I remembered Lucy was dead." I think we can agree that it is most extraordinary that anyone should forget that their best friend is dead! A slip of the tongue? In which case, what knowledge, what impossible desire, is the subject trying to keep from herself? Were Mina already under the Count's influence, she would not have mentioned Lucy so as not to arouse the men's suspicions, so I would argue that we must interpret her remark as indicating a desire to repress Lucy's death because she knows what it *means*. Or rather, she is in the possession of an unconscious knowledge of what this death, and hence what the vampire itself, signifies. Bryan Senn has done us the great service of drawing our attention to an incoherency of a similar kind in *Mark of the Vampire*. Irene is first attacked on the terrace of the mansion by Luna, with Count Mora looking on approvingly. The second attack occurs in her bedroom, and Irene recounts it to Zelen and the others in these terms: "Then I saw *her*, just like she was on the terrace." Senn quite rightly stresses "her," as Irene does, adding that the shadow of the vampire we see in Irene's bedroom is clearly that of the Count, not Luna (Senn 265, 276*n*1). From the spectators' point of view, what is interesting is that we see Luna peering through the bedroom window, but Irene cannot see her, as she is asleep. It is therefore logical that we should assume it is Luna who enters the bedroom when the door opens; but the film has just included a shot of Count Mora inside the mansion, so his shadow comes as no surprise: it is not illogical that it should be he who attacks Irene. What is illogical, however, is that Irene should see Luna and not her father, the Count. Unless, of course, we propose another logic — that of the unconscious, of desire itself. The alert reader will have noticed the deliberate ambiguity contained above in the words I used: "her father" could refer to Luna's father, Count Mora, and to Irene's dead father, Sir Karell. In other words, if Irene claims she was vampirized by Luna, it is because of a desire, a desire that cannot say its name because of the concomitant dread it evokes. For Irene's secret desire is to be reunited with her father, for reasons too abominable to admit to, let alone to name. *Mark of the Vampire* turns on the closely-related themes of pre–Oedipal desire and incest.

Let us now take a few steps backwards from theory and textual analysis and examine, in the cold light of dawn, exactly where all this has got us. Bryan Senn reproduces a production still of Bela Lugosi to which he appends the following information:

> Note the prominent bullet wound in his temple. The original screenplay [by Guy Endore] stipulated that Count Mora carry on an incestuous relationship with his daughter Luna before murdering her and then killing himself with a revolver (thus condemning the pair to eternal damnation as the undead). No mention of these sacrilegious acts made it to the finished film, however.[6]

Senn also insists on a fact which is patent for anyone keeping their eyes open, although the fact of seeing does not necessarily coincide with the meaning of what one sees: the spectator is caught up in some very particular events upon seeing this film. There is indeed cause for wonder, as Senn puts it, all the more so since the MGM Pressbook (reproduced by Senn on page 270) not only portrays Lugosi with said bullet wound on his temple but carries the eloquent caption: "YOU WON'T DARE BELIEVE — WHAT YOUR EYES SEE!" Curiouser and curiouser. The fact that in every shot of Lugosi in profile can be seen on his temple a bullet wound and a trickle of blood can only mean that this aspect of the screenplay was actually filmed. Which in turn suggests that the decision to eliminate both the supernatural elements and the references to incest in favour of an ending which turns the film into a sort of thriller came very late in the day. More interesting information is forthcoming on this from Senn:

> Carroll Borland [Luna] remembered that Browning's ending ... incensed the actors — when they were finally allowed to read it. "You see," she explained, "Browning didn't give any of us the final scene, so neither Bela nor I knew exactly how it would end. We were playing it straight horror — which is exactly what Browning wanted us to do, but when he gave us the ending everyone protested.... No one wanted the gimmick ending, but Browning insisted" [Senn 271].

We are not, of course, obliged to take Borland's testimony at face value, just as seeing is not always believing. However, I suggest we would be advised to take seriously the revealing formula that she and Lugosi "were playing it straight horror." In that case, and given what we have already seen about the incest theme being maintained (the bullet wound remains its literal trace within the text as from Count Mora's very first appearance), the "horror" expressed must perforce refer to this theme as much as to that of vampirism, whose "real" significance we have explained above. As I shall show below, the themes of incest and vampirism are inextricably bound together. Nor do I wish to suggest any criticism of Bryan Senn. Quite the contrary: both he and I, not to mention the readers of this article, must be firmly placed in the category known as "the spectator." And the shots of Count Mora watching Luna inscribe us into the logic of spectators watching a performance: the Count, Luna (whom, I remind readers, we see looking in at Irene in bed) and Irene herself are all actors performing in a play of which we are the spectators and of whose ruses we are the unconscious effect.[7] Characters looking at other characters and the precise spectatorial point of view involved in each case will also concern us when discussing the film's narrative strategies. Prior to that, however, I wish to return to aspects of the *mise en scène* which are to be found in both *Dracula* and *Mark of the Vampire,* and to offer a psychoanalytic reading which will hopefully enable us to go further with our investigation.

It is the question of "slowness" that I wish to address here first, along with its opposite, "speed," which, as we shall see, is linked to "immobility." Bryan Senn has most pertinently pointed out that *Dracula* has always been found wanting by critics, ever ready to accuse Browning of directing it in a static or theatrical manner. This is partly true, but can just as easily be put down to the film's need to rely on dialogue in order to put over a certain number of facts. The "theatrical" can hardly be considered a valid criticism of *Mark of the Vampire,* which is deliberately "staged." It is as if the critics had chosen to forget (i.e. repress) early scenes in *Dracula* which are highly cinematic: the Count's three wives moving about in the crypt; the wives advancing on Renfield until Dracula insists on his male prerogatives; Dracula advancing on Lucy; Mina and the usherette at the theater moving as if in a trance. Another scene shows Renfield on all fours moving slowly and deliberately towards a nurse who has fainted. It is interesting to note that, in the first version of the film, he was shown to be after a fly, but the excision of this — for reasons of "bad taste," no doubt — only helps to reinforce a certain unconscious logic at work here and elsewhere. In *Mark of the Vampire* the first time we see Count Mora and Luna they are moving very slowly indeed and in the scene where Irene claims to have heard the dead voice of her father, her descent of the staircase is similarly slow and deliberate.

This phenomenon is not limited to the two films under discussion here, and I would like to refer to a little-known film of the period, *The Crime of Dr. Crespi* (John H. Auer, 1935), to help elucidate my thesis.[8] The "crime" referred to is that of burying alive the man who was preferred to Crespi by the woman the mad doctor loved. Crespi deliberately bungles an operation meant to save the husband's life in order to leave him in a state akin to death (no breathing, eyes closed), whereas he is in fact in a drug-induced state where he is capable only of hearing, and from which he will emerge only after he has been buried.[9] However, the man's colleagues suspect Crespi of murder and dig up the body in order to prove their thesis; they leave it by itself in a room while they prepare an autopsy. There then occurs one of the most chillingly effective scenes in the whole of '30s horror, due precisely to the placing of the camera and the implication of us, the spectators. The door of the room where the body is lying is situated in the far background. In the foreground, close to the camera and therefore to the spectators, is a desk behind which sits a nurse working, her back to the corridor and therefore to the door of the room. Suddenly the door opens and the form of the man buried alive appears. He advances slowly, ever so slowly, until he finally appears to the nurse out of the corner of her eye. This approach of the "living dead" has been recorded by the camera without any movement or change of point of view, thus rendering the scene almost unbearable. For, if we know that the man has not died, we also know that he has been treated as dead and is believed to be so by the nurse. We can therefore identify with her subject position. Not knowing the real fate of the victim, her reaction on seeing him return, as it were, from the dead in a context from which the supernatural is absent — (in no way can the unfortunate nurse appeal to any such "explanation") cannot but give her the terrifyingly uncanny feeling of encountering death itself. Before drawing any conclusions, however, let us turn first to the notion, already raised above, of immobility.

In a strikingly written description, Bryan Senn has revealed how the interdependent opposites of frenzied movement and total immobility coexist and are over-determined semantically by point-of-view shots. He is referring to the sequence in *Mark of the Vampire* in which two peasants driving their cart towards the abandoned castle where the "vampires" hide out suddenly find themselves confronted with Luna in the middle of the road:

> While the rate of approach is smooth, [James Wong] Howe wisely jostles the camera as it tracks closer (just as if it were riding on the bumpy cart), creating a sense of immediacy and an air of realism. Luna simply stands still, performing no action whatsoever. The elevated camera angle and rushing, unsteady movement place the viewer in the driver's seat and so create the terror as we move inexorably toward this frightful figure [Senn 267].

Luna represents the Real, that which cannot be known directly and which is outside linguistic expression: "an unknowable *x*, beyond symbolisation" (Evans 205). A desire to reach beyond life to death, to know what mortality "is," crops up frequently in tales of horror and fantasy. One of the most striking examples is to be found in *The Walking Dead* (Michael Curtiz, 1936), where John Elman (Boris Karloff), executed for a crime he did not commit, comes back from the dead as a result of experiments carried out by Dr. Beaumont (Edmund Gwenn) and pursues the gangsters responsible. They all die as a result, although Elman does nothing physically to harm them. Beaumont is anxious to find out what Elman has experienced in his life after death. At the end, Elman is killed for a second time, and Beaumont desperately tries to get him to speak, but as he tries to formulate the words necessary to explain, Elman succumbs. Beaumont, of course, could never know, for Elman is the stand-in for "the Thing," which "is characterised by the fact that it is impossible for us to imagine it" (Jacques Lacan, quoted in Evans 205).

Such is also the function of Luna, an excessive proximity to whom can only induce starkest horror. The fact that the cart with the peasants (and the spectators) comes ever closer to Luna without actually reaching her is an eloquent expression of the fact that there is a sort of invisible barrier between the Real and the human subject that cannot be broached. The closer one gets, the more unbearable the tension, the more unspeakable (literally) the horror. We are in the presence of that desire to go "beyond the pleasure principle" that for Freud constitutes the basis of humanity. The pleasure principle is that of constancy, but constancy leads to stasis and death, so the subject is condemned to strive to go beyond it: "The pleasure principle is the law which maintains the subject at a certain distance from the Thing, making the subject circle round it without every attaining it" (Evans 205). Clearly Evans had in mind the scene under discussion in *Mark of the Vampire* when defining thus the pleasure principle. However, it is essential here to grasp the psychoanalytic significance of this desire to go beyond. The Thing is the object/cause of desire, that which the subject seeks eternally to find again, that which precipitates the subject on its endless and headlong search: "It is the lost object which must be continually refound, it is the prehistoric, unforgettable Other — in other words, the forbidden object of incestuous desire, the mother" (Evans 205). The mother is the person one strives to rejoin, but to do so would result in unspeakable suffering and evil. Let me give a simple example, taken from another horror film, *The Shining*. Readers will remember that uncanny sequence where Jack discovers the beautiful young naked woman in the bath. She emerges, slowly (of course!) and seductively, from the bath and advances, just as slowly, towards him. They embrace and, as they do so, she turns into a cackling, putrescent old hag. The "ideal woman," the mother, the Sublime object, becomes the obscene "Thing" when that necessary distance is transcended. The fact that the perfectly visible pubic hairs on the body of the young woman have disappeared draws attention to that area of the female anatomy, the genitals, which are the object of the most intense case of disavowal: the gaze is drawn inexorable to this particular part of the anatomy, only to be displaced elsewhere.

Referring to Dracula's first attack on her, Mina cannot be sure whether it really happened or whether she dreamt it. What is important, however, is how she describes the "visit," first saying how he came "closer and closer," then referring to how she feels now, the following morning: "the life drained out of me." This surely symbolises the aftermath of orgasm, what the libertines of the eighteenth century called "la petite mort," a sort of death, perfectly summing up at one and the same time the drop in tension that has become unbearable, the return to a state of constancy and stasis, and the striving to be beyond, together with the potentially mortal consequences of such striving. This striving Lacan refers to as "jouissance"— what is sought for in an impossible union with a figure representing the incestuous dimension of desire, for characters of both sexes. In what ways, then, does *Mark of the Vampire* communicate, in ways that the text cannot consciously assume or symbolise, the concept of incest which lingers on after the revelation that it's all been a hoax? With the possible exception of the doctor, whom we shall discuss separately, only one of the main characters in the plot is unaware of what is being concocted: Fedor, the fiancé of the murder victim's daughter. At one point he tries to find out what's wrong and reiterates his wish to get her away from the house where she is still brooding over her father's murder a year before. Hence Fedor's being kept in ignorance: without Irene, the charade cannot possible succeed. There ensues the following conversation where he speaks first — "I want to know why you're acting this way. You're not yourself"—"Forgive me for what I'm doing."

At this juncture in the film the spectators cannot possibly interpret the word "acting" as meaning other than "behaving," as they adopt the same subject position as Fedor. Nor can they interpret the reply as an address of the heroine-as-actress to a person ignorant of the charade rather than that of a distraught victim of a vampire trying to elicit the understanding of her lover. If we now place the conversation in the context of other exchanges between characters, the form of the film represents an unconscious desire that cannot say its name, is literally "unspeakable." Almost immediately after this confrontation the daughter breaks down and the film reveals the truth. She gives as her excuse the fact that the actor chosen to play her dead father and to convince the Baron that the father has returned as a vampire bears too close a likeness to her father. "To act as if you were my father, alive and with me, don't you see the horror of it?" Earlier in the film she had played her role most convincingly, claiming that she had heard her father's voice and that she had to go to him. The Inspector had played his part by dismissing her claim as "hysteria," adopting a skeptical attitude so that the Baron would not become suspicious and could thus be led gradually to believe, just like the Inspector himself, once the "evidence" became too substantial to be ignored. What I find surprising in her remark is the use of the word "horror."

The word is far too strong for what is happening consciously to Irene: repeating the mourning she has undergone after the murder of her father. Joan Copjec has referred to the fact that it is essential not to confuse "the first and the second death. The first is the real death of the biological body, after which there is usually another, the second, exemplified by the various rituals of mourning that take place in the symbolic" (Copjec 46). For Irene, taking the actor for her father while going back to a time prior to the latter's murder is a question of repeating the sorrow she suffered and has already worked through via the rituals of mourning. This, however, can hardly be said to induce "horror." However, things take on a very different complexion if we turn to the seemingly innocuous word "alive" in the statement she makes to the actor.[10] "Alive" is in fact the condensation of two contradictory unconscious desires, inasmuch as, whereas the actor is very much alive, it is "as if" her dead father still were. These desires are: she wants her father to be alive in order to continue her special (incestuous) relation with him; and she wants him dead so that she can have a normal relation with Fedor. The place of incest in the film is here complicated by the fact that she is glad that her father is dead. Thus re-living the past, albeit through a game, is re-living the *guilt* caused by her unconscious desire. Whichever way she turns, she is "guilty"— of desiring her father; and of wanting him dead.[11] It is surely most revealing that when the actor playing her father says, "Be brave, my child," she should reply, "I'll try, father." Why "father"? In order to maintain the act under all circumstances? Perhaps, but in that case role-playing has triggered off a linguistic manifestation of another role, unconscious this time, the one she is playing in relation to her real father.

To this we must add another unconscious element. If, at some time in the past prior to his murder she wished him dead, then her most secret and horrible unconscious fear can only be that he will return, in the time-honored tradition of the living dead, to collect a symbolic debt and to *punish* her for her desire to get rid of him.[12] Since incest flows in both directions, however, he could also be returning from the dead to carry on the relationship, to impose himself upon her. This, then, is why she said it was Luna who attacked her in her bedroom, while knowing unconsciously that it was the Count, the father-figure (after all, he has a daughter who seems to be Irene's age...). Her horror at desiring the attack finds its equal only in the horror of being attacked: the incestuous desire is mutual. Irene's case would seem to correspond to the situation described by Freud in *Totem and Taboo*: "In the course of psycho-analyses of neurotics who suffer (or who suffered in their childhood) from fear of ghosts, it is often possible to show without much difficulty that the ghosts are disguises for the patient's parents" (*Totem and Taboo* 65n3). Similarly, when she was play-acting and claiming to hear her father's voice, her unconscious desire was precisely that he *should return* and call her to him so that their forbidden relationship could continue. Her words to her fiancé—"Forgive me for what I'm doing"—are thus the manifestation of a conscious dismay at deceiving him because of the game, and an unconscious attempt at an excuse which I propose to rewrite as follows: "Forgive me for deceiving you with another man, my father." Whether we interpret the conversation as an admission to play-acting on the first level, the one enounced by the film, or as an admission to indulging in incestuous fantasies, then the conversation is a complex example of Lacan's fundamental insight that human beings are the only creatures which can deceive by telling the truth. Whichever way the fiancé or the spectator interprets the conversation, they are being deceived, for the unconscious desire will remain repressed.

This, however, is far from being all there is to the incest theme. Immediately after the sequence where she claims to hear her father's voice, the Inspector barks: "Hysteria!" This is not simple male prejudice, nor must it be put down to part of the charade. For hysteria is indeed present in the film—at the moment she breaks down in the presence of the actor. Her loss of control is the effect of a particular cause: that of the truth of her desire suddenly being revealed in the remark which she makes to the actor, and in the slip of the tongue involving "father." Her inability to control her words, gestures and body movements is surely a sign of the repressed desire inscribing its traces on her body and through her words in the form of symptoms. No further displacement is possible at this point. If such a displacement was still possible after the Inspector pronounced the word which now returns to haunt the daughter, then this is due to the fact that in the charade the father-daughter encounter had not yet taken place. The film cuts at this point to a large close-up of Irene looking adoringly off-screen right, in the direction of Professor Zelen, the film's stern patriarch and obvious father substitute (an acceptable one, unlike the Count, for the reasons we have already seen). If only she can convince herself that by admiring (i.e. loving) him she will escape punishment; if only the symbolic debt can be collected in this displaced form — accepting the authority of the substitute patriarch — then she will be able to rest in peace, as will her father.

Yet another twist is added through the character of the Baron. At the end of the film Zelen hypnotizes him so that he will obey instructions and repeat the gestures leading to the murder of Sir Karell. At this point, then, the audience realizes what has been happening and what the scheme is: to have the Baron repeat before the key witness of the butler how he murdered Sir Karell. The actor/Sir Karell reveals to the spectator that the Baron is to be Irene's guardian should anything happen to her father. He then adds: "You've spoilt her since the day she was born." What transpires here is that the Baron was, and still is, in love with Irene and killed the father so as to gain access to her and her fortune. In which case the plot surely thickens. The final section of the play is a repetition of the murder of Sir Karell, so if we now see how the Baron killed him, then this is the acting-out of the desire of another person, namely the daughter. She desired to kill her father, and the Baron unconsciously assumed that desire as his own by identifying with it. Consciously he could hide this from himself with the argument that, by killing Sir Karell, he would obtain both Irene and her fortune. Unfortunately, he could not reckon with Irene's desire, which was to use Fedor as a bulwark against the Real of her desire. This is all the more credible as Fedor is a far more suitable fiancé, ideologically speaking, than the much older Baron.

The incest theme, then, remains in the film embodied in another father-daughter relationship, which means that the little matter of sexuality is not really resolved, despite the heterosexual pairing of Irene and Fedor (as essential ideologically to the horror film as it was generally in Hollywood). It is in this context of textual/sexual instability that the character of the doctor plays his part. I have already referred to his ambiguity over the question of vampires in the scene which takes place at the inn and which constitutes, along with the scene involving the peasants and the scene with the old crone in the cemetery, a sort of Prologue. We have seen that he scoffs at the very notion of vampires but nevertheless is frightened at the thought of being out at night. Thus he appears in the film *prior* to the events that comprise the plot to confound the Baron. These events take place either in the mansion of the late Sir Karell (where we see the Baron in the very next scene informing the servants of the murder of their master/employer) or in the old abandoned castle. There is reason, therefore, to assume that he is not part of the plot, since he maintains (once he has examined the corpse) that a vampire is responsible. Moreover, there is a scene where the doctor, the Inspector and the butler are present, but where the Baron is absent; this means that it is not necessary to try to convince him that vampires exist. The butler states that he couldn't sleep because of a bat, which provokes immediate skepticism on the part of Neumann. It would be more logical to read this scene as an attempt to hoodwink the doctor, who is adamant over his diagnosis. This is reinforced by Zelen who, on meeting the doctor, tells him that he agrees with him. We can therefore interpret these elements as tending to indicate that the doctor must be encouraged by those privy to the plot to believe in the truth of his diagnosis, the better to get the Baron to adopt the same viewpoint.

If this be the case, it indicates that the doctor is not considered as someone the plotters can count on, unlike the butler (devoted to Sir Karell). Rather, the doctor, like Fedor (who, being in love with Irene), might upset the applecart in the name of the male protecting the female. Which is why I am paying attention to the doctor, whose behavior is that of a coward and who, apart from his insistence on his scientific competence (where he brooks no hints to the contrary), is a passive character. He is, after all, played by the character actor Donald *Meek*. Moreover, the Inspector — portrayed very much as a nononsense individual — responds contemptuously to the medico's fear of going out at night by calling him a "morning glory," a flower.[13] He makes this remark to belittle the doctor in the course of a discussion between the two men. I would suggest, therefore, that he is being connoted as homosexual, in keeping with a major theme of the horror film of the 1930s.[14] The doctor is visibly vexed and humiliated, as well he might be, for the flower was a Hollywood signifier connoting effeminacy, which, as we know, was the code name for homosexuality.[15] It is, for instance, striking to note how he takes refuge in the bosom of the butler — whose own cowardly behavior is very much part of his act — just as Irene does in the arms of Fedor. This kind of visual parallel is certainly not coincidental, and is over-determined retroactively by certain ambiguities, both on the level of language and behavior, that structure the entire film. We can also add that the doctor's credulity from the outset, in the Prologue, will tend to *undermine* our belief in vampires, as he is not a positive character: we too have to be convinced. That the doctor should disappear from the film before the ending indicates that he has served his purpose.

We have already shown how the use of the word "acting" in Irene's conversation with Fedor cannot be interpreted as such by the spectator without the film actually cheating; we are deceived, but this is part of the plot and is most skilfully done. An identical example occurs when Fedor pursues Irene, who he thinks is in terrible danger from Luna. Irene shouts desperately, "Go away, Fedor!" which can obviously be interpreted in two ways: she does not want him to face the danger of being vampirized to save her; and she is trying as hard as she can — which is her brief as an actress in the Inspector's play — to prevent him from seeing through the game (of which he is a victim). What, however, are we to make of the scene where Fedor staggers into the mansion, revealing what seems to be a bite on his neck? He claims he fell, struck his head and returned to consciousness only when it was dark. The spectator, in his ignorance, can only interpret this as a vampire attack on Fedor. Now it would be easy to suggest that the Inspector knocked Fedor out and made the marks on his neck in order to convince him of the danger from vampires should Fedor prove unreliable, or over-anxious to protect Irene. But Fedor says he fell and struck his head, a claim which he would hardly make if he had been knocked unconscious while standing! After all, he has no reason to lie, so we are perforce led to see in this scene a deliberate cheat on the film's part to convince us the vampire tale is true.

The fact that Fedor is not part of the plot places this little narrative of his in a totally different category from that of the butler and the maid, who, pretending to be terror-stricken, recount that when they were placing batthorne everywhere, Count Mora suddenly appeared. The film cunningly resorts to a strategem within the overall narrative, one that is purely visual. As the butler starts to relate the event, the film cuts to him and the maid in a corridor. We are therefore seeing what they claim to have seen and are spectators to the visual representation of the events they narrate. A bat appears at an open window at the other end of the corridor and turns into the Count. The two servants flee for their lives. This most carefully realized little scene is not therefore the representation of a real event but of *the way the butler narrates it*. Its status is therefore subjective, but since the spectators have no reason to doubt the man's word, they have no reason to doubt the truth of the image. Thus *Mark of the Vampire* gives us a little lesson in the inherent artificiality of the image: seeing is believing when we want to believe or when the codes of the genre, be it the *fantastique* or neo-realism, give us what we *expect*.

The problem with the Fedor incident, then, is one of *motivation*. This notion is fundamental to traditional realist fiction and dominant filmmaking. If a minor element is to play a key role later in the work, it must be motivated at some early stage by being introduced "naturally"; the spectator must not feel cheated when a later event appears in the narrative in an artificial and unconvincing fashion. Belief, like a vampire, takes many forms. This feeling is likely to accompany the Fedor incident once the spectator starts reading backwards. One could, of course, be as cynical as the makers of *Mark of the*

Vampire may have been and assume the spectator will be too stupid or indifferent to do so; they might even forget! In an attempt to render the vexed matter of motivation in terms chosen by the film itself, I remind readers of the scene where Irene is attacked in her bedroom by Count Mora and claims it was Luna. Zelen has asked the maid always to be present, but she leaves momentarily, thus leaving the way wide open for a vampire attack. Zelen, significantly, calls her a fool when she explains that she left the room to get some coffee to keep her awake. This cunningly hides the fact that she left deliberately in order for the attack to take place and thus further the plan of the plotters. For what could be more "natural" than going to get coffee, especially as Browning has included a shot of the maid nodding off, then being jerked awake by the fact that she is seated uncomfortably on a chair? The film has thus included in its own narrative an element which, like the verbal ambiguities of Irene's statements to Fedor, can be given simultaneously two different interpretations without lying to the audience. We have been deceived, not lied to.

I would argue also that all the business with candles going out in the crypt functions in a like fashion, albeit less successfully than the question of the maid going for coffee. Zelen, the Inspector and the Baron visit the crypt with lighted candles in an attempt to locate the vampires and stake them. They come across the third man (part of the professional act of Count Mora), and the Baron grabs an axe, only to be stopped by Zelen. Clearly the plotters cannot allow one of those involved to be decapitated! To convince the Baron, Zelen has recourse to the lore of the vampire: kill one and the others will pursue the killers to the end of eternity with their vengeance. Strong stuff for the Baron! So he submits to the impeccable logic of Zelen, who insists all three must be staked together—and the spectator, well versed in such lore, goes along with this. When they find the Count, the candles suddenly go out, and the very next shot reveals him and Sir Karell outside, as well as Luna walking about. Cut to the two men looking off-screen, but who are they watching—Luna, as the Count did earlier when she went after Irene on the terrace, or the inside of the crypt to monitor the Baron's actions? Clearly the candles going out was a ruse on the part of Zelen and the Inspector to prevent the Baron from doing anything untoward, and to give the Count and the actor playing Sir Karell time to escape. Thus the film takes over as part of its own narrative logic the candles going out, passing this off as "the sort of thing that can happen." If it could be claimed that a certain "suspension of disbelief" on our part is essential for the ruse (on the part of the film and of the plotters) to work, then this is arguably also the case with the maid leaving the room, especially as Zelen had insisted that she do so under no circumstances.

Let us return, for the last time, to our friend the doctor, for there exists a scene after the Prologue which at once makes his role even more difficult to ascertain and suggests just to what extent the film is cheating us. During the inquest, scorn is poured on the idea that vampires are involved, both by the coroner and the Inspector, with the doctor defending his position. It is during this inquest that the names of Count Mora and Luna are evoked, and that a peasant reminds the coroner of the mysterious death at an earlier date of a farmer whose body was found drained of blood. Unless we conclude that the coroner and the peasants are involved in the Inspector's scheme, this smacks very much of deliberately leading the spectator astray — and in a manner as useless as it is stupid, for the care with which Count Mora and Luna are introduced visually by Browning removes any need for them to be introduced as if they had been terrorizing the district since time immemorial.

I have mentioned more than once that the Count, Sir Karell and Luna, separately or together, are seen looking. This particular strategy is also exploited by Browning in the case of the Inspector and the Baron, who are searching for the vampires' lair. We see them approach the old castle and hoist themselves up to the level of a window in order to have a good view of the inside. Cut to a shot of them taken from the inside, looking in. Cut to a shot where we see the Count, Sir Karell and the third vampire. Luna then descends from the rafters, visibly equipped with bat's wings. This last shot has aroused Senn's ire as an instance of the supernatural elements not being explained and therefore of the film's cheating. I shall argue now that, not only is this untrue, it fails to take into account the (f)act of looking that also implies the spectators, and that this sequence goes to the heart of the unconscious logic of the film. It is crucial that we see the Baron and the Inspector moving into position to look, followed by a shot of them looking, as this places us in their position — we adopt their point of view of what is happening within the castle — while allowing us to adopt a certain distance: we "are" the characters, but we are also spectators watching a spectacle, a theme of crucial importance to the film. Let me remind readers here of the way we are placed on the cart as it rushes headlong towards the motionless Luna, and where we not only see what the peasants do but also interpret the vision in the way the codes of the genre expect.

We must not forget the specific cinematic code Browning uses at this point: Luna floats eerily down from the rafters, touches the floor and starts to fold her wings. There then follows a *cut*, and we see Sir Karell at the organ. When next we see Luna, the bat wings have disappeared and she is simply wearing her shroud, as in all other scenes. What is important here is that we see no reaction from the Baron and the Inspector. In other words, we see what Browning has chosen to let us see. Nor must we overlook a piece of information Senn himself gives us: Count Mora, Luna and the third man are part of a team called "The Flying Moras." Nothing could be more simple. The bat wings are part of their usual act; Luna "flies" thanks to invisible strings that are destined to make the spectators present at their shows, like the Baron and the spectators of the film, take for supernatural what is a simple "special effect," another trick like those used by magicians. By employing a cut, Browning simply uses a cinematic device whose function, among others, is to pass from one scene to another and thus choose what the spectators see. What they do see is always a question of choice and can always involve a certain amount of subterfuge on the director's part. Here, therefore, the issue is one of making us believe what we see, just as the plotters have sought to make the Baron believe what he sees. Moreover, the cut from Luna to Sir Karell at the piano can be interpreted as being a cut *for the Baron too*. Or, to be more precise, the Inspector has always functioned as the "director" of the spectacle and thus as a stand-in for Browning within the fictional world. Thus the Baron now shifts his gaze to Sir Karell at the behest of the Inspector so that he won't see Luna divest herself of the phoney wings. Consequently, the Inspector controls the Baron's vision and point of view much as Browning controls those of the spectators.

In an attempt to sum up and draw certain conclusions, I shall examine one detail in *London After Midnight* in the light of the insightful remarks made by Jean-Marie Sabatier about role playing in Browning's cinema (see note 2). The film of 1927 is both more coherent than *Mark of the Vampire* and considerably less elaborate. Thus it eschews all references to the supernatural that cannot be put down to the play concocted by the central character, Inspector Burke of Scotland Yard, played by Lon Chaney, who also plays the role of the phoney vampire. The details of the plot are substantially the same, including a young man who is in love with the daughter of the murder victim and whom Burke keeps in ignorance so as not to compromise the game. The vampire is accompanied by a young "bat girl" called Luna,[16] and hypnosis is used by Burke, both to neutralize the young man at a crucial moment of the plot and to trap the murderer, the close friend of the victim, into betraying how he killed the man who is supposed to have committed suicide. Similarly, the butler and the maid are involved in the Inspector's charade. However, the unconscious dimension of incest is totally absent. Unfortunately, the only version available (the last print known to exist was destroyed in a fire in the 1960s) consists of stills that have been edited to enable spectators today to have an idea of the plot, in the sense of the story of the film and the Inspector's play within a play. This inevitably eliminates how Browning moved from one scene to the next, and the revelation of how it was all a play contains so little information that we are entitled to wonder what is missing. Certainly the crucial missing element is *movement*, both that of characters within the frame and of the camera itself.

Before looking at the detail in question, however, it is useful to compare the scene in *Mark of the Vampire* where the butler tells of how he and the maid encountered Count Mora in the corridor with the corresponding scene in *London After Midnight*. In the silent film it is the maid who narrates. One major difference is how the vampire materializes — not by turning from a bat into a human but by a sort of fade-in where the vampire suddenly appears in the corridor. It is interesting to note that this is the only scene where he is endowed with wings like a bat, whereas the "bat girl" at no time is so endowed, unlike Luna in *Mark of the Vampire*. Thus we see an image of him, his wings open like a huge bird of prey, towering over the cowering maid. Given that she is revealed to be part of the plot, Browning at one and the same time insists on the vampiric traits of the character and renders the encounter as much parodic and "overacted" as purely terrifying. Looking at the film a second time and with the benefit of hindsight, we can notice just how "stagey" it is. We shall see why below.

The detail in question would, on the face of it (and taking many of Browning's scenes at their face value is most unwise indeed), introduce the same incoherency that we have shown to be sometimes a case of cheating in *Mark of the Vampire*. On nearly every occasion we see the "vampire," Browning not only shows his staring eyes and pointed teeth but insists on them by the use of huge close-ups. On three occasions, however, we see him with his back turned to us. The film proceeds most skilfully here, for the first occasion cannot be interpreted as other than our seeing the vampire from behind, with Luna looking into the camera. The other two instances, however, could be read as cases of Browning being downright dishonest, although this interpretation is possible only after the film has ended and the Inspector's ploy revealed by the policeman himself. One of the last shots of *London After Midnight* shows Burke holding in his hands a wig and the vampire's hat, obviously indicating that the vampire was no such thing but simply a man dressed and made up to look like a vampire. The interesting element here is that the audience is encouraged to assume that it was Burke himself who played the role of the vampire, and this is certainly how Sabatier interprets the film. It is a perfectly valid interpretation, but if we leave things there, then we must perforce accuse Browning of cheating us, as he was to do in 1935 in certain scenes of *Mark of the Vampire*.

Things, however, are not that obvious, nor that simple. One shot shows Burke and the other characters looking out of a window. First they see only Luna, down in the garden, but the next shot of the characters together in the home of Sir James (who will be revealed as the murderer) is followed by a shot of Luna and the vampire *with his back to us*. In a later scene — corresponding to the scene in *Mark of the Vampire* where Zelen and the Baron peer through the window of the abandoned house where Sir Karell and Count Mora are united, and where Luna flies down on her bat wings — Burke and Sir James peer through a window and we see the murder victim (whom both we and Sir James consider to be a vampire) sitting facing us; he is in the company of the vampire, again seated with his back to us. Now the editing in both cases is such that it is clear that both Burke and the vampire are present at the same time but in two different spaces: the former outside looking in, very much like the spectator of a play, the latter seated within. So if Burke plays the vampire, the film is simply lying to us, since Burke cannot be with the other characters or with Sir James and simultaneously the object of everyone's gaze as the mysterious vampire.

Indeed he cannot, but that assumes that it is indeed Burke playing the vampire! Or rather that he *and he alone* plays that role. But there is nothing to stop Burke from resorting to another person, a professional actor (much as Luna is part of a professional troupe of acrobats in both *London After Midnight* and *Mark of the Vampire*) called upon to play the vampire when Burke is prevented from doing so by being/playing himself. Or, to put it differently, when Chaney is playing Burke he cannot be playing the vampire at the same time. Burke deceives everyone, including the film's spectators, by pretending at the outset to be a private investigator, not a Scotland Yard Inspector, so even there he was playing a role and reveals his true identity only at the end. Thus what we have seen on the second and third occasions when the vampire is shown with his back to us is an actor playing the vampire, which is precisely what Chaney was, whether in the role of Burke or the vampire! The shots of the vampire with his back to us simply deceive us, they do not lie to us. The fact that it was Burke himself dressed up as the vampire on the first occasion beautifully brings home to us that the very concepts of role playing and make-up are inherently deceptive: we can be made to believe what the film's makers, or the play's director, want us to believe. Despite the incoherencies of *Mark of the Vampire*, this is surely the lesson to be learned from this quite fascinating movie.

Notes

1. We shall see which characters and how they participate in the charade in due course.
2. In his incisive analysis of Browning's work, Jean-Marie Sabatier points out that role playing, make up, the double and the world of the circus are central elements in his films from *The Unholy Three* (1925) to *The Devil Doll* (1936). *The Black Bird* (1926), *Freaks* (1932), *London After Midnight* (1927) and *Mark of the Vampire* are all concerned with this over-arching theme of acting (see Sabatier 81–87). We shall return to *London After Midnight* and how it can help us appreciate *Mark of the Vampire* in our concluding remarks.
3. Peasants and villagers play a crucial role in *Dracula*; it is they who welcome Renfield,

then warn him not to continue to Borgo Pass, where Dracula's castle is situated, as it is now night. We shall return to their role in the earlier film and to the character of Renfield later.

4. Such a cart plays a crucial role much later, involving Count Mora's daughter Luna, as we shall see.

5. At the end of the film he turns out to be one of the team of actors engaged to confound the Baron, but no information is given at any time prior to this as to his role; he is just presented as a vampire.

6. The still is reproduced in Senn 268.

7. Of all the main characters, only Fedor is unaware of the charade, for reasons we shall return to later. The case of the doctor is as ambiguous as everything about him and demands special analysis.

8. I have dealt in detail with the various themes raised here in my book *The Hollywood Horror Film, 1931–1941: Madness in a Social Landscape* (Lanham, Maryland: Scarecrow Press, 2006), particularly in chapter 1, "Curse of the Superstitious Script."

9. The film is (very) loosely based on Poe's "The Premature Burial."

10. The importance of the meaning of the word is, as it were, hidden or repressed by the presence of the word "horror."

11. This, then, is "the horror of it."

12. The most perfect instance of this is the cemetery sequence that opens *Night of the Living Dead* (George A. Romero, 1968). The zombie that suddenly appears when the brother tries to frighten his sister by saying "They're coming to get you, Barbara" is the manifestation of unconscious desire: the dead father returning to punish the children, in particular his son, for their insufficient devotion to his memory. Similarly, towards the end of the film the brother returns "to get" Barbara, thus punishing her for her moralizing attitude.

13. An interesting detail. The French for "morning glory" is "belle de jour," the name given to the heroine in Bunuel's film of that title dating from 1967.

14. I have analyzed this phenomenon in detail in my book (see above, note 9), in particular when discussing the character of Henry Frankenstein in Whale's two films. However, so many films involve sexually ambiguous male characters — not to mention the arguably lesbian central character of *Dracula's Daughter*— that it is patent that the question goes far beyond Whale's homosexuality to embrace the genre as a whole. For different but complementary approaches, see Benshoff and Berenstein. See also Humphries "The Semiotics of Horror."

15. In *Laura* (1944), director Otto Preminger insists on a certain number of details in order to connote Waldo Lydecker as gay, including the way he chooses a carnation for his buttonhole. Moreover, the word "pansy," whose polysemy I hardly need to comment on, was bandied around from one film and context to another in the horror films of the 30s. See Humphries *The Hollywood Horror Film* 67–68.

16. The character is referred to as "bat girl" in the end credits only.

Works Cited

Benshoff, Harry M. *Monsters in the Closet: Homosexuality and the Horror Film.* Manchester and New York: Manchester University Press, 1997.
Berenstein, Rhona J. *Attack of the Leading Ladies: Gender, Sexuality, and Spectatorship in Classic Horror Cinema.* New York: Columbia University Press, 1996.
Copjec, Joan. *Read My Desire: Lacan Against the Historicists.* Cambridge, MA: Massachusetts Institute of Technology, 1994.
Evans, Dylan. *An Introductory Dictionary of Lacanian Psychoanalysis.* London and New York: Routledge, 1996.
Freud, Sigmund. "The Uncanny." *The Standard Edition of the Complete Psychological Works of Sigmund Freud.* London: The Hogarth Press and the Institute of Psycho-analysis, Vol. XVII, 217–52.

_____. *Totem and Taboo. The Standard Edition of the Complete Psychological Works of Sigmund Freud.* London: The Hogarth Press and the Institute of Psycho-analysis, Vol. XIII, 1–161.
Humphries, Reynold. "The Semiotics of Horror: The Case of *Dracula's Daughter.*" *Interdisciplinary Journal for German Linguistics and Semiotic Analysis* 5:2 (Fall 2000), 273–89.
_____. *The Hollywood Horror Film, 1931–1941: Madness in a Social Landscape.* Lanham, Maryland: Scarecrow Press, 2006.
PCA file on the film, Academy of Motion Picture Arts and Sciences, Margaret Herrick Library, Special Collections, Beverly Hills, California.
Sabatier, Jean-Marie. *Les Classiques du Cinéma Fantastique.* Paris: Balland, 1973.
Senn, Bryan. *Golden Horrors: An Illustrated Critical Filmography of Terror Cinema, 1931–1939.* Jefferson, NC: McFarland and Company, 1996.

An Incident in the History of Surrealism
On a Sequence in The Devil-Doll

ADRIAN MARTIN

> *One doesn't decide to make a Surrealist film; one is either Surrealist or not.*
> — Robert Benayoun [48]

In 1998, an intriguing essay appeared in *The Journal of Popular Film and Television*. Exploring the topics of women, violence, and disability in two Tod Browning films, *The Devil-Doll* (1936) and *Freaks* (1932), its authors, Martin Norden and Madeleine Cahill, argued that there is something unusual, for the historical period, in these works: the depiction of disabled women (circus performers in *Freaks*, Rafaela Ottiano as Malita in *The Devil-Doll*) as active agents, not simply the "saintly innocent"—that stereotype of the disabled as children which *Freaks* very cunningly evokes in its opening scenes, only in order to invert it, with such savage fury, by the end.

But what sort of action do these fictive women take? In both cases, it is violent revenge. This causes some difficulty for Norden and Cahill, because it catches them up in an ideological double-bind: if Browning's films make a progressive move by de-pacifying the figure of the disabled person, they also make a regressive move by assimilating the figure of the feminine to a code of psychotic revenge! So the disabled woman, à la Browning, is no longer the mimsy wallflower of silent cinema, but she is already on her way to becoming the Glenn Close *femme fatale* of *Fatal Attraction* (1987). In an ultimate rhetorical move that is familiar from twenty years of a certain kind of "cultural studies" analysis of cinema, Norden and Cahill conclude that Browning's films "paradoxically both rupture and reinforce traditional views of female roles in films" (94). It's paradox which, however critically well-intentioned, leaves us in something of a stalemate.

This is a very typical kind of intellectual ambivalence, but it does not get us very far when confronted with the great "extreme" films — whether they be by Browning or, over sixty years later, Gaspar Noé, Bruno Dumont, Claire Denis, and Philippe Grandrieux. In the particular case of Browning, his films invite us to adopt a very strange and compelling ethical position; they are, we might say, *celebrations of revenge*, where this revenge is always wielded, in all its confronting horror, by the marginal, the oppressed, by "fanatics" and by the impassioned. Browning rarely recodes this revenge-kick, in the conventionally moral way, at some key turning point of his narratives — as the sign of an obsession, a sickness or a fatal character flaw (as do, for example, literally hundreds of cop-revenge movies in the *Big Heat/Dirty Harry* tradition). He leaves us no room for that fence-sitting response which tries to equilibrate his films around a comforting paradox (like the story both ruptures and reinforces the dominant values).

There is, in fact, only a single choice for the spectator: he/she, for the length of the film and perhaps beyond it, either joins in the celebration — no matter how contrary it might be to their own previously assumed moral code (hence the immense disquiet generated by these films in many viewers) — or refuses it altogether. This is the very logic of Browning's cinema that has often brought forth the label of *perverse* — for it has the power (if we allow this power to work on us) to truly "lead us astray," seducing us away from standard ways of thinking, feeling, and evaluating. It is little wonder that a recent commentator finds that "for sheer perverseness, Browning's films have never been equaled," and that "revenge is taken in a way that is as dizzying as it is justified" (Richardson 67).

Where *Freaks* builds to its revenge plot over the better part of an hour, *The Devil-Doll* begins from the fierce intention to avenge a personal injustice. Paul Lavond (Lionel Barrymore) has done time on Devil's Island, framed by his three business associates. He escapes prison with the aid of a scientist, Marcel (Henry P. Walthall), who (as Paul learns upon arriving at Marcel's house in the film's opening moments) has developed a method of shrinking living beings. Lavond disregards Marcel's purpose, once he keels over dead, and embarks on his plan of revenge: shrinking people, who he then uses as assassins. Much of the film is taken up with this implacable, one-by-one schema of revenge. In the course of this plan, Lavond disguises himself — mainly as a little old woman. In what is evidently the most conventional and sentimental part of the film, Lavond comes to reconcile himself with his daughter, Lorraine (Maureen O'Sullivan), hence giving up, at last, his evil ways and rejoining the social order.

This attempt to synopsize *The Devil-Doll*, like all attempts, can signal one of two options, according to the sensibility and intent of the analyst.

Boiled down this way, the story is revealed either as an immensely silly, incoherent absurdity or it takes on the lineaments of a dream — in the same way that the narratives of Luis Buñuel, David Cronenberg, David Lynch, or Raúl Ruiz do. Is it important to dwell, in a narratively normative fashion, on the contradictions generated by the film's half-supernatural, half-scientific premise (e.g. how does a brain-shrink "wipe memory" and erase will?)? It is better to accept this "drift" of logic and sense, and to plunge in elsewhere, to the places where the film really affects us. For instance, what could be more perverse, finally, than *The Devil-Doll*'s "happy ending," after all the atrocity that has preceded it? Something latent is stirring here under what is manifest — the surest sign of the dream-work.

This ending raises many issues about the status of *The Devil-Doll* as precisely "a film by Tod Browning." If it is an endlessly fascinating work, it is also, unquestionably, a compromised one; and if it is a "penultimate film" for Browning, it is so in the same way that *Big Trouble* (1986) is the "last film" for John Cassavetes — in other words, far from the transparent testament that auteurists would like it to be. Here, however, we may need to rescue Browning from some of his most fervent champions — those who, inadvertently recycling the hoariest old value of high-art judgment, praise the supposed "subtlety" of Browning's convulsive artistry, and lament the "dumbing down" destruction wreaked upon it by insensitive producers, studios, censors, etc. (as if all trace of the original work and its intent have been irretrievably lost). But *The Devil-Doll* cannot be rejected as an utterly foreign body in relation to the directorial career that preceded it.

In the miasma of dim but intense recollections that this film calls forth in scholars and ordinary fans alike — even as the title is mangled (the French translation gives us *The Devil's Dolls*) and the plot misremembered — it is the power of certain images, incidents, and situations that insists, like the deepest unconscious material in a dream. "*The Devil-Doll* captured me with its superb special effects and its casual acceptance of Lionel Barrymore in drag," wrote Vivian Sobchack in 1974 (22). And everything that spins out from those spectacular effects (such as the tiny assassins bent on revenge), and the disquieting apparitions of gender and sexuality, belongs wholly to Browning; the narrative context may be deformed, but the signature and its phantasmic charge can hardly be watered down by outside interference.

Therefore, *The Devil-Doll* is one of those movies that is best approached as a palimpsest — as notable for the intertextual network comprising what it filters from key earlier films and what it prophesizes of crucial future films, as for how it manages to negotiate (with no small amount of difficulty) its own variously written-over but only partially erased layers. Indeed, from a psychoanalytic angle, the greater the "psychic interference" — here translated into the literal interference of the studio and its various related agencies — the greater the effort and work of the dream must be in investing energy and intensity into the "traces" that will be allowed to remain.

The research into the film's troubled production history carried out by Bret Wood (1992) has established that, as intended by Browning, *The Devil-Doll* (or, rather, *The Witch of Timbuctoo*) — would have been, in the long view of cinema history, far closer to the overt subversiveness of Jacques Tourneur and Val Lewton's *I Walked with a Zombie* (1943) than *Bride of Frankenstein* (1935), as well as those prior horror hits that *The Devil-Doll* "rechannels" at moments. In Browning's initial script (subsequently recast by many other hands), the character of Malita was Nyleta, a black African woman from the Belgian Congo who practiced voodoo and witchcraft. It is this kind of "active agency," by way of black magic, which was to have been the motor of the revenge scenario. This element led to direct political censorship from the British distributors and exhibitors with which MGM was associated at the time; they did not want any such imaginable "resistance" propaganda stirring up the native subjects of the Empire!

But *The Devil-Doll*, in however censored a form it comes to us, is the kind of film that the Surrealists would — and indeed did — enjoy watching; and such Surrealism, as we will see, is far from being a dead dinosaur of cultural history. *The Devil-Doll* hinges, as already mentioned, on the visionary plan of Marcel, a Dr. Frankenstein–style mad scientist who dreams of shrinking the population of the entire world (with an ecological, resource-maximizing goal in mind). That is the first irresistibly Surrealist slant to *The Devil-Doll*: this mad, magnificent obsession to shrink "the whole world!" (starting with Paris because, as Malita says, "There are many people there"). And why not? Supposed scientific rationality has gone completely over the edge into quasi-mystical irrationality; this is science as voodoo, or as circus magic tricks.

The indelible sequence devoted to Marcel's demonstration of his ingenious shrinkage technique, beginning five minutes into the film, is among the summits of Browning's career; it is this sequence, essentially, which my comments in this essay circle in an attempt to bring out its full historic and aesthetic significance. The sequence bridges two lab scenes, separated by the exposition of Paul's "backstory." As always, Browning's narrative and thematic construction is logical, rigorous, and systematic, building by steps or (as I will call them) phases. Even before the entry into the house, the film literally "scatters" figures through the frame — a pack of dogs and a woman who is "an inbred peasant half-wit" (as Malita describes her) — that will soon become central to the film's bizarre and singular "economy" of normal versus abnormal and large versus small (a semantic structure systematized even more thoroughly, but using different physical elements, in *Freaks*).

The first lab scene offers us an introduction to the shrinkage process through its "failures," or only halfway successful attempts. In the first phase of the scene, Marcel and Malita fondle what Paul takes to be "toy dogs"— which is, on the level of filmic fact, exactly what they are. Thus, objects of reduced size become the first figural, cinematic means to convey or signify the sequence's "unnatural" concept. The next phase of the scene covers a verbal elaboration of this concept, as explained zealously by Marcel to an incredulous Paul. The scene's third phase, in which the shrunken animals are stirred into animate life and directed by the willpower of another's guiding brain, at last unveils what any spectator would regard as the film's central "special effect": the placing of people made photographically small within a composition that compares them to normal-size bodies and domestic fixtures (as in the simultaneity, within the same frame, of the domestic pet dog and the shrunken canines). However, in a very real sense, everything that Browning manages in his figural economy of small/large and normal/abnormal is truly an "effect" of one kind or another: the cinema of Tod Browning is, in the most profound and far-reaching sense, a cinema of effects.

Another option is available to Browning to convey the play of sizes and scales, and he uses it as surely as every other teller of "incredible shrinking" stories on the screen (including Ruiz in his inspired short *Snakes and Ladders*, 1980) has used it ever since: shots in which huge sets (or simply sides, parts, or aspects of specific objects) have been built to give the illusion of a vast, oversize world dwarfing the shrunken figures — who this time are actors appearing in the frame at their "normal" height — the concept now conveyed via the resources of *mise en scène*. Of course, it becomes dizzying trying to precisely specify sizes and scales within such a thoroughly artificial schema of fantastic representation. Browning also employs, as an economic shortcut, images where no attempt is made whatsoever to convey the size differential: for instance, when Marcel is seen placing cotton wool balls just below the screen, upon the unseen shrunken body.

When we return to the lab for the second half of the sequence, everything is taken up a notch. Now the experiment is being carried out on a human, not an animal; and the work requires greater, and queerer, elaboration: the body must be wrapped in cotton wool and "enchanted" into its complete state of being by a "mist" (so Marcel scientifically calls it) created through the action of various interconnected chemical bottles. The montage that brings this creature to life (I shall say more about its sense in a moment) is a superbly Eisensteinian passage: as the cutting-rate of the shots quickens, the framings click into a pattern of starkly-angled graphic contrasts. Browning was a master at such montage sequence inserts, which he was able to integrate effortlessly into the scenic flow of the narrative (whereas, so often, they stand out as the "extras" they are); a later sequence of this kind rivals Fritz Lang in its rapid "identikit" interplay of documents, still photographs, and standard figures-in-motion images.

In the shrinkage sequence we clearly see the legacy of George Méliès' early "trick films." But let us be clear on this: it is not that the special effects of 1936 are laughable because they are not as seamless and digital as the effects of modern CGI blockbusters. I am suggesting something quite different: that when you can see the bits and pieces of artifice and illusion, then the uncanny, dreamlike, poetic effect — the Surreal effect — can be enhanced tenfold. Claude Ollier once praised the slightly clunky special effects in the original *King Kong* (1936) by observing, "So true is it that the world of dreams is one of spatial effects, optical dislocations, ruptures between shots and generalised 'difference'" (270). Ollier went on to evoke "(a) visual universe which perfectly realizes the 'collage' basic to any nightmare vision — stippled space and stippled time, gaps, fringes, scenic overlaps and incompatibilities, zones of imponderable duration, void, into which apprehensions of unreality tumble headlong" (271). Stippled space and stippled time: this phrase reminds me of an "inscription" by Louis Scutenaire in 1945, who mused, "My taste for *Popeye the Sailor*, in the cartoons by Max Fleischer, owes much to the liberties he takes with those cherished beliefs of humanity: space and time" (102). It is a very cinematic idea that space and time should be regarded as cherished human beliefs, and accordingly derailed and subverted.

In *The Devil-Doll* there is the very Surrealist theme of *animation*, the "illusion of life"— the idea of an animating force, some emotion or desire that breathes life into the too-fixed objects of the real world. Surrealist stories are so often about a form of rejuvenation, a revival, a reawakening to life, a re-opening up to the wonders of the everyday world, from René Clair's merry sci-fi comedy *Paris qui dort* (aka *The Crazy Ray*, 1926)— in which a laser can freeze and then unfreeze the world in its tracks — to the political visions of the Taviani brothers, such as *The Night of the Shooting Stars* (1982) and *Kaos* (1984), where the sound of music, traveling magically across land or sea, can stir an individual, a community, or a whole nation into instant song and dance and revolutionary action, as in a feverish trance of possession. In fact, it was precisely this image of infectious song that Walter Benjamin used to sum up the positive charms of Surrealism (embodied by André Breton's novel *Nadja*) as he saw them:

> Breton and Nadja are the lovers who convert everything that we have experienced on mournful railway journeys (railways are beginning to age), on godforsaken Sunday afternoons in the proletarian neighborhoods of great cities, in the first glance through the rain-blurred window of a new apartment, into revolutionary experience, if not action. They bring the immense forces of

"atmosphere" concealed in these things to the point of explosion. What form do you suppose a life would take that was determined at a decisive moment precisely by the street song last on everyone's lips? [210].

And what life this animation brings in *The Devil-Doll*! Who is this woman named Lachna (Grace Ford), half human and half doll, stretching out her arms and yawning as if she has just awoken from the voluptuous sleep of some unearthly beautification treatment? Indeed, Browning's treatment of Lachna's awakening is striking for its total distance from the "Expressionist nightmare" model familiar from the horror classics of the '30s: no stormy night, flashes of lightning, or melodramatically ominous music; instead, a lulling score, rays of light, and the soothing, poetic effects of woolen texture and enveloping mist. The close shot of Lachna stretching — like the shot of her body wrapped in wool and then energized by a mist — is one of those striking, disconnected, excessive images that Surrealist cinema loves to film, and that Surrealist taste loves to discover — images that wander off from the film at hand, sabotaging the plot, arresting the situation, freezing the psychological interrelationships of the characters in order for something incandescent and truly phenomenal to emerge, phenomena of absolute or maximum strangeness and intensity. These are moments when the film itself seems itself to become an unconscious brain, fallen asleep and dreaming, offering up some moment of its plot or world from a deeper, subterranean logic.

Let us take a detour here into the history of Surrealism itself, especially in its connections to cinema, as a means to enrich our appreciation of Browning's achievement in this sequence in particular, and in *The Devil-Doll* in general — a reminder that is needed today, more than ever, now that Surrealism is blanketed in so many misconceptions, whether intended positively or negatively. On the one hand, Surrealism is pulverized into any imagery that is vaguely "weird" or incongruous; on the other hand, a line of formidable intellectuals, including Roland Barthes, have dismissed (misguidedly, in my view) Surrealism as banally "psychologistic" or purely mystical. A popular myth has it that Surrealism was a purely French-based art movement of the 1920s which died out — depending on which account you read — either at the start of the '30s or the end of World War II. But Surrealism is not an aesthetic style (like Pop Art); it is, above all, an *attitude*, a philosophy, a way of seeing the world and experiencing life. And as such it both begins long before and endures long after the lives and times of those we identify as the most famous Surrealists.

Breton's close collaborator, Jean Schuster, once made an important distinction between *eternal* and *historic* Surrealism. Historic Surrealism encompasses finite careers and biographies, and documents the activities of those who invented the term Surrealism and called themselves Surrealists. Eternal Surrealism, on the other hand, has a much broader and far-reaching life — it is the history of that attitude or *impulse* which has expressed itself in the acts or works of many. Eternal Surrealism takes in wonders ranging from the sexual treatises of the Marquis de Sade to Lewis Carroll's *Alice in Wonderland*, from the trance rituals of African tribes to the Warner Bros. cartoonists of the '30s and '40s. This Surrealism, as Schuster puts it, "belongs to no other patrimony than that of the human heart and mind" (23), and constitutes (as so many Surrealists have reminded us) a *permanent revolution*.

The avowed political program of Surrealism can seem a little Utopian and old-fashioned these days — this invocation of permanent revolution on the plane of everyday life. The idea of permanent revolution is itself a paradox, hiding a melancholic afterthought. The revolution is permanent, ongoing, but it *never truly arrives*. Philosophers of a profoundly radical political persuasion, from Benjamin to Giorgio Agamben, have long pondered this "fulfillment" which never comes — which never *can* come, almost by definition. That does not mean that it is not worth experiencing, but it puts a strange bracket around its "real world" efficacy, its practicality. In a way, that lack of real-world reference *is* the political point of Surrealism: there is always something more, something better, to hope for, to strive for, always a new pleasure to be found where you are, always a new transformation to be achieved, some new potential to be mined. Such Utopianism is profoundly critical — a veritable negation — of the world as it is. In this sense, as in many senses, Surrealism is a philosophy of the *virtual*, an art of the virtual, a vector of the virtual — if we do not restrict the realm of the virtual to its literal, new-fangled, cyberculture sense.

We can see this enabling power of the virtual in a familiar trope of Surrealist discourse (as in much film theorizing of a Utopian persuasion): the disappointed lamentation that, everywhere, cinema is in chains, able to realize only a fraction of its true possibilities. For over eighty years Surrealist artists, writers, critics, and sympathizers have embraced the cinema as the ideal dream-medium while also, in virtually the next sentence, expressing regret that a film industry run on and by money wants to sell us only formulaic, compromised dreams and fantasies, commercialized and commodified desires. Individuals follow, to the end of their days, this restless logic of perpetual disappointment fighting with irrepressible, impossible hope. But another, happier secret is hidden inside this logic. To take an example at a close tangent to official historic Surrealism: in the '20s, Jean Epstein praised cinema for its magical qualities of *photogénie*— when magnified faces and gestures onscreen become unreal, timeless, sublime (1977) — but, as he once admitted, it is hard to find more than one whole minute of *photogénie* in an average movie (hence the Surrealist taste for fragments, "privileged moments" in a film — such as the revivification demonstration in *The Devil-Doll*). This melancholic realization, however, served a positive effect: it spurred Epstein's own rich filmmaking experiments.

Since Surrealism has an historic dimension, some of its most familiar gestures and images have inexorably become repetitive, congealed, vulgar, and empty. Long before slick television ads and music video, the Situationist philosopher Guy Debord was already complaining in 1957 — in a highly critical but deeply informed commentary — "that automatic writing is monotonous, and that the whole genre of ostentatious Surrealist 'weirdness' has ceased to be very surprising" (19). We must separate what Ruiz calls the purely "decorative and stereotypical aspects" of Surrealism (Buci-Glucksmann 103) — the banally monstrous or magical imagery that today floods television, graphic design and films — from the deeper and more fertile Surreal impulse.

Surrealism, in the truest sense, is not a mere immersion in fantasy life — the world of dreams, or pure imagination. It seeks what Breton called *absolute reality* or the *marvelous*. The properly Surreal realm is that of daily life — but daily life freed from the stranglehold of the reality principle, and invaded by the forces of love, the unconscious, and what Schuster calls "the indestructible nature of the interior poetic voice" (23). Surrealism is not about *escaping* into the imaginary (which would align it with the worst tendency of Hollywood fantasy); it celebrates the (sometimes fleeting) *triumph* of the imagination in a world so battened down by misery, oppression, and repression. It would take a true artist of Surrealist sensibility, the Czech-French poet-essayist Petr Král, to eventually produce, many years later, perhaps the only cogent critical "transcendence" of this Surrealist code from within the movement itself:

> Surrealism uses an *a priori* formula in order to declare the presence of mystery. Now, for me, what is proper to the unveiling of mystery is the "unforeseen encounter." ... My withdrawal from Surrealism came more profoundly from the fact that my walks, my journeys through cities, had the consequence of separating me from the Surrealist practice of the image — which is a sort of spasm, the sudden appearance of the incredible. It was while walking that the intimate texture of reality hit me.... Working with the things all around you takes you somewhere — even if it's simply the street where you live — whereas the Surrealist image is a sudden "hole" that leaves you exactly where you began [Laugier].

Král's oscillation between an "other world" as revealed by Surrealist practices of the image, and the daily, concrete world as it must be divined and celebrated takes us to the very heart of the attraction of cinema as a Surrealist medium. Filmmakers have always been torn — sometimes with great unease — between two extreme poles of the cinematic medium. If they try to make a film of pure, synthetic fantasy, there is always too much heavy, material reality on display, something too common or unglamorous mercilessly magnified by the camera's cold, photographic eye. Conversely, attempts at making the bleakest, grittiest, "kitchen sink" drama on film are invariably betrayed by something inherently, inescapably magical in the *photogénie* of which Epstein spoke, which is so characteristic of cinema — this capacity to take even the most banal object and make it seem abstract, weightless, and boundlessly mysterious on the big screen. Ultimately, for the Surrealists and their various spiritually sympathetic "fellow travelers," this very *impurity* of the cinematic medium destined it to capture the messy, vital interpenetration of reality and the marvelous.

Surrealist cinema bears little relation to most of the classic *avant-garde* movements of the last century. It is not a film form tempted by total abstraction or impressionism, nor is it drawn to neatly Expressionist or Symbolist modes where visual "weirdness" is accompanied by an esoteric, analytic key. (The films of Jean Cocteau, Sergei Paradjanov, and Roman Polanski, while influenced by Surrealism, lean more towards this Symbolist mode.) Much Surrealist cinema is — surprisingly — remarkably wedded to photographic representationalism of a fairly conventional kind, at least as a baseline premise for many of its operations. In Surrealist cinema, quite simply, *reality surprises us*. That is why Surrealist filmmakers are just as fond of making kooky documentaries (like Jean Vigo's *À Propos de Nice*, 1930; Buñuel's *Las Hurdes*, 1932; or Peter Greenaway's *Act of God*, 1980) as fictional fables.

A true map of the relationship between Surrealism and cinema must show two intertwining paths. The first path embraces those films made under the historic sign of Surrealism. One must avoid restricting this list to a handful of official classics, however, like *Entr'acte* (Rene Clair, 1924), *La Coquille et le Clergyman* (Germaine Dulac and Antonin Artaud, 1927), *Rose Hobart* (Joseph Cornell, 1939), and *Anemic Cinema* (Marcel Duchamp, 1925). The net must be spread far and wide enough to gather films by lesser-known latter-day Surrealists such as Robert Benayoun (*Paris n'existe pas*, 1969), Ado Kyrou (*The Monk*, 1972), and the important feminist filmmaker Nelly Kaplan (*The Pirate's Fiancée*, 1969; *Néa*, 1976). Also in this group are the animated and live-action features of Walerian Borowczyk (*Les Jeux des Anges*, 1964, *Goto, the Island of Love*, 1969); the Japanese *avant-gardist* Toshio Matsumoto (*Funeral Parade of Roses*, 1969); and the prodigious œuvre of the radical anthropological filmmaker and "dancing Socrates," Jean Rouch (*Les Maîtres Fous*, 1955; *Jaguar*, 1971).

The second path is of those films which have been (or can be) viewed in a Surrealist manner. The history of the Surrealist *experience* of movies is a grand one indeed. Exploring this history widens our perception of what Surrealism was (and still is) about — not just paintings, sculptures, drawings, and films, but reviews, homages, ravings, poems, and games. Surrealism proposes a *theory of experience*— a set of suggestions about how to perceive the world in a suitably intoxicated manner (whether intoxicated by love, drugs, poetry, or political rage). It is here that Tod Browning enters, through the side door, as it were, into the history of Surrealism. His films were flagged as something to see by the original Surrealists who admired *Dracula* (1930), through Jacques Brunius who belatedly enjoyed *Freaks* and *The Devil-Doll* on UK television, and the literary critic Michael Richardson in his recent survey *Surrealism and Cinema*, for whom Browning is the only filmmaker to "ever come close to giving form to the sort of glacial cruelty which Lautréamont's Maldoror specializes in" (68).

In one of the most famous texts of Surrealism, Salvador Dalí in 1930 advocated a practice of *paranoiac criticism*. "It is enough that the delirium of interpretation should have linked together the implications of the images of the different pictures covering a wall for the real existence of this link to be no longer deniable" (98). The critic or viewer creates the meaning and being of a work through the prodigious exercise of his or her imagination, in a kind of projective delirium; the result is not mere delusion but an apprehension of the truer, deeper, more marvelous reality lying dormant within the work. Dalí's idea was the basis, twenty years later, for the Surrealist game of *irrational enlargement* applied to random films: asking each other all manner of inventive questions (such as "At what moment should a snowfall take place?" and "How and when did you come into the film?"), a group of Surrealists would compile their various responses into an *objective-internal* account of the film (Hammond 74–80). Roger Cardinal has called these various Surrealist methods "a kind of errant dream-criticism" (114).

Ultimately, the best picture of Surrealist cinema can only be formed from an imaginative amalgam of the films that Surrealists make with those that they love and eulogize. Four key elements of this "dream-cinema" can be usefully emphasized:

> 1. *Artificiality.* Surrealists have always worshipped "tacky," cheaply made B films, whose tricks and bursting seams are completely evident — not in a derisive, camp fashion, but in a quite sublime way. Schuster warned the world in 1951 that "the better a film is made the more dangerous it becomes" (Shadow 80). B films — particularly in popular genres like fantasy, horror, film noir, science fiction, and the musical — can reach the heights of dream-like abstraction precisely *because* they are so blatantly artificial. Moreover, they are Surrealist in (usu-

ally) an *involuntary*, not self-conscious manner. And — best of all — they are virtually *anonymous* works in the eyes of official culture, filling DVD shops today the way they filled the cinemas of Paris immediately after the end of World War II, silently and prolifically.

2. *Hyperlogic*. According to Schuster, "At Surrealism's origins was a quest for ... a *meta-reason*— the need to draw on the most secret wellsprings of thought to disengage a new logic founded on the ruins of rationalism" (23). Thus, Surrealism is not a form of irrationalism or pure absurdism, but a search for a *hyperlogic*, a dizzying, revelatory version of psychoanalytic free association. Narrative cinema, with its ceaseless movements between discrete shots, scenes, times and spaces, tips easily into a deranged hyperlogic. *Un Chien Andalou* is based entirely on such a logic; so, too, is Resnais's *L'Année Derniere a Marienbad* (*Last Year at Marienbad*, 1962).

3. *Intensity*. Even when Surrealism is at its most light-hearted, it embodies a seriousness of purpose — a deep investment in the signs of a free imagination, whenever and wherever it breaks out. Searingly serious emotional intensity — bordering on complete paranoia and psychosis — governs many Surrealist favorites, from the astonishing Hollywood romance *Peter Ibbetson* (Henry Hathaway, 1935) to the sole film directed by Charles Laughton, *The Night of the Hunter* (1955). And, although realist or naturalist cinema rarely offers much to Surrealist taste, a newer form of mainstream *hyper-realism* has refound a certain crazy, high-pitched, near-hysterical intensity — for instance, in the unbridled excess of an Oliver Stone.

4. *Innocence*. Surrealism's interest in the naive or "outsider" art of children and the mentally disturbed (as well as the related interest in primitive art) is well known. All these creative expressions are characterized by a much longed-for innocence. So, too, with cinema, where such a passion is often accompanied by a pointed nostalgia. In 1949 Brunius celebrated the "childlike naiveté of yesterday's pioneers" in silent cinema, and lamented that "it is becoming almost impossible to compose a programme for children" (109–110). In our cynical, hyper-self-conscious postmodern age, innocence is even harder to come by; jaded Western filmgoers today inevitably find themselves fleeing, in their imaginations, to the popular cinemas of Bollywood or Hong Kong for a dose of what they are sorely lacking.

This listing of attributes points to why *The Devil-Doll* was able to become an incident in the history of Surrealism. Disreputable genre, artificiality, hyperlogic, intensity, innocence: it is all there, in varied, shifting combinations, with its center constantly displaced or suddenly condensed, as in a dream. It offers (intentionally or not) a species of free association between artificial bits and pieces — a kind of crazy montage between nominal pieces of plot, character, tone, and idea — and an opening to unconscious processes of various sorts. Let us add that one final piece of interference, occurring far beyond Browning's death, which might be regarded as the ultimate indignity visited upon *The Devil-Doll*, but in fact ensures the film's Surrealistic veneer: a garish, inconsistent, and hyper-fake colorization for television of Leonard Smith's black-and-white cinematography!

My emphasis on innocence will give some connoisseurs of Surrealism ground for debate. Several commentators have noted a fundamental, dialectical opposition at the heart of Surrealism's history: the opposition between Breton and Georges Bataille (author of *Story of the Eye*), who rallied his own dissident Surrealist group in the '30s. Schuster remarks, "You could say that a common desire to accede to the sacred proceeded along different paths: in Bataille the path of sacrifice, with representations of mutilation, ritual murder; and in Breton via a cult of the marvelous, a provocative openness towards poetry, be it aided by objective chance, amorous passion or simply artistic emotion" (23).

Much discussion of Surrealism since the '70s has taken the form of a fervent rehabilitation of Bataille — and a wider tradition that includes Antonin Artaud's asylum writings, Jacques Vaché's black "umour," Hans Bellmer's pornographic dolls, Michel Leiris's autobiography *Manhood*, Jacques Lacan's psychoanalysis of the alienated human condition, and even the counter-cultural fantasies of American novelist William Burroughs. Such work has emphasized the perverse, Gothic, violent, and monstrous aspects of the free imagination; in Surrealism's artificial night, this tradition is its black sun. It is seemingly under the sign of Bataille that many dark, contemporary Surrealist films have appeared, from those of Cronenberg (*Naked Lunch*, 1992) and Lynch (*Blue Velvet*, 1986) to Ruiz's *City of Pirates* (1983). Such works enact the bleak politics of Surrealist transgression — a tearing open of bodies, and a voyage of no return into furiously alienated minds.

In entering this black Surrealist tradition, however, we are perhaps in danger of entirely overlooking Breton's "provocative openness towards poetry" — and its particular resonance within movies and popular culture generally. The Surrealism of George Herriman's *Krazy Kat* comics, Daffy Duck cartoons, *Mad* magazine in the '50s or Sam Raimi's delirious horror film *Evil Dead II* (1987) offers a special kind of imaginative liberation. While often blackly humorous and full of social rage, this Surrealism is also light, airy, and supremely comic. It urges us to let go of brutal reason and a consistent ego. Surrealists have always loved the "walking undead" of the cinema, from

Boris Karloff to the zombies of George Romero's *Night of the Living Dead* films. This is doubtless because the merry undead live out the fine Surrealist message once delivered by Ado Kyrou — that "with everything possible, everything is fundamentally simple" (45).

So let us turn back to Browning with this credo in mind: everything possible, everything simple. The bodies in *The Devil-Doll* are a strange assortment: shrunken bodies, transvestite bodies ... what are we to make of them? It would seem logical to place Browning within the Bataille tradition, especially given the emphasis on perversity. But if Surrealism, across the full gamut of its aesthetic and philosophical possibilities, can teach us anything, it is surely that cinema imagery, however apparently black or perverse, cannot justly be probed, diagnosed, or attacked too literally. If one takes a literal approach, if one reads purely what one sees at first glance, then it is easy to fall into a moralistic, disapproving intolerance, finding evidence at every turn that Surrealism is (variously) repressive, punishing, and death-driven, the privileged libertine pastime of an exclusivist social cult — powered solely by anxiety, homophobia, misogyny, and alienation (the usual suspects). We are soon back with the "problematic" equivocations and precarious intellectual-agenda balancing acts with which we began....

But this line of attack is hard to sustain once it is grasped that Surrealism sets out to teach us, first and foremost, that appearances are never merely appearances: that they are, in fact, often veils, pretexts, metaphors, fleeting incarnations or simmering apparitions of some deeper, broader feeling or impulse. Another great, playful, and quizzical Surrealist slogan, this one borrowed from a Romantic era of art, literature and philosophy long predating Surrealism is that *life is a dream*, meaning that this world, the waking world, is the illusion, the temporary housing, while the dream world is the truly real and collective realm that we only get to glimpse and frolic in while sleeping. Like the happiness of Lachna as she awakes and stretches ...

It is along this fugitive path that we must explore *The Devil-Doll*'s spontaneously Surreal depictions and evocations of eroticism, violence, and transgression — the stuff that is so often labeled sick or suspicious by an ideologically-driven contemporary critique. No doubt there are some very murky things stirring in Browning's imagination, stoked as it was by the "blackouts" of his alcoholic experience. As in the films of Abel Ferrara, an only dimly-acknowledged phantasy of incest stalks *The Devil Doll*'s scenario in which a father makes himself known to his daughter only via another guise, another body and identity (in this especially devious case, as a woman!). But the harm done to bodies in art and culture — at least when seen from the eternal Surrealist view — is less literal violation than a more figurative escape and abandonment, a less "heated" realm of psychic fantasy.

We hear a lot these days about the classical storytelling principle of the journey: the need for the hero to make a definite trip — often a literal, physical, action-based journey in which the hero wins something, gains something, and finds him or herself in the process. The motif of the journey, however, can be rescued and rewritten from a Surrealist perspective. *The Devil-Doll*, after all, is quite a journey: escape from prison, trip to Paris, going underground, change of identity....

Surrealists have always loved certain kinds of mythic journeys and adventures: Alice's voyage in Wonderland, the Pilgrim's Progress, the Odyssey, the Stations of the Cross, or *Fantastic Voyage* (1966), in which a miniaturized spaceship travels through the inside of a human body. But the Surreal journey is one that is inflected in a particular way, with a certain aspect played up: the element of transformation, metamorphosis. And the character arcs so beloved of conventional screenwriting wisdom also hold Surreal possibility, since the more characters change, the more likely they are to "get out" of themselves and escape their sanctioned social roles. That is what being "transported" as a spectator by a film — taken somewhere within the emotional and imaginary ride created by a feature narrative — is (or can be) all about.

Once, trying to formulate the particular philosophy, the world-view, of Surrealism, I found myself pondering the usual options. On the one hand, Surrealism is definitely not religious; it has always proudly, fiercely held to the creed of "no God the Father." And its metaphysic is very particular, very concrete; in a fundamental sense, it is grounded in the world, in reality. And it is political in nature, more left-wing political than anything else; in its different forms and phases around the globe it has been anarchist, socialist, Marxist.... So, could we call Surrealism *materialist*? Well, yes, but then again no, because that sounds like not much fun, too dour, too strict, too rigid.

Surrealism is about the invisible world, the other world, as much as it is about the visible world. It is about the invisible inside the visible, the invisible that charges up the visible. And because Surrealism is about this animating force of feeling, of desire, of emotional investment, it can also be said that it is an *ecstatic* philosophy. Not about religious spiritualism, but certainly about trances and transport, dreams and visions, the unconscious. If there is a mysticism in Surrealism — and many Surrealists have been drawn, theoretically or practically, to phenomena like drugs, voodoo, and magical ritual — then it is a proudly secular or earthly, earthy mysticism. And if there is materialism in Surrealism, it surely has to be an *ecstatic materialism*. This is the way that cinephilia participates in the eternal, ongoing adventure and experiment of Surrealism — and Tod Browning is one of the finest traveling companions for the trip.

This essay draws upon work on cinema and Surrealism first presented in a catalogue for the Australian National Gallery in 1993, and in a lecture at the Brisbane International Film Festival in 1999.

Works Cited

Benayoun, Robert. "Le Cinéma et Nous." *Positif* 240 (March 1981), 48–50.
Benjamin, Walter. "Surrealism." *Selected Writings Volume 2: 1927–1934*. Cambridge: Harvard University Press, 1999, 207–21.
Brunius, Jacques. "Experimental Film in France." *Experiment in the Film*. Ed. Roger Manvell. London: The Grey Walls Press, 1949, 60–112.
Buci-Glucksmann, Christine, and Fabrice Revault D'Allones. *Raoul Ruiz*. Paris: Éditions Dis Voir, 1987.
Cardinal, Roger. "Pausing Over Peripheral Detail." *Framework* 30/31 (1986): 112–30.
Dalí, Salvador. "The Stinking Ass." *Surrealists on Art*. Ed. Lucy R. Lippard. New Jersey: Prentice Hall, 1970, 97–100.
Debord, Guy. "Report on the Construction of Situations and on the International Situationist Tendency's Conditions of Organization and Action." *Situationist International Anthology*. Ed. Ken Knabb. Berkeley: Bureau of Public Secrets, 1981, 17–25.
Epstein, Jean. "Magnification and Other Writings." *October* 3 (1977), 9–25.
Hammond, Paul (ed.). *The Shadow and Its Shadow: Surrealist Writings on the Cinema*. Ed. Paul Hammond. San Francisco: City Lights Books, 2000.
Herzogenrath, Bernd (ed.). *The Films of Tod Browning*. London: Black Dog, 2006.
Kyrou, Ado. "The Marvelous Is Popular." *Surrealism and Its Popular Accomplices*. Ed. Franklin Rosemont. San Francisco: City Lights Books, 1980, 45.
Laugier, Emmanuel. "Detours par l'Antichambre de Petr Král." *Le Matricule des Anges* 23 (June/July 1998). No longer archived online.
Norden, Martin F., and Madeleine A. Cahill. "Violence, Women, and Disability in Tod Browning's *Freaks* and *The Devil-Doll*: The Shows of Violence." *The Journal of Popular Film and Television* (Summer 1998): 86–94.
Ollier, Claude. *Souvenirs Ecran*. Paris: Cahiers du Cinéma/Gallimard, 1981.
Richardson, Michael. *Surrealism and Cinema*. London: Berg, 2006.
Schuster, Jean. "Specialists in Revolt." *New Statesman*, 2958 (December 4, 1987), 23–24.
Scutenaire, Louis. "Inscriptions." *Surrealism and Its Popular Accomplices*. Ed. Franklin Rosemont. San Francisco: City Lights Books, 1980, 102.
Sobchack, Vivian. "Tod Browning: An Overview Long Past." (Herzogenrath 21–40).
Wood, Bret. "The *Witch*, The *Devil* and The Code." *Film Comment* (November–December 1992), 52–56.

Miracles for Sale and Other Films of Detection and the Occult

MARCEL ARBEIT

Miracles for Sale (1939), Tod Browning's last directorial item, is definitely one of his most underestimated and least analyzed movies. Even the most comprehensive sources devote only a few unsubstantial remarks to it. Stuart Rosenthal, in his study for *The Hollywood Professionals* series, labels the film "a fairly routine mystery against a background of the occult" (50). Save the introductory scene with its original sawing-a-woman-in-half stunt, it is, for Rosenthal, in the pejorative sense "the only Browning production that really looks like an M-G-M studio job" (49). David J. Skal and Elias Savada give several interesting facts concerning the movie (for example, the complaint from the Pacific Coast Association of Magicians against the revelation of stage-magic techniques, and the censor's rejection of the film in Sweden), but otherwise dismiss it as "a rather transparent comedy melodrama" (203). Only Stefanie Diekmann and Ekkehard Knörer give it some justice, praising it as "a marvelous swan song ... which in the farcical form of a screwball comedy conjures up a world of traps and sleights of hand, of crookery and trickery" (76).

Vivian Sobchack, in her overview of Tod Browning's films, singles out three main genre categories: crook melodramas, exotic melodramas and bizarre melodramas. As an addition, she gives a fourth, minor category: mystery melodramas "that deal with solving a crime (usually a murder), often debunking supernatural exploitations in the process" (22). This fourth category connects *Miracles for Sale* with another neglected Browning movie, *The Thirteenth Chair* (1929), as well as with his *Mark of the Vampire* (1935).

However, *Miracles for Sale* does not fit the pattern of melodrama, the genre which Browning mastered so flawlessly, very well. It is a mystery, and of a specific type — the locked-room story of detection. In a locked New York hotel room the body of Cesare Sabbat, a famous occultist and sorcerer who planned to evoke a demon in front of his skeptical audience, is found by three of those invited to watch the experiment: Michael Morgan (played by Robert Young), who designs and sells equipment for professional magicians; Colonel Watrous, a British expert on various psychic phenomena; and Madame Rapport, an internationally acknowledged spirit medium. Later, several other masters of magic appear at or near the place of the murder: Mr. Tauro, the Card King; Zelma LaClaire, the woman with the radio mind and Sabbat's lover; and her jealous husband Alfred, who performs the mind-reading stunts with her. The suspects also include David Duvallo, the master of escape, and Judy Barclay, a young lady who tries to persuade Morgan to keep Madame Rapport out of the business, and in the course of the story is found to be Madame Rapport's younger sister. The major twist in the story occurs when the prime suspect, Tauro, who managed to elude the police, is found dead in his flat, and the investigation shows that he was killed even before the man he was supposed to have murdered.

Miracles for Sale is a loose adaptation of *Death from a Top Hat* (1938), the first novel by Clayton Rawson (1906–1971), a commercial artist, illustrator and practicing magician who regularly performed at the evenings of the Society of American Magicians. As his son Hugh recollects, "it occurred to Rawson that since a murderer trying to escape detection must use the same principles of deception that a magician employs, a magician would make the perfect fictional detective" (6). Browning himself seemed to have rich experience with the world of tricks and magic. As Skal and Savada note, as a young boy he was employed as a handcuff-escape artist, and at the turn of the century he even performed as the Hypnotic Living Corpse. In this act, which was a part of a river show, he was put into a trance by a hypnotist and buried several feet under the ground for as long as two days. During that time people could watch him through a wooden shaft through which fresh air could get to him. Around 1905 Browning was claimed to have performed with the magician and illusionist Leon Herrmann, whose routines, like those of his uncles Carl and Andre, were described both in Browning's movies and Rawson's novels. According to some (albeit not very reliable) sources, Browning also cooperated with a popular Chinese or Mongolian magician in an act involving a mysteriously appearing and disappearing goldfish bowl (see Skal and Savada 24–29).

As is common in the detective genre, the crime in *Death from a Top Hat* is investigated at the same time by the police and by an amateur sleuth who has the advantage of being familiar with the world of the victims and the murderer, even knowing most of the suspects personally. While in some stories in the genre the investigations are parallel and there is animosity between both parties, here the official and unofficial arms of the law act in accord and, despite occasional problems, learn from each other. The amateur detective is The Great Merlini, the owner of a New York magic shop, inventor of numerous magic tricks, and chairman of the American Scientists Psychic Investigating Committee, the aim of which is to expose fraudulent psychics, clairvoyants and mediums.[1] He collaborates with law enforcers on a daily basis; at the Police College he lectures on card tricks and the methods of con artists. Merlini's major police force ally in *Death from a Top Hat* is Inspector Homer Gavigan (in the movie renamed Marty), a neurotic and skeptical Irishman for whom the environment in which he must investigate is completely alien; in spite of that, however, his scientific methods contribute to the solution of the mystery more than it seems at first. In the film, the energetic and rational Gavigan, who fires questions at suspects in rapid succession and hates any cracks about the supernatural, even betrays in an unguarded moment that his grandmother believed in ghosts, and he now surprisingly fears that during a staged séance the medium might produce a real one.

The novel literally swarms with policemen: besides Gavigan, there are three members of his team, three other detective investigators, a dactylographer named Brady, and coroner Hess (whose hobby, appropriate under the circumstances, is card tricks). Browning left Gavigan with only one assistant — the clumsy and scarcely competent Detective Quinn. Their team includes a grumbling coroner who, facing the task of examining a corpse in the dark, complains that he is "not a bat," and a technician who briskly finds out why no lights in the room are in order, having discovered pennies in every bulb socket.

The annals do not betray why The Great Merlini was renamed Michael Morgan by Harry Ruskin, Marion Parsonnet, and James Edward Grant, who are credited for the film script. In any case, the change of the name deprived the film not only of Rawson's allusion to Merlin of the Arthurian legends, but also of a nod to Lon Chaney, the favorite Browning actor, who was as early as 1919 dubbed by an anonymous journalist "the Merlin of the Movies" (see Solomon 56).

A much more crucial change from the novel is the absence of the third investigator and the narrator of the story, Russ Harte, an unsuccessful journalist who serves as a Dr. Watson–like foil to Merlini. The reason is obvious — Harte's questions directed toward his magician friend are mostly identical to those of Inspector Gavigan, and their mutual thirst for information must be quenched by long explanatory passages covering the fields of occultism, demonology, alchemy, magic, and witchcraft (as well as book-collecting, physics, geometry and psychology), which considerably slows the pace of the story.

In the elimination of Harte, Browning's trio of screenwriters was, three years later, followed by Arnaud d'Usseau, who adapted for the screen the last of Rawson's four novels, *No Coffin for the Corpse* (1942), to be directed by Herbert I. Leeds under the title *The Man Who Wouldn't Die* (1942). Besides the disposal of the poor journalist, d'Usseau also considerably diminished the role of The Great Merlini, making him a mere one-time advisor, and employed as a private investigator a sleuth from a completely different world: Michael Shayne, the redheaded Irish detective introduced by Davis Dresser, writing at that time under the pen name Brett Halliday, in his 1939 novel *Dividend on Death*.[2] The presence of Shayne (played by Lloyd Nolan) required not only the change of setting from New York to Florida, but a thorough revision of the plot. The incompatibility of Rawson's fictional world and d'Usseau's scipt is obvious from the film's very first frames: while the novel's introductory chapter gives a comic description of Harte's falling in love, the movie starts with a burial scene — heavy rain and a storm reflect the mood of the characters and create from the beginning a macabre, horror-like atmosphere, one only later alleviated by Shayne's Irish airs and crude jokes. Even though *No Coffin for the Corpse* is a much more cinematic novel than *Death from a Top Hat*, the comparison of Leeds's *The Man Who Wouldn't Die* with *Miracles for Sale* only underscores Browning's mastery in making a relatively static and verbose story extremely lively and amusing.

Like *Death from a Top Hat*, Rawson's *No Coffin for the Corpse* features magicians and fake mediums, but in its focus is the story of a man who could successfully pose as dead and, when buried alive, was able to survive more than one hour in the grave due to his mastering of the technique of "shallow breathing." This man, an Algerian fakir named Zareh Bey, became the pivotal element in the blackmail and murder plot of the wife of the fabulously rich Dudley Wolff; Zareh Bey is double-crossed by the wife and finally dies in a cleverly arranged car accident. Among the supporting characters is the director of the American Psychic Research Laboratories, hired to find what is after death, and at the same time investigate rationally unexplainable psychic phenomena and expose fraudulent mediums.

The novel offers many opportunities for stunning cinematic tricks, from several appearances of a fake ghost to a few examples of poltergeist effects — a vase falling off a mantelpiece, furniture moving or china mysteriously smashed. On top of that, the female villain used to be a medium famous for spirit lights and cold breezes of astral origin. Leeds did not use anything from this promising assortment, and what was left of Rawson's story could not provide any rational justification for the characters' behavior. That is why the screenwriter chose a different victim — a medical doctor instead of the millionaire husband — and abandoned any technical explanation of the few tricks preserved; even the dark figure with shining eyes and a gun in his hand does not remotely look like a ghost.

Strangely enough, d'Usseau and Leeds ignored the romance in *No Coffin for the Corpse* as well. While in the novel Russ Harte dates the tycoon's daughter, wanting to marry her against the will of her father, in the film Mike Shayne is Kay's friend, hired by her to pose as her husband to investigate the mysterious shooting in her bedroom. The Great Merlini, for reasons unknown, is given the civilian name Gus, and, as an elderly magician stereotypically producing rabbits from his hat, is only there to identify the mysterious Zareh Bey. The source of comedy in the film is a bumbling local police chief who repeatedly falls into Shayne's little traps, but later is always patted on his back or shoulder and made to believe that it was his idea which brought the case to a successful conclusion. The result, not even vaguely true to the original book, exposes the ambiguity of what Rawson himself wrote about movies in *No Coffin for the Corpse*: "Anyone who has ever seen a motion picture knows very well that the camera can tell far better lies than anything Ananias ever dreamed up" (115).[3]

The difficulty of Browning's task arose from the fact that Rawson made his *Death from a Top Hat* not only a thrilling and amusing story of detection, but also a popular survey of contemporary and historical magic and occult practices; Rawson even uses footnotes containing bibliographical data and additional facts.[4] Among other explanations and comments, it also paraphrases a lecture about the basic rules of locked-room mystery stories given by John Dickson Carr in his novel *The Three Coffins* (1935). In this part of Carr's novel, generally known as "The Locked-Room Lecture," the author explains seven ways of solving the mystery of a hermetically sealed room, all of them seemingly improbable but, under closer scrutiny, logical. One of the variants employs illusion and impersonation:

> [T]he victim, still thought to be alive, is already lying murdered inside a room, of which the door is under observation. The murderer, either dressed as his victim or mistaken from behind for the victim, hurries in at the door. He whirls round, gets rid of the disguise, and instantly comes out of the room as *himself*.... In any event, he has an alibi; since, when the body is discovered later, the murder is presumed to have taken place some time after the impersonated "victim" entered the room [279, Carr's italics].

This description reads as a skeleton of Rawson's novel, but Browning did not elaborate much on the manner in which the murderer tampered with the door to the locked room (although Gideon Fell, the investigator in Carr's *The Three Coffins*, offers no less than five alternatives of this activity, each of them comprising several options). The greater emphasis of Browning and his screenwriters on the magic aspects of the story even led to the omission of another sealed-room murder. In the novel the second victim is also found in a locked room. This time a window is open and a ladder leaning against the wall is right under it, but this does not make the investigation any easier, as the foot of the ladder is buried in the snow and, although it was not snowing after the deed, there is not a single footprint.

In the film, even the roles and importance of some of the characters are different from the source novel. Not taking into account the change of the names of Tarot into Tauro and Madame Eva Rappourt into Rapport, as well as the inconsistency in the use of the name "Sabbat" (in the phone directory shown on the screen its spelling is the same as in the novel, but in the film credits it is given with "tt" in the end), the most crucial change from the novel was the elevation of the young and beautiful damsel in distress, Judy Barclay, a minor character in Rawson's book, to the leading female character.

Judy, a niece of the murdered Sabbat, turns up in the novel late, in Chapter 16, emerging suddenly in Duvallo's flat while the police are investigating the murder of Tarot, whose body was found there not long ago (in the movie, Tauro was found dead in his own flat). She is held under suspicion, having worked with the late illusionist as his assistant, but seems to have an alibi — she attended the Music Hall movie theater where she saw a "mystery thriller, full of policemen that barked" (Rawson, *Death* 166). In Browning's version, a taxi cab brings Judy in front of Morgan's "Miracles for Sale" shop, and the girl claims that she is being followed, begging Morgan for assistance. This early introduction of Judy into the story brought romance and humor into the film. In the presence of Judy, Morgan is at first uttering cynical remarks like a hard-boiled detective, but in no time he changes into a courteous protector who amuses her in a club by making several sugar bowls vanish right before the eyes of a startled waiter, a version of the "Vanishing Gold Fish Bowl" trick from Browning's youth, and comforting her by joking, "Nothing is ever so bad as it seems; not even that coffee."

Judy's hasty arrival also enabled Browning to include scenes not to be found in the novel, like the one with a mysterious assailant in her hotel room who gets inside through an open window, seen only as a shadow on the wall, or another one in which she can see through the same window the figure of the murdered Dr. Sabbat pointing a revolver at her and, a moment later, vanishing in a cloud of smoke after a blast. After the first of these seeming encounters with the world of the supernatural, Morgan alleviates the tension with another tough-guy cliché: "It's funny, I've never been able to walk out on a woman who is crying."

The opportunity to use more special effects and scare the audience sympathizing with the frightened girl is, however, not the only reason for plot alterations. If Browning and the screenwriters had used the book without considerable changes, they would have had to recycle some of the major themes and techniques used in the director's previous films. In addition to that, some passages in the novel betray that its author was familiar with Tod Browning's earlier films and was influenced by them.

Cesare Sabbat, an expert in demonology and primitive magic, and a collector of rare books on the occult, is described in the novel by the first-person narrator in the following way: "He had an annoying habit of looking suspiciously back over his shoulder when I passed him in the dark hall that made me think of Count Dracula" (Rawson, *Death* 16). Browning takes the hint and stylizes the only two scenes with Sabbat (including the ghost scene in which Sabbat is impersonated by his murderer), neither of which appears in the book, accordingly—after his masterpiece. Bela Lugosi as Dracula is suggested by Sabbat's posture, attire, and foreign accent—and in the novel it is explicitly mentioned that Sabbat had spent ten years in Hungary, not very far from the vampirish Count's Transylvania. In another passage, Merlini compares Sabbat with Lon Chaney: "He even had the traditional sword and sprigs of garlic on his door as a vampire preventive. Odd, because he looked a bit vampirish himself. There was a Lon Chaney–Boris Karloff feel to him" (61). This clearly alludes to another of Browning's vampire movies that is also a story of detection—*London After Midnight* (1927), now lost, with Chaney in the triple role of detective, Colonel and Mooney the vampire. Another subtle allusion to a Browning film can be found near the end of Rawson's novel where The Great Merlini clarifies to Gavigan that even the most famous magicians and impersonators learned some methods "from the old-time carnival freaks" (285). To substitute Rawson's namedropping in other scenes, Browning let Mike Morgan appreciate Gavigan's performance when he was throwing bait to the suspects as so compelling that "Barrymore wouldn't lose any sleep over it." In the book, Barrymore is not mentioned in this context, but Merlini comments at one point: "The Inspector is something of an actor, himself.... That was a very good exit" (155).

In *Death from a Top Hat*, Rawson drew a comparison between magicians and filmmakers—both equally deceive their audience, using their knowledge of science and psychology: "Even a trained observer cannot possibly see more than a portion of the things within his view at one time, nor can he look in more than one direction at a time. It only remains to place the device or stratagem that works the trick among those things that are not seen, or if seen, not properly observed" (104). In detective stories and horrors, a change of the camera angle or the use of a different kind of shot can increase or decrease suspense, show the audience what protagonists are not able to see, or, conversely, hide some important details from the viewers. Rawson takes the parallel further when Merlini explains to Gavigan the principle of ventriloquism: "The ear depends on the eye for the localization of sound, and when the dummy's mouth is synchronized with his patter it *looks* and, thus, sounds as if he were speaking. Talking pictures utilize the same principle...." (197, Rawson's italics). Sometimes Rawson seems to mock Browning alone — for example, when he attributes the performance of the Buried Alive stunt for which the director used to be famous to the murderer who, when young, enjoyed enormous self-confidence until something went wrong during the act. The motives that make, according to Merlini, great magicians might be the same as those producing great actors and directors: "I've a little theory ... that conjuring as a hobby appeals most to people with inferiority complexes. And the more they overcompensate the better magicians they make" (264).

All three of Browning's films of detection have a common denominator: the murderers cannot be brought to trial, as there is no direct evidence against them, so the only way to catch them is to make them confess. In the world of magic and the occult, it can be done in three ways: (1) through hypnosis, (2) through a cunningly staged performance that makes the villains believe in supernatural forces able to punish them more severely than human justice could, or (3) by pushing them into a monitored attempt at a new crime during which they could be caught red-handed and immediately arrested. However, hypnosis or staged performances implying the existence of the supernatural might be used by the criminals as well, and not only if they are magicians themselves, as is the case in *Miracles for Sale*. Lynn Biederstadt, analyzing another of The Great Merlini novels, notices:

> Criminals and magicians have more in common than is immediately apparent. Magic is the art of misdirection. The magician is the ultimate thief: he steals from time, from sight, from attention.... Murder — premeditated murder — is the supreme attempt at misdirection. The sleight-of-hand which relieves the subject of his life must be flawless..." [v–vi].

Maybe this is the reason why Browning, a magician at heart, focused more on crooks than on men of law. If there are policemen, they are shown as ardent but not very efficient, and definitely as no match for the villains with whom they often communicate without being able to disclose their true identity. Most of them are flat comic characters, dangerously close to stereotypical cops in slapstick comedies, the genre that ruled the early stage of Browning's career.[5] For example, in the silent version of *Outside the Law* (1920), Molly, a gangster's daughter and skillful pickpocket and thief, performs with her accomplice a daring theft of a necklace from a rich man's house. The police know about the planned robbery well in advance, as Molly is to be framed by her father's enemy, but do not care much about the aristocrat's possible loss, as the owner did not ask police to protect the valuables, hiring private guards instead. In the melodramatic end, the thieves return the necklace and promise to lead a rightful and decent life. It is surprising how easy it is in Browning's film to undo a crime.[6] In another Browning silent, *The Unholy Three* (1925), Professor Echo, a ventriloquist who invents a clever scheme to rob rich people, avoids a prison sentence through a public confession — as the intertitle says, "the Law can be kind," and nobody seems to mind that his plan has cost a human life.

The Unholy Three shows more of police work than any previous Browning film. Investigating policemen interrogate occupants of the house where an expensive necklace with precious red rubies was stolen and its owner brutally murdered, and later question the prime suspect, an innocent shop assistant selected by the unscrupulous criminals as a scapegoat, at police headquarters. The room where the cross-examination is held has a surprisingly cozy atmosphere; we can see peaceful-looking bookcases and two detectives casually talking, the shadow of one of them projected on the open door into the next room. However, the dominant scene involving a police investigator — he even gets a name, Regan, for this purpose — takes place in the pet shop that serves as a cover for criminal activities of the "unholy" threesome.

Regan comes to question the owner of the shop, not having the slightest suspicion that the old lady is a male ventriloquist in drag, and the little child sitting on the floor, playing with a small wooden locomotive, is a treacherous and vengeful dwarf named Tweedledee. While Regan talks to the "lady," the dwarf exposes the stolen necklace, hastily hiding it inside a toy elephant. The policeman does not notice the clever maneuver, but later compulsively touches the head of the elephant with his shoe. The suspense culminates when he takes the animal and finds out that something rattles inside. Despite all odds, the robbers manage to fool him, and the toy is swiftly returned to the dwarf, who pretends to put a candy in his mouth. The fake father of the "baby" even threatens the investigator, telling him, "I hate to see anybody tease a baby."

An almost identical situation, demonstrating the slow wit of policemen, can be seen in *The Devil-Doll* (1936) — according to Boris Henry, "a hymn to the ridiculousness of the police force" (Henry 43). In this blend of science fiction, criminal drama and revenge melodrama, Paul Lavond, a former banker and an escaped convict who wants to retaliate against three former associates of his who framed him seventeen years ago, joins forces with the wife of his fellow prisoner, who discovered a formula for miniaturizing people. While in *The Unholy Three* it was the dwarf who, posing as a baby in a pram, found where the jewels were kept, in *The Devil-Doll* the thefts are performed by minuscule humans controlled by the domineering wills of their masters. The investigator from the prefecture (the story is set in Paris) visits the toy shop that sells miraculously life-like dolls, one of which was, on the previous day, delivered to a man who several hours later became mysteriously paralyzed. Again, the stolen jewels, including a rare green sea emerald, are hidden in a toy, and again the criminals pretend that there are candies inside. In this case, the policeman wants to buy a rattling toy, a painted clown with a removable head, and the danger is averted only after Lavond persuades him that his daughter will definitely prefer a toy animal to a clown. Against tricks and misused science the police are helpless: four guards are unable to protect the last intended victim of Lavond's against his former accomplice turned miniaturized assassin. Lavond, as the elderly Madame Mandilip, gives his opinion of the police: "I always thought policemen were terrible men who went around with pistols in their pockets, always ready to drag somebody to prison." Like Professor Echo, Lavond never returns to jail, although his revenge left one person miniaturized and another crippled — as if his previous, undeserved punishment were a subscription for the future crimes.

Those who considered Browning's crook melodramas morally dubious were much happier when tricks and elaborately staged performances were finally used by the "good guys" against the villains. Detective stories may be free of moralizing, but at least the rules of the genre demand that evil be condemned and properly penalized. In Rawson's *Death from a Top Hat*, the murderer, who is himself a very skilled magician and master of escapes and impersonations, is led by Merlini to believe that his unwitting partner in crime (who was hypnotically pre-programmed to switch on the light in the corridor at a particular time) will tell the truth during a police-observed hypnotic session scheduled for the next day. Then the murderer is given an opportunity to kill the witness during an evening performance at which the desired victim is supposed to present the dangerous "Great Bullet Catching Feat" (i.e. catch a flying bullet between his teeth).

This trick, in the past a climax of the Herrmann family's performances, required a swift replacement of live shells marked by randomly chosen members of the audience by blanks. The danger of this act lay in the necessary involvement of several people, the failure of any single one of them meaning a sure death for the person being the target (see Skal and Savada 27–28). In the movie, the one who is being shot at is Judy, who could at any moment remember that the false prestidigitator posing as Tauro fanned cards during a card trick from left to right, and not vice versa as the real Tauro would have done. This simplifies the plot substantially — there is no necessity to dwell too long on the locked room mystery and reveal exactly how the murderer performed the complicated trick (with a handkerchief pulled into the keyhole via a piece of string). Rawson explains the elaborate trick at great length and in considerable detail, but if it were shown on the screen, viewers without technical talent and skill would have missed the point and become bored, while those more practically oriented and gifted would have been given an instruction that could easily be abused.

The present, more intelligible ending also completely rules out hypnosis as the means of conquering people's wills by both criminals and investigators, probably because Browning did not want to use it again after *Mark of the Vampire*, where Professor Zelen (Lionel Barrymore), the amateur helper of fast-talking and resolute Inspector Neumann of Prague, hypnotized the suspect to make him reenact his crime. It might be just a coincidence that in Rawson's *Death from a Top Hat* two important characters are also Czech: the real name of Sabbat is Josef Vanek; while Eva Rappourt, his wife and the fake medium, lived in London as Mrs. Svoboda ("Liberty" in Czech).

In *Mark of the Vampire*, both the hypnosis and the performance preceding it were equally important, as the goal of the plot which demanded the participation of seven people, including the main female protagonist and a faithful butler, was to plant in the mind of the murderer the idea that vampires might really exist. He who branded his victim, Sir Karell, with fake "vampire marks," having "sucked" his blood by means of a heated glass over the wound, relied on the power of superstition within the Carpathian Czech and Slovak community, but eventually became even more susceptible to a belief in supernatural evil than the villagers.[7] *Mark of the Vampire* became an elucidating example of the detective/crime movie that combined all three "magic" methods of convicting a murderer who could not be brought to justice any other way.

In *Miracles for Sale*, an additional simplification was achieved by getting rid of all plot twists connected with ventriloquism for the benefit of other magic and occult tricks. In *Death from a Top Hat* there are as many as five ventriloquists, including the amateur sleuth and the criminal, and one of the characters (Mr. Jones, who was hypnotized by the murderer) even performs under the name of Signor Ecco, which again brings to mind the Lon Chaney character of Professor Echo from *The Unholy Three*. Consequently, the screenwriters completely disposed of the character of Mr. Jones, who in the novel was set as the third victim. On the other hand, they give much more space to a séance as the most efficient method of convicting a murderer.

The séance, during which communication with the victim through a medium is supposed to take place, plays a more important role in the film than in the novel, which corresponds with the more flexible approach of Browning's Morgan, in comparison to Rawson's Merlini, toward the occult. In the movie, Mike Morgan expresses his admiration for good magic tricks and illusions, immediately followed by contempt directed at mediums advertising their abilities to contact the dead: "But I hate these fakers that trade on human suffering and get money from heartbroken widows and mothers." When Colonel Watrous, usually very skeptical about the supernatural powers of humans, refers to Morgan as "a famous unbeliever," the magician-detective laconically states: "I just don't believe in ghosts, that's all." To Madame Rapport, the medium who designates Morgan as a man "who has done more in America to ridicule our [psychics'] efforts," he replies: "Sincere workers I gladly help, but you're a fake."

In spite of this harsh statement, Morgan organizes an impromptu séance in which Madame Rapport evokes the ghost of the murdered Sabbat, who tells the participants (by rapping the usual one for "yes" and two for "no") that the man who killed him was, and at the same time was not, Tauro (who, as the investigation showed, was really killed before Sabbat), and that the one who holds the key to the murders is Judy. During the séance, which was an addition to Rawson's story, there is absolute silence as Sabbat's astral body gradually becomes visible and, only after all those present can clearly recognize him, the medium shrieks and collapses causing the image to vanish. Morgan then, without any further elaboration, explains to Gavigan: "It was not real. I've been working on a ghost illusion for months." A better comment on the seeming incongruity between the magician's contempt for mediums and the esteem in which he holds some of them, can be found in the novel: "But you mustn't forget that the great majority of mediums are female and that the magic profession has the fraudulent ones among them to thank for some of the best and subtlest conjuring devices in the whole field of deception" (*Death* 228).

For Morgan, exposing mediums does not mean that he cannot use them for stage performances when needed. For Browning it was also an excuse for one more use of visual effects that could surprise and scare the audience. The visual imagery of the scene corresponds, for instance, with descriptions of séances in Robert Dale Owen's (1801–1877) classic book on spiritualism *Debatable Land Between This World and the Next* (1872), especially the chapter "A Near Relative Shows Herself, Throughout Five Years, to a Surviving Friend." There Dale, who considered communication between the two worlds a result of hard scientific work, gave detailed accounts of numerous séances in the course of which a Lord Livermore successfully contacted his deceased wife Estelle through a medium in the years 1861 through 1866. Although Dale presented all the procedures and their results in a serious, scholarly fashion, he undermined the effect when, in all earnestness, he described a séance during which, instead of Livermore's wife, Benjamin Franklin appeared, looking exactly like he did in textbooks. Of course, when the occult turns into the comic, there is no way to make it serious again.

On the other hand, rules of the movie business dictate the necessity to add a funny character to alleviate the tension in an occult or horror movie, and for the detective genre it was doubly true. Richard Mealand, a story editor for Paramount Pictures, explained in his article aptly called "Hollywoodunit" that "Hollywood wants to do, in mysteries, either one of two things: scare the living daylights out of the audiences, or roll 'em in the aisles" (299). This makes any film version of a detective novel extremely difficult, as their plots are too intricate and clever, and instead of humor and action, there are descriptions and explanations. Mealand gives, as a prime example of a first-rate detective author whose works are unsuitable for the screen, none else but the master of locked-room mysteries John Dickson Carr, and he also gives a piece of advice to both screenwriters and directors who cannot be talked out of the idea of shooting a detective story: "[A]udiences don't like trickery — unless it's funny" (300). In the case of *Miracles for Sale*, Browning and his screenwriters definitely took this advice to heart, especially after the box-office failure of *Mark of the Vampire*, which disappointed the audience by turning at the last moment from a horror into a crime story.

In *Death from a Top Hat*, the main source of humor is short parodies of the styles of well-known detective authors, starting with Sir Arthur Conan Doyle and E. Phillip Oppenheim, and ending with authors from the hard-boiled school. The humor in *Miracles for Sale* is primarily visual, not verbal. For this reason, the screenwriters created a brand new character, Morgan's father, who journeys, for the first time in his life, from Indiana to New York. The widowed Dad Morgan, who is sixty-two, mistakes a sightseeing tour minibus for a taxi and, not happy that the driver took him to the same place where he boarded the vehicle, makes him proceed to his son's magic shop. Pointing to the inscription on the bus reading "All Over Town for $1," he even refuses to pay the additional fifty cents the desperate driver requires. Such a "country bumpkin" type endowed with natural intelligence and a heart of gold appears frequently across different genres of American literature (and later cinematography) from the mid–19th century, but in Browning's movie he struggles less with the advances of modern technical civilization than with his son's magic machinery, such as the automatic barber, the secret door that opens and closes by uttering the names of Cagliostro and Robert-Houdin, and the levitation machine (which makes a person fly through a ring and keeps them in the air with a halo around their heads and a flag bearing the inscription "The Magic Marcos"). Although at the beginning Dad Morgan claims that New York is the only city he learned to hate in only one day, and for some time cannot get used to the idea of walking the streets armed with a gun, in the end he finds New York his legitimate home and even calls himself a New Yorker.

As I mentioned earlier, Morgan, who sells these miracles and is proud of them, does not believe in ghosts and demons; but when the real skeptics, like Inspector Gavigan, ridicule everything that cannot be explained by reason, Morgan asks them not to laugh too loud: "There is an awful humbug about the occult and the psychic, but plenty of things happen that can't be explained by any of the rules of this world." He is against fake fortune tellers and laughs at the magic power of poison ivy, but "don't kid yourself, for several thousand years the human race has been trying to step across the threshold of the darkness of the unknown — call it the other world if you like — because there's something there once in a while somebody gets pretty close to." Such statements cannot be found in the novel. There, when Colonel Watrous claims that he has discovered "several genuine instances of psychic phenomena, inexplicable on any materialistic basis," Merlini's comment is merely, "He's right when he says that science should take the field of psychical research a bit more seriously" (*Death* 77–78). Surprisingly, his monologues in the movie are remarkably close to the statements of Rosalie LaGrange, the medium in Bayard Veiller's (1869–1943) play *The Thirteenth Chair* (1916, published in 1922), which was the basis for Browning's first talking picture of the same title.[8]

In this play, Rosalie, who is invited to the Crosby home (in the play a rich New York family, in the movie a British family residing in India) to stage a séance that would disclose the name of the murderer of a local high-society womanizer and rascal, answers Mrs. Crosby's question about whether communication with the dead is really just trickery by saying:

> I tell you, madame, most of the time it is tricks, with even the best of us. But there 'ave been times in my life when it was not tricks.... There is a power — a wonderful power — that come to us. But you never can tell when it is coming. And if you waited for it you would starve to death. So when it is not there we use tricks" [Veiller 14].

Rosalie La Grange is not the first medium in Browning's films. In *The Mystic* (1925), a medium named Zara, together with her gypsy colleagues, is hired by an American criminal to cheat a rich young woman of her jewels. Even though Zara is a fake, the séance uncovers another criminal plot and results in her remorse. The pattern is similar to the one in other crook melodramas: the petty criminals realize the monstrosity of someone else's conspiracy, reform themselves, and even save their original mark from being embezzled. However, *The Thirteenth Chair* is Browning's first film, using the occult, that focuses on detection and police investigation, as well as his first locked-room mystery. The gentleman-like but imperious Inspector Donohue uses common methods of investigation, although in the movie he loses most of the humor he is endowed with in the play ("I'm not going to employ the usual police methods. There is to be no threatening or badgering" [Veiller 35]). His amateur counterpart is Rosalie the medium, but only after her daughter Helen is accused of the murders. Browning's version of the story has a completely different ending — even the murderers are not the same, which brings some confusion into the movie because, while Veiller's murderer, a man, was known to be able to throw knives skillfully, the female assassin from the movie could hardly be expected to drive a knife, the murder weapon, into the high ceiling inside the space of a few seconds.

In *The Thirteenth Chair* there are two séances. Before the first one, which ends with the murder of the man who invited her, Rosalie, whose "spirit control" is supposed to be a child she calls Laughing Eyes, reveals to the stunned participants some commonly used tricks. For example, the medium can easily leave the closed circle of people holding hands in the dark, joining the hands of the two people sitting on either side of her, which is a trick mentioned in Rawson's novel as well (see *Death* 201). To hide the fact that the séance has a carefully prepared written script, Rosalie gets her hands tied to the arms of the chair and her ankles to its legs. In *Death from a Top Hat*, Madame Rapport makes the performance even more sophisticated by sitting in a canvas bag drawn around her neck, with the drawstring tied to the back of the chair. Merlini, after hearing a description of the procedure, immediately questions her alibi, since within magic "real facts are just the opposite of what they seem." This séance did not make it into *Miracles for Sale*, as it only had marginal importance in solving the crime, and at the same time it would mean Browning would be recycling material already exploited by him in the past, this time second-, maybe even third-hand.

In *The Thirteenth Chair*, Rosalie's methods of detection are more those of a psychologist than those of a mystic, which makes her similar to Merlini/Morgan. In the movies, they both have personal reasons for solving the crime (although Morgan's love for Judy is missing in the original novel), and they both need the consent of professional police investigators for their experiments—Bela Lugosi, as the skeptical Donohue in *The Thirteenth Chair*, tells Rosalie, who asks him for permission to stage another séance: "What you ask me to let you do is insanity—unheard of." Comparing the two séances that help the amateur sleuths prove the murderers' guilt, Rosalie's is more successful because the murderess confesses immediately after the arm of the corpse "magically" points at the knife in the ceiling, having no idea that the fiancé of the wrongly accused girl put a cane into the dead man's sleeve. Rosalie, at least for one moment, believes that she acquired a supernatural power that helped her locate the murder weapon. It is a disappointment when she finds out that the tappings were not signs from the other world, but ordinary knocks on the door. In the play the séance strikingly resembles that in *Miracles for Sale*. Rosalie makes the spirit of the victim visible, and the murderer, as the production notes say, "follows the spirit he sees moving across the stage until he is C. [in the center] and a little above the table" (Veiller 69). The criminal is frightened, crying desperately, "I can't fight the dead"

(69). Although the murderer in *Miracles for Sale* is much tougher and more intelligent, the atmosphere of the séance grips him and makes him take the information he received as granted, which causes his downfall.

As shown, the similarity between *The Thirteenth Chair* and *Miracles for Sale* goes beyond the genre affinities, the similar layout of the characters and the related methods of deduction; some ideas, details and scenes from the source of the former movie were even used in the latter. As *The Thirteenth Chair* might have been one of the sources that influenced Rawson's novel on which *Miracles for Sale* was based, it made the adaptation an even more challenging task and was, among other reasons, responsible for several changes, omissions and additions in the script. The two movies form points of two triangles in Browning's oeuvre. With *The Mystic*, they form an "occult trilogy," a subcategory in the broader group of his films exploiting the mysterious and supernatural. Together with *Mark of the Vampire*, they form a loose "detection trilogy" that unjustly ranks among the most underestimated of Browning's works, but brought new wind into the director's sails, driven by his usual melodrama of strong emotions, mild perversion, and revenge.

Notes

1. After *Death from a Top Hat* Merlini appeared in three more novels — *The Footprints on the Ceiling* (1939), *The Headless Lady* (1940), and *No Coffin for the Corpse* (1942). The investigating magician also appeared in numerous short stories collected in the volume *The Great Merlini* (1979). In the 1940s Rawson created another amateur private eye of this sort, Don Diavolo, whose cases he introduced under the pen name Stuart Towne.
2. Even before Dresser's death in 1977 the name Brett Halliday became used as a byline for other ghost writers who (from 1958) joined Dresser in spinning Mike Shayne's new cases. See (Green and Finch 636–37).
3. Ananias died for lying to God. See Acts 5:1–11.
4. Footnotes can be found even in *No Coffin for the Corpse*, but there are only seven of them, while *Death from a Top Hat* has nineteen.
5. The exploitation of this genre in Browning's mature movies is discussed in Boris Henry's article "Tod Browning and the Slapstick Genre." See (Henry 41–47).
6. Sobchack draws attention to the fact that criminals escape imprisonment or death in no less than thirteen Browning movies. See (Sobchack 24).
7. For thoughtful and relevant notes on this film see (Sweney 201–07). But although Sir Karell's (in correct Czech it should be Karel; in Slovak, Karol) servants speak Czech, it does not place the setting of the story anywhere near Prague, as Sweney suggests. When there was a serious crime, it was a common practice in Czechoslovakia between the world wars to summon an investigator from Prague even to the remotest regions of the country. At the beginning villagers sing a Slovak folk song, the lyrics of which, not captioned into English, are crucial for the story. The translation is: "I'll die / I'll die / But I don't know which day / I'll die / I'll die / When it comes I don't care // And when I die / I'll stay that way / hop skip tra la la." The refrain of that song is supposed to be fast and cheerful, but villagers in the film sing it very slowly and mournfully, replacing the final line with some unintelligible words, ending with

a cryptic "jako ja" (like myself). While the song is supposed to praise that after death there come rest and peace, the Browning country folk rather seem to regret having been deprived of the privilege of an eternal life, even though as bloodthirsty vampires.

8. *The Thirteenth Chair* was simultaneously released in a silent version as well.

Works Cited

Biderstadt, Lynn. "Introduction." *No Coffin for the Corpse*. v–viii.
Carr, John Dickson. "The Locked-Room Lecture." (Haycraft 273–86).
Diekmann, Stefanie, and Ekkehard Knörer. "The Spectator's Spectacle: Tod Browning's Theatre." (Herzogenrath 69–77).
Green, Joseph, and Jim Finch. *Sleuths, Sidekicks and Stooges: An Annotated Bibliography of Detectives, Their Assistants and Their Rivals in Crime, Mystery and Adventurous Fiction, 1795–1995*. Cambridge: Scolar Press, 1997.
Haycraft, Howard, ed. *The Art of the Mystery Story: A Collection of Critical Essays*. 1946. New York: Carroll & Graf Publishers, 1983.
Henry, Boris. "Tod Browning and the Slapstick Genre." (Herzogenrath 41–47).
Herzogenrath, Bernd, ed. *The Films of Tod Browning*. London: Black Dog Publishing, 2006.
Leeds, Herbert I. *The Man Who Wouldn't Die*. 20th Century–Fox, 1942.
Mealand, Richard. "Hollywoodunit." (Haycraft 298–303).
Owen, Robert Dale. *Debatable Land Between This World and the Next*. 1871. N.p.: Trübner, 1874.
Rawson, Clayton. *Death from a Top Hat*. 1938. New York: International Polygonics, 1986.
_____. *No Coffin for the Corpse*. 1942. Boston: Gregg Press, 1979.
Rawson, Hugh. "About the Author." *Death from a Top Hat*. [5]–[8].
Rosenthal, Stuart. "Tod Browning." *The Hollywood Professionals: Tod Browning and Don Siegel*. London: Tantivy Press, 1975.
Skal, David J., and Elias Savada. *Dark Carnival: The Secret World of Tod Browning, Hollywood's Master of the Macabre*. New York: Anchor Books, 1995.
Sobchack, Vivian. "The Films of Tod Browning: An Overview Long Past." (Herzogenrath 21–39).
Solomon, Matthew. "Staging Deception: Theatrical Illusionism in Browning's Films of the 1920s." (Herzogenrath 49–67).
Sweney, Matthew. "Mark of the Vampire." (Herzogenrath 201–07).
Veiller, Bayard. *The Thirteenth Chair: A Play in Three Acts*. London: Samuel French, 1922.

Filmography

Since different sources give different information, sometimes contradictory, on Tod Browning's involvement, the following is a "consensus list" rather than a complete list of Browning's credits.

1909
Ethel's Luncheon (actor)

1913
Bill Joins the Band (actor)
Scenting a Terrible Crime (actor)
A Fallen Hero (actor)

1914
An Interrupted Séance (actor)
After Her Dough (actor)
Victims of Speed (actor)
The Fatal Dress Suit (actor)
Nearly a Burglar's Bride (actor)
Izzy and the Bandit (actor)
The Scene of His Crime (actor)
A Race for a Bride (actor)
The Man on the Couch (actor)
Neil's Eugenic Wedding (actor)
An Exciting Courtship (actor)
The Last Drink of Whiskey (actor)
Hubby to the Rescue (actor)
The Deceiver (actor)
The White Slave Catchers (actor)
Bill's Job (actor)
Wrong All Around (actor)
How Bill Squared It with His Boss (actor)
Leave It to Smiley (actor)
Bill Takes a Lady Out to Lunch (...Never Again) (actor)
Ethel's Teacher (actor)
Bill Saves the Day (actor)
A Physical Culture Romance (actor)
Bill Organizes a Union (actor)
The Mascot (actor)
Business for Himself (actor)
Foiled Again (actor)
Bill Manages a Prize Fighter (actor)
The Million Dollar Bride (actor)
Bill Spoils a Vacation (actor)
Dizzy Joe's Career (actor)
Bill Joins the W.W.W.'s (actor)
Casey's Vendetta (actor)
Ethel's Roof Party (actor)
Out Again, in Again (actor)
Ethel Has a Steady (actor)
A Corner in Hats (actor)
Mr. Hadley's Uncle (actor)
The Housebreakers (actor)
Bill and Ethel at the Ball (actor)
The Record Breaker (actor)
By the Sun's Rays (director)

1915
The Lucky Transfer (director)
The Slave Girl (director)
An Image of the Past (director)
The Highbinders (director)
The Story of a Story (director)
The Spell of the Poppy (director)
The Electric Alarm (director)

232 FILMOGRAPHY

The Living Death (director)
The Burned Hand (director)
The Woman from Warrens (director)
Little Marie (director)
The Queen of the Band (story)
Sunshine Dad (story)
The Mystery of the Leaping Fish (story)

1916

Puppets (director)
Intolerance: Love's Struggle Throughout the Ages (actor, assistant director)
Everybody's Doing It (director)
The Fatal Glass of Beer (director)
Atta Boy's Last Race (story, scenario)

1917

Jim Bludso (director, scenario)
A Love Sublime (director, scenario)
Hands Up! (director)
Peggy, the Will o' the Wisp (director)
The Jury of Fate (director)

1918

The Eyes of Mystery (director)
The Legion of Death (director)
Revenge (director)
Which Woman? (director)
The Deciding Kiss (director)
The Brazen Beauty (director)
Set Free (director, scenario)

1919

The Wicked Darling (director)
The Exquisite Thief (director)
The Unpainted Woman (director)
The Petal on the Current (director)
Bonnie, Bonnie Lassie (director, scenario)

1920

The Virgin of Stamboul (director, scenario)
Outside the Law (director, producer, story, scenario)

1921

No Woman Knows (director, producer, scenario)

1922

The Wise Kid (director)
Man Under Cover (director)
Under Two Flags (director)

1923

Drifting (director)
The Day of Faith (director)
White Tiger (director, story, scenario)

1924

The Dangerous Flirt (director)
Silk Stocking Sal (director)

1925

The Unholy Three (director, producer)
The Mystic (director, producer, story)
Dollar Down (director)

1926

The Black Bird (director, producer, story)
The Road to Mandalay (director, producer, story)

1927

The Show (director, producer)
The Unknown (director, producer, story)
London After Midnight (director, producer, story, scenario)

1928

The Big City (director, producer, story)
West of Zanzibar (director, producer)

1929

Where East Is East (director)
The Thirteenth Chair (director, producer)

1930

Outside the Law ("remake" of Browning's 1920 version)
(director, producer, story, scenario)

1931

Dracula (director)
Iron Man (director)

1932

Freaks (director, producer)

1933

Fast Workers (director, story)

1935

Mark of the Vampire (director, producer)

1936

The Devil-Doll (director, story, scenario)

1939

Miracles for Sale (director, producer)

About the Contributors

Marcel Arbeit is associate professor in the Department of English and American Studies, Palacký University, Olomouc, Czech Republic. He is the current president of the Czech and Slovak Association for American Studies, and an EAAS board member. His main fields of research are contemporary southern literature, American and Canadian independent film, and popular culture. His recent publications focus on Harry Crews, Richard Ford, Lewis Nordan, and the South in film. He also translated a number of books by American and British writers. He is the main editor of the three-volume *Bibliography of American Literature in Czech Translation* (2000). In 2006 he co-edited *Vypravěči amerického Jihu* [Narrators of the American South], an anthology of southern fiction after 1945, and published a monograph on Fred Chappell and Cormac McCarthy.

Eugenie Brinkema is a Ph.D student in modern culture and media at Brown University in Providence, Rhode Island. Her articles on cinema, psychoanalysis, and feminism have appeared in *The Dalhousie Review*, *Camera Obscura*, and *Paradoxa*. Forthcoming projects include an essay on Catherine Breillat for *Women: A Culture Review* and an article on Michael Haneke for an anthology on New German Cinema.

Sarah Dellmann studied theater, film and media science, philosophy and sociology at the University of Frankfurt (Germany) and the Université Paris 8 (France). She wrote her master's thesis on body representations and carnival traditions in Tod Browning's films with Lon Chaney and *Freaks*. Sarah is volunteering in the cinema initiative "pupille" at the University of Frankfurt. She coaches weekends and seminars in the political youth education on the subject of antiracism, feminism and popular culture. She loves seeing projected film at the movies.

Bernd Herzogenrath is a professor of American Literature and Culture and teaches at Goethe-University of Frankfurt am Main. He is the author of *An Art of Desire: Reading Paul Auster* (Rodopi, 1999), and the editor of *From Virgin Land to Disney World: Nature and Its Discontents in the USA of Yesterday and Today* (Rodopi, 2001), and *The Films of Tod Browning* (Black Dog, 2006). Bernd's fields of interest are 19th and 20th century American Literature, critical theory, and cultural media studies. Currently he is working on "Deleuzian History of the American Body|Politic." Future publications include a collection of essays on *Deleuze/Guattari & Ecology*, and on the work of Edgar G. Ulmer (to be published by McFarland). Bernd is also the organizer and "inventor" of the *ulmerfest*, a biannual conference series devoted to Edgar G.

Ulmer that takes place in Ulmer's hometown of Olomouc in the Czech Republic (see *www.uni-koeln.de/phil-fak/englisch/abteilungen/berressem/herzogenrath/ulmer/index.htm*).

Reynold Humphries is the author of *The American Horror Film: An Introduction* (Edinburgh University Press, 2002) and *The Hollywood Horror Film, 1931–1941: Madness in a Social Landscape* (Scarecrow Press, 2006). His study of early Mario Bava appeared in *Monstrous Adaptions*, and he wrote for the online journal *Kinoeye* and the special horror issues of *Post Script* and *Paradoxa*. He has written for French publications on Tobe Hooper, George A. Romero and Jacques Tourneur. Other publications include two books: *Film Noir Reader 4* and *The Gangster Film*. He has written chapters for forthcoming anthologies devoted to John Huston and Edgar G. Ulmer. His contributions to *Docufictions, Stanley Kubrick: The Legacy* and to several volumes published in France concern Cold War politics and Hollywood. His latest book, *Hollywood's Blacklists: A Political and Cultural History*, will be published by Edinburgh University Press in September 2008.

Hioni Karamanos is an independent scholar, with a master's of library and information science degree and a BA with distinction in cultural anthropology from the University of Washington. Hioni maintains an active interest in the politics and academics of disability, particularly in promoting the understanding of disability as human variation and cultural construct, through work with the University of Washington's Disability Studies Program. As a person with a disability, Hioni remains engaged in a lifelong study of disability representation, especially in the realms of popular culture and visual media, including everything from the films of Tod Browning to episodes of *South Park*.

Ekkehard Knörer is a film and literature scholar, as well as a film critic. He wrote his dissertation on *wit* and *ingenium* in 17th and 18th century poetics and aesthetics, from Baltasar Gracián to Jean Paul. He has published articles on desert movies, Robert Bresson's aesthetics of transsubstantiation and various aspects of Hollywood movies. Hundreds of reviews and essays can be found in *Jump Cut* (*www.jump-cut.de*), the online movie magazine he has been editing since 1998. He is currently working on a book-length study of (seemingly) identical copies and remakes.

Frank Lafond teaches film studies at the University of Lille's Faculté Libre de Sciences Humaines in France. He has written (in French and in English) mostly on the horror genre in journals such as *Post Script, Positif, Simulacres, Iris/Les Cahiers du Gerf, CinémAction, La Licorne*, and *Kinoeye*. He has notably contributed to *Le Crime organisé à la ville et à l'écran (États-Unis, 1929–1951)* (Ellipses), *24 Frames: Cinema in the Low Countries* (Wallflower Press), *Japanese Horror Cinema* (Edinburgh University Press), and *Roman Polanski, l'art de l'adaptation* (L'Harmattan). He has edited a collection on the modern American horror film (*Cauchemars américains: fantastique et horreur dans le cinéma moderne*, Les Editions du Céfal), and is the editor of a journal dedicated to horror and science-fiction films (*Rendez-vous avec la peur*). In 2007 Frank published *Jacques Tourneur, les figures de la peur* (Presses Universitaires de Rennes) and edited a book on George Romero. His homepage is *http://frank.lafond.free.fr*.

Michael Lawrence is a doctoral candidate at Middlesex University, London, where he is completing his thesis on the films of Atom Egoyan. He has taught film studies at a number of universities, and specializes in world cinema and film theory.

F. Gwynplaine MacIntyre, born in Perthshire, Scotland, was one of the thousands of "child migrants" taken from postwar Britain and sent to rural Australia. He currently lives near Minffordd in northern Wales, but spends several months of each year in New York City. MacIntyre has been a professional author and journalist since the early 1960s. He was a London crime reporter and police liaison in the 1970s; from 2002 through 2005 he wrote about arts and sport for the *New York Daily News*. He is now writing a nonfiction book about the U.S. Army officer who oversaw executions of Nazi war criminals. His home page is http://www.sff.net/people/fgwyn/

Hugh S. Manon (Ph.D in cultural and critical studies, University of Pittsburgh) is an associate professor in the English Department and Screen Studies Program at Oklahoma State University. He is currently writing a book that employs the psychoanalytic notion of fetishism to link the rise and decline of classic American *film noir* with the advent of television. He has recently taught courses on Lacanian psychoanalysis, international *Film Noir*, and Lo-Fi aesthetics.

Adrian Martin is a senior research fellow in film and television studies, Monash University (Melbourne, Australia). He has won the Byron Kennedy Award (Australian Film Institute), the Pascall Prize for Critical Writing, and the Mollie Holman Medal for Doctoral Excellence. He is the author of *Phantasms* (1994), *Once Upon a Time in America* (1998), *The Mad Max Movies* (2003) and *Sublimes Obsesiones* (2004), and is co-editor of *Movie Mutations* (2003) and the Internet film journal *Rouge* (*www.rouge.com.au*). His essays and reviews appear in publications including *Cahiers du cinéma*, *Film Comment*, *Sight and Sound*, *Trafic*, *Miradas de cine*, *Film International*, *Tren de sombras*, and *Ekran*. He has contributed chapters to books on Godard, Minnelli, Romero, and Hou. His forthcoming projects deal with De Palma, Malick, and the "cinema of poetry" today.

Lars Nowak is a teaching assistant in media philosophy at the Bauhaus-University at Weimar, where he is also currently working on a dissertation called *Deformation and Difference: The Films of Tod Browning*. He has published essays and given talks about Browning, Federico Fellini, William S. Burroughs, the connections between film and Taylorism, and psychoanalytic and poststructuralist film theory. He also serves as an editor at the electronic film journal *Nach dem Film* (*www.nachdemfilm.de*).

Björn Quiring studied comparative literature and philosophy in Berlin and Paris. He was a member of the Graduiertenkolleg "Representation — Rhetoric — Knowledge" in Frankfurt/Oder and has just finished his dissertation on the aporias of ritual cursing in Shakespeare's histories. His current research interests include the connection between theologico-juridical discourses, economics and literature. He has also published articles on film, comic art and experimental music. Publications include "Die Repräsentation von devianten und normativen Körpern in Tod Brownings Film *Freaks*" in *Körperlichkeit und Tabuisierung* (eds. Matthias Rothe und Hartmut Schröder, Berlin: Weidler, 2004).

Index

Academy of Motion Picture Arts and Sciences 116
Adorée, Renée 90, 91
Agamben, Giorgio 205
amputation 105–7
animal/animals 3, 11, 15, 40–41, 45, 48, 67n16, 107, 142–46, 202, 222–24
Apocalypse Now (1979) 136–37
The Art of Make-Up for Stage and Screen (1927 book) 94
At the Sign of the Story (1927 play) 86

Bakhtin, Mikhail 3, 11, 140–41, 146
Barrymore, Lionel 224
Bataille, Georges 210
Baudrillard, Jean 96, 104
Bazin, André 108–9
Benjamin, Walter 137, 203–4, 205
Best, Peggy 93
Betz, Matthew 92–93, 120, 131
Beyond the Rocks (1922) 116
The Big City (Browning) 91, 92–93, 95, 116–31
Birds of Rhiannon (1930 play) 86
The Black Bird (Browning) 84–95, 121, 123
The Black Room (1935) 89
Blake, Michael 44, 48
Breton, André 204
Brodie, William 87–88, 91
Broken Blossoms (1919) 90
Burke, Thomas 90

Cameron, Kenneth 132
carnival 1, 8, 11, 1–20, 38, 96–97, 106, 121, 139–41, 143, 147, 220
Carr, John Dickson 218, 226
Chaney, Lon, Sr. 20, 26, 31, 42, 43, 44, 46, 48, 49, 51–52, 54, 64–66, 70, 79, 85–95, 97–98, 102–8, 110, 114, 117, 120, 121, 123, 124, 127, 128, 129, 131, 133, 139, 141–42, 145, 147–48, 158, 167, 170, 193, 195, 216, 220, 224
Chemers, Michael 39, 49

Christianity 60–61, 67
Cinecon 41, 116
cinema of attractions 5–6, 21–23, 109
Compson, Betty 122
Conan Doyle, Sir Arthur 226
Conrad, Joseph 133, 136–38

Dalí, Salvador 208
Darke, Paul 34, 35, 49
Dauphin, Gary 42, 49
Day, Marceline 120, 124, 125, 126, 128
Debord, Guy 206
de Lauretis, Teresa 11, 143, 147
Deleuze, Gilles 2–3, 50–69
The Devil Doll (Browning) 95, 123
disability/Disability Studies 33–49
Dismuki, Peter 44
Dracula (Browning) 51, 58–60, 66, 111, 151–57, 175–80, 182–83, 185, 195–96, 208, 220
Dracula (Melford) 151–57
Dresser, Davis 217, 229n2
d'Usseau, Arnaud 216, 218

Earles, Harry 70
Epstein, Jean 205–6, 207

family 11–12, 15, 77, 87, 133, 142–48, 223, 227
Fassbinder, Rainer Werner 54
Fay, Larry 119
feminist/feminism 11, 53, 62, 147, 150, 164, 167, 207
fetishism 33, 37, 39, 43, 45, 46, 56–57, 60–63, 67
"flash prints" 118
Fort, Garrett 84
freaks 158–72
Freaks (Browning) 2–3, 41, 119, 120, 122, 126, 135, 198, 199
Freud, Sigmund 11, 14, 53, 62, 135, 142–43, 147–48, 158–60, 177–78, 184–85
Freund, Karl 152
The Fuel of Life (1917) 120

Garland-Thomson, Rosemarie 34, 38
Gaycken, Oliver 45, 49
George, John 120, 129
Giornate del Cinema Muto 116
The Golden Feathers (1939 play) 86
Grant, James Edward 216
Griffith, D.W. 90
Guattari, Félix 3
Guinan, Mary "Texas" 119–20
Gunning, Tom 5, 21–22, 109

Halliday, Brett (pen name) 217, 229n2
Harlow, Jean 94
Hilton, Daisy 122–23
Hilton, Violet 120, 122–23
His Majesty, the Scarecrow of Oz (1925) 121
Hitchcock, Alfred 166, 167
Hochschild, Adam 133–34
Holland, Cecil 94
Hope, Bob 123
Hugo, Victor 48, 49
human body 97–98, 102–7

incest 181, 182, 185–88

"Jack the Ripper" 91
Jacobsen-Hodgkinson Corporation 84

Kaite, Berkeley 33, 49
Kamiyama, Sojin 93
Kant, Immanuel 3–5
Karloff, Boris 220
Kohner, Paul 151
Král, Petr 206
Kyrou, Ado 211

Lacan, Jacques 97–100, 106–8, 160–61, 163–72, 184–85, 187
Lang, Fritz 152
Leeds, Herbert I. 217–18
Lévi-Strauss, Claude 135
Linton, Simi 33, 49
London After Midnight (Browning) 90, 118, 121, 124, 128
Longmore, Paul 36, 49
"lost films" 116–17, 131
Lugosi, Bela 110, 152, 154, 156, 167, 175, 181–82, 220, 228

magic 19–32, 109–10, 112–13, 119, 221–30
Mark of the Vampire (Browning) 121
masochism 50–69
McCarty, John 39, 49
Mealand, Richard 225–26
Melford, George 151, 152, 153, 155, 156

Metro-Goldwyn-Mayer 84, 91, 94, 117, 126, 127
MGM *see* Metro-Goldwyn-Mayer
Miracles for Sale (Browning) 6, 15–16, 20, 28–30, 111–13, 119, 156, 214–16
Mockery (1927) 117
The Mocking Bird (novel) 84–85, 86, 88–89, 95
Moore, Owen 85
movement 182–85
Movieola flatbed 119
Murnau, Friedrich W. 2, 152
Murray, James 122, 123, 125, 128, 129
The Mystic (Browning) 119, 121

Nederlands Filmmuseum 116
Norden, Martin F. 37, 42, 44, 49

oedipal/Oedipus 11, 12, 14, 52, 54, 56, 133, 142–43, 146–48, 158–60, 180–81
Oppenheim, E. Phillip 226
Out Yonder (1919) 116
Outside the Law (1920 film and novelization) 84
Owen, Robert Dale 225

Paramount Pictures Corporation 117
Parsonnet, Marion 216
Pearson, Virginia 120
Poe, Edgar Allan 1, 121, 123
point of view 175, 181, 182, 183, 184, 192–93
Pointon, Ann 36, 41, 49
Poor Jake's Demise (1913) 117
Popular Plays and Screen Library 84, 85
psychoanalysis 200, 211
"The Purloined Letter" (Poe) 123

Rawson, Clayton 215–29
Rawson, Hugh 215
realism 97, 102, 104, 108–10, 114
Reynolds, Harry 127
The Road to Mandalay (Browning) 93, 94
Robbins, Clarence Aaron "Tod" 70
Rohmer, Eric 16
Rohmer, Sax 16
role playing 175, 185–86, 193, 194–95, 195n2
Rosenthal, Stuart 40, 42, 49
Ruiz, Raúl 202, 206, 210
Ruskin, Harry 216

Sacher-Masoch, Leopold von 56–58, 66
sadism 56–59, 62–63, 66–67
Sharp, Henry 127

The Show (Browning) 1, 5–7, 20–22, 51–53, 99, 119, 121, 145, 158
Sidney Street siege (1911) 90
Sojin (actor) *see* Kamiyama, Sojin
Solomon, Matthew 38, 49
Sorrell and Son (1927) 116
"Southern Gothic" 1
special effects 202–3
Steenbeck viewer 118–19, 131
Sternberg, Josef von 53–54, 56, 60–61, 64
Sting (1973) 131
Stroheim, Erich von 53
Studlar, Gaylyn 51–54, 58, 60–61, 63, 64–65, 78, 145, 147–48
Sturgis, Eddie 122
Sun, Gus (vaudeville impresario) 122
Sunrise (1927) 2
Surrealism 201, 203–12
suspension of disbelief 10, 26–27, 29, 75, 80–81, 103, 191
Swanson, Gloria 116
symbolic castration 54–56, 60

Thalberg, Irving 79, 127
Thomas, Olive 116
Thunder (1929) 117, 123
Tichenor, Edna 121, 126
Todorov, Tzvetan 156, 157
trompe-l'oeil 96–110

The Unholy Three (Browning) 88, 95, 122, 123, 124, 128, 130
The Unholy Three (Jack Conway) 78–82
Universal Pictures 84
The Unknown (Browning) 33, 36, 38, 42, 43, 44, 46, 47, 48, 49, 86, 94, 116, 118

Valentino, Rudolph 116, 151
Vampire 152–57
vaudeville 6, 19–21, 93, 122, 133, 134, 139
Veiller, Bayard 227–29
Villar Carlos 154, 155

West of Zanzibar (Browning) 6–7, 10, 20, 26–28, 51–53, 90, 110–12, 119, 122, 132–38, 141, 145, 153
White Tiger (Browning) 119, 121, 123, 128, 130
Wild Party (1929) 124
Williams, Tennessee 2, 5
Wittgenstein, Ludwig 5
woman 158–72
Wood, Sam 116

Young, Brigham 85
Young, Waldemar 84, 85–86, 91, 93, 123

Žižek, Slavoj 69, 107, 115, 161, 172, 173

www.ingramcontent.com/pod-product-compliance
Ingram Content Group UK Ltd.
Pitfield, Milton Keynes, MK11 3LW, UK
UKHW041940140426
5217IPUK00014B/582

9 780786 434473